Running the Race

Devotionals Encouraging Discipleship

William T. Blount

Running the Race
Devotionals Encouraging Discipleship
by William T. Blount

Printed in the United States of America

ISBN 978-1514870747

Unless otherwise indicated, Bible quotations are taken from The New American Standard Bible. Copyright © 1977 by The Lockman Foundation.

Order book in paperback or Kindle ebook through amazon.com.

Contents

Acknowledgments

I am deeply grateful to my wife, Patricia, for using her God-given talents in editing this work. She has improved my sentence structure, corrected my poor grammar, and suggested better words or phrases. Patricia has been my constant companion throughout this effort and I have used her as a sounding board for many of the devotionals ideas I have had. She has been invaluable to me by discussing doctrinal ideas and Biblical examples for various topics.

I am also indebted to my friend, Dr Charles Young, who reviewed many of my devotionals for doctrinal correctness. He was also helpful in navigating me through the mechanics of self-publishing. He self-published his first book, <u>Charging Hell with a Squirt-gun,</u> in 2009, the same year I started writing these devotionals.

Introduction

In summer 2009 I had a thought that led to this book: Wouldn't it be good to have something to show for teaching Bible studies for forty years other than just reams of paper representing my lesson plans? I recognized that I had benefited spiritually from my times of preparation and I also trusted that the Word taught benefited those who heard the lessons. Nevertheless, I wanted something even more tangible. I decided to write a devotional whenever I had a thought with merit from a Bible study. That narrow source of input soon expanded to also include thoughts from my own devotional times, thoughts from sermons I heard, and thoughts from Scripture memory verses I reviewed. After six years I arranged the devotionals I had written by topic and you have the results in your hand.

The theme at our church for 2015 was "Be Disciples, Make Disciples". As I looked at my devotional topics, I realized they all related to discipleship. My favorite Biblical metaphor for living the Christian life is that of running a race. So, I entitled this devotional book Running the Race with a subtitle: Devotionals Encouraging Discipleship.

By discipleship I mean what we need to know and do to become mature followers of Jesus Christ, to include leading others to Christ and helping them grow to maturity. I trust this devotional book will help new believers grow and keep mature believers mindful of their spiritual race.

I grouped devotionals topically in sets of five. For the last two days in the week, I included two application/thought questions and the first sentence or two of a prayer related to the topic. Please allow the Holy Spirit to guide you in finishing the prayer as you relate the topic to your life.

Six of the 52 weeks address the topic of witnessing. Four topics are allocated two weeks each; the remaining 38 topics each have one week assigned. I did not intentionally focus on witnessing as I was writing the devotionals. Rather, I personally sense a need to share my faith more and thus passages on evangelism speak to my heart more often than other topics. Perhaps you will also benefit by being challenged on a regular basis regarding sharing Jesus with others.

Now the Lord said to Moses and Aaron in the land of Egypt, this month shall be the beginning of months for you; it is to be the first month of the year to you.   *Exodus 12:1-2*

A fresh start always seems to be uplifting and invigorating. The past is history and you are plotting a new course. That is precisely how the Israelites must have felt when they left Egypt with all its struggles and disappointments. The Lord encouraged this positive attitude toward the future when He designated their exodus month as the first month of a new year. He also instituted the Passover celebration that same month as a reminder of His goodness to the children of Israel in setting them free from their oppressors.

The Apostle Paul was also no stranger to fresh starts. His life was forever changed one day on the road to Damascus when he heard the words: *I am Jesus whom you are persecuting.*[1] Gone were days of persecuting Christians; ahead were days of being persecuted for Jesus. Behind were years of only knowing about God; before were years of knowing God personally and intimately. In the rear was emptiness; forward was an abundant, joyful life.

Paul could have spent his future years dwelling on past failures, recalling when he imprisoned and persecuted the innocent. However, he chose to accept Jesus' forgiveness and focus on a future lived for God. Paul looked forward and upward, not backward and downward. The best way to atone for the past was to invest his future in growing God's kingdom on earth.

For the believer in Jesus, any moment can be a fresh start. Jesus stands ready to forgive us when we sin and the indwelling Holy Spirit is ready to lead when we are ready to follow. However, there is nothing wrong with a fresh start at the beginning of a new year. If God did it for Israel, He will also do it for you. God wants to lead you on an exodus from your bondage to sin into a Promised Land of His provision and fulfillment.

[1] Acts 9:5b

Therefore, since we have so great a cloud of witnesses surrounding us, let us also lay aside every encumbrance, and the sin which so easily entangles us, and let us run with endurance the race that is set before us, fixing our eyes on Jesus...   *Hebrews 12:1-2a*

The longest race I ever ran was the 15K (9.3 miles) Gasparilla Distance Classic in Tampa, Florida. I prepared, I started, I endured, I finished. If you are a follower of Christ, you are in a race. The race began when you accepted the gift of eternal life through the Lord Jesus Christ. At that moment, Jesus set your race before you. Unlike my foot race, preparation for our spiritual race takes place during the race. Our race ends at death.

The best preparation for our race is to daily fix our eyes on Jesus. He gives us strength, direction, motivation, and endurance to finish our race. As we abide in Christ through His Word and prayer, we are less likely to get entangled in sin which always detours us from our given track. As we are led by the Spirit, we will be able to discern among the good, the better, and the best, thereby identifying what can be laid aside to lighten our load.

The biggest tragedy of the Christian life is to not recognize you are in a race. *Do you not know that those who run in a race all run, but only one receives the prize? Run in such a way that you may win.*[1] The race occurs on the track that God has laid out for you. If you are not running the race, then you are not on God's track. Instead you are on your own track and at the race's end you will give an accounting to the Race-Master.

As we start a new year, let's rededicate ourselves to running the race well that God has laid out for each of us. At the end of our race, may we say with Paul: *the time of my departure has come...I have finished the course...in the future there is laid up for me the crown of righteousness.*[2]

[1]I Corinthians 9:24   [2]II Timothy 4:6b-8a

But I say, walk by the Spirit, and you will not carry out the desire of the flesh. For the flesh sets its desire against the Spirit, and the Spirit against the flesh; for these are in opposition to one another, so that you may not do the things that you please.   Galatians 5:16-17

I help teach a systematic theology class to a group of inmates in a local prison. One topic taught deals with the essential nature of mankind represented by two viewpoints. The view that man is comprised of three distinct parts (body, soul, and spirit) is called trichotomy. The view that man is made of two parts (body and soul/spirit) is called dichotomy. In the latter, soul and spirit are seen as interchangeable terms which are synonymous. Most men in the room supported trichotomy whereas the author of the textbook favored dichotomy. A lively discussion ensued.

Prior to the group reading and discussing the chapter dealing with this topic, I read the above verses as an introduction. I sensed the lesson would be controversial so I wanted to put the lesson in the proper perspective before discussion began. The truth is that it doesn't matter if I am made up of two or three parts. What matters is that however many parts I have, they are all involved in a battle that must be won. The key to victory is that I walk by the Spirit and not walk in the flesh.

As we listen to sermons, read, study and memorize Scripture, we must remember that the main objective is a changed life, not knowledge gained. Scripture encourages us to increase in knowledge, but knowledge is not the end state. If we focus on walking in the Spirit daily, that objective will result in personal spiritual growth and a desire to share our faith with others.

Let's start each day with a prayer to be sensitive to the Holy Spirit within us.

And indeed if they had been thinking of that country from which they went out, they would have had opportunity to return.

Hebrews 11:15

The faith hall of fame in Hebrews 11 gives central billing to Abraham. He is described as one who embraced God's promises in the present and looked to the future awaiting their fulfillment. There is no record of Abraham ever considering a return to his homeland after he obeyed God's call to leave.

By contrast when his descendants, the Israelites, were miraculously delivered from bondage in Egypt they often contemplated the life they left behind.[1] When threatened by Pharaoh's army or when lacking food or water, they complained, wishing they had never left Egypt. They forgot God's promises to Abraham and to them. When circumstances got tough, they were mindful of easier times.

As we mature down the road toward Christ-likeness, the journey does not get easier. God-given responsibilities increase, more sacrifice is required, and Satan's opposition intensifies. When obstacles and discouragement loom, we will be tempted to think of former days when times were easier.

If we allow our minds to dwell on the past, Satan will provide an opportunity to return there. The Israelites never did physically return to Egypt but their backward gaze caused them to not trust God. The result was that they wandered in the wilderness forty years as those of accountable age expired one by one. They experienced the bondage of Egypt while confined in the desert.

Let's acknowledge that following Christ is not without struggles and disappointments. Let's also ask God for a promise to cling to during those challenging times that we may look to Jesus, not to the past!

[1] Exodus 16:3

Let the word of Christ richly dwell within you.   Colossians 3:16a
Therefore do not let sin reign in your mortal body that you should
obey its lusts.   Romans 6:12

     "Let me drive your car." Two factors are at work in this request. First, the requester has a desire to drive the car but needs permission. Second, the owner of the car must decide whether to grant the request.

     If you are a Christian, the Holy Spirit within you is requesting that you to let the word of Christ richly dwell in you. *Like newborn babes, long for the pure milk of the word, that by it you may grow in respect to salvation.*[1] The Holy Spirit gives us a thirst for the word of God as believers, but we have to act and schedule time in the Bible. We must say yes to that desire.

     Unfortunately, Christians still have a sin nature and it is asking permission to act out. However, in Christ we no longer have to be slaves to the old man. We can choose to serve Christ instead. We have the power to say no, but we must exercise that power.

     Perhaps you have heard the illustration of the two dogs confined in a cage. The dogs were always fighting. The dog that won was the dog that the owner fed. In the same way, we have two opposing natures within us and the battle is joined. Each Christian determines which nature wins when he or she decides which nature is fed.

     For the Christian, the word of God is food for the soul. It helps us keep God's perspective when we are bombarded with Satan's worldview. It provides strength to resist the temptations this world sends our way. You have a choice. Choose to immerse yourself in the word of God through hearing, reading, studying, memorizing and meditating. To the degree you choose the Word, there will be a corresponding decrease in the number of times you permit your sin nature to reign.

[1] I Peter 2:2

1. As you run your race this year you will want to set realistic goals and actions for spiritual growth. However, let your primary focus be a direction rather that the individual steps toward the goal. Throughout the year, press toward "the upward call of God in Christ Jesus". Don't be discouraged if you fail to complete some actions along the way. Keep pressing toward godliness in Christ Jesus.

Brethren, I do not regard myself as having laid hold of it yet; but one thing I do: forgetting what lies behind and reaching forward to what lies ahead, I press on toward the goal for the prize of the upward call of God in Christ Jesus.   Philippians 3:13-14

2. Name one area in your life where you are letting the old nature have its way. Confess that specific area to God and ask for an awareness of God's presence the next time you are tempted in that area.

Prayer Starter: Lord Jesus, thank you that this week is a new beginning in my spiritual life. Thank you that through the Holy Spirit's power I can say "no" to my old nature and say "yes" to your Spirit within me. Father, I pray that you would help me have victory over…

Therefore, say, 'Thus says the Lord God, "Though I had removed them far away among the nations, and though I had scattered them among the countries, yet I was a sanctuary for them a little while in the countries where they had gone."'   *Ezekiel 11:16*

Picture this. Your nation has been conquered by a foreign power. You are separated from family and have been deported to a faraway land. You must learn a new language and a new culture. Are you hopeful or discouraged?

The answer depends on how real God is in your life. If you are godly men like Ezekiel or Daniel who were exiled, you are probably hopeful. If you are an ungodly person who contributed to God's judgment of the Babylonian conquest on Judah, then you are probably discouraged.

It is not uncommon for godly men and women to be tempted to lose hope when confronted by the harsh realities of life. God doesn't place his people in a protective bubble that is impervious to sickness, unemployment, disaster, or calamity. However, God always does provide Himself as a sanctuary during the tribulation.

While in Babylon, Daniel was thrown in the lion's den because he was caught praying three times a day to His God.[1] He had purposely disobeyed the law of the land because he refused to give up his daily time with God in his private sanctuary. Daniel's private time with God not only provided hope to Daniel but God used it to bring glory to Himself when he shut the lion's mouths to protect Daniel.

For Thou art my hope; O Lord God, Thou art my confidence from my youth.[2]

[1]Daniel 6   [2]Psalm 71:5

But he himself went a day's journey into the wilderness, and came and sat down under a juniper tree; and he requested for himself that he might die ...   *I Kings 19:4a*

Most of us can identify with Elijah as we encounter situations in our lives where we become discouraged and wonder if life is worth living. Elijah was fearful when he learned that Queen Jezebel had vowed to kill him for his role in killing 450 of her prophets of Baal. We can learn some lessons about coping with discouragement from Elijah and God's response to him.

When discouraged we tend to over exaggerate the negative aspects of our situation. Elijah saw himself as the only prophet left since many others had been killed. But God told him that there were 7,000 people in Israel who had not bowed to Baal. Many times in discouragement we want to be alone as Elijah was in this situation. But friends can help us keep things in perspective when we may not be thinking rationally.

In times of discouragement God is with us. God sent an angel to minister to Elijah and He will care for us as well. *Call upon Me in the day of trouble; I shall rescue you, and you will honor Me.*[1] To be mindful of God's presence we need to be proactive in seeking Him in the Word and prayer.

We must recognize in these low points of life that God is not finished with us yet. In the midst of Elijah's discouragement and self-pity, God sent him to Damascus to anoint three men: a new king over Aram, a new king over Israel, and Elisha as his successor. Meaningful activity is often good to help us get our focus off self and on eternal matters.

Why are you in despair, O my soul? And why have you become disturbed within me? Hope in God, for I shall again praise Him for the help of His presence.[2]

[1]Psalm 50:15   [2]Psalm 42:5

If we have hoped in Christ in this life only, we are of all men most to
be pitied.   *I Corinthians 15:19*

    Hope is defined by Webster as a feeling that what is wanted
will happen. This definition has to be refined somewhat to capture
the Biblical meaning of hope. At some point I have said: "I hope I
have enough money one day to buy _____". More than likely, I
was not considering God's will when I made the statement and that
omission disqualified it as Biblical hope. Biblical hope is the
confidence that God will do what is right for me.

    Hope for the believer in Christ focuses both on the here-and-
now and the by-and-by. It seems that hope is sought after in life's
tough times. When circumstances are good, we thank God for the
blessings of life and don't think much about hope. However, when
our world is turned upside down, we wonder if we will survive and
need hope to get us through the upheaval. Hope will sustain us as
we realize that *all things work together for good to those who love*
God and are called according to His purpose.[1] If we can grasp the
idea that God promises to use our tribulation for good in His
Kingdom, then we can persevere with hope in the here-and-now.

    Hope is also needed for the by-and-by, especially at the death
of a loved one. *But we do not want you to be uninformed, brethren,*
about those who are asleep, that you may not grieve, as do the rest
who have no hope.[2] Paul is not saying that we will not grieve at the
loss of a loved one who knows Christ. Rather, our grief will not be
as deep and desperate as those who don't have hope in Christ. Since
God raised Jesus from the dead, we know that we will one day be
reunited with believing relatives and friends in heaven. That hope
provides needed comfort during times of physical separation through
death.

    Because of the resurrection of Jesus Christ from the dead,
believers in Christ have hope in this life and for the life to come.
Those who cannot say that need our prayers and the gospel.

[1]Romans 8:28   [2]I Thessalonians 4:13

But as for me, my feet came close to stumbling; my steps had almost slipped. For I was envious of the arrogant, as I saw the prosperity of the wicked.   Psalm 73:2-3

When was the last time your faith was shaken during a time of difficulty because you envied those who were ungodly and prosperous? Asaph, the author of Psalm 73, knew the feeling first hand. Asaph was appointed by King David as the chief chorister during a time when the ark was being brought into Jerusalem.[1] Yet even with his musical focus and abilities, Asaph was discouraged and sang the blues.

We all have an innate sense of fairness. When we try to live for God and things don't seem to go our way, we wonder where God is. During this time, if we see others shun God while living the "good life", we conclude that life is not fair and we feel sorry for ourselves. Surely this is the way Asaph must have felt.

So did Asaph ever emerge from the doldrums? Yes, we read: *It was troublesome in my sight, until I came into the sanctuary of God; then I perceived their end.*[2] The remedy was a fresh encounter with God. Asaph had gotten his focus off God and started to compare his situation to that of others. In so doing, he had forgotten that God was still sovereign in his life as well as the lives of the ungodly.

Perhaps the best known verse in this psalm is verse 25: *Whom have I in heaven but Thee? And besides Thee, I desire nothing on earth.* That is the statement of a man who has found his contentment in God, and God alone.

Asaph concludes his psalm with*: But as for me, the nearness of God is my good; I have made the Lord God my refuge, that I may tell of all Thy works.* When we find ourselves discouraged and envious of others, let's follow Asaph's lead and draw near to God as our one true refuge.

[1] I Chronicles 16:4-5   [2] Psalm 73:16b-17

And as for me, I know that my Redeemer lives, and at the last He will take His stand on the earth. Even after my skin is destroyed, yet from my flesh I shall see God.   Job 19:25-26

Over one million people die by suicide worldwide each year. Many more attempt to take their own life. Hopelessness is the primary cause of suicide. I think of three Biblical incidents of suicide.

King Saul requested that his armor bearer kill him as the enemy was about to capture him. When the armor bearer refused, Saul fell on his own sword and the armor bearer did likewise. Ahithophel counseled Absalom to immediately pursue David who had fled Jerusalem after Absalom's coup. When his counsel was rejected, Ahithophel went home and strangled himself. Finally, Judas experienced guilt after betraying Jesus and he hanged himself.

In all three incidents, hopelessness was evident. From an earthly perspective, no one has ever been in a more hopeless, suicidal situation than Job after losing his ten children, his possessions, and his health. In fact, his wife advised him to curse God and die. But Job had hope in that he knew his Redeemer lived, was sovereign, loved him, and had his best interests at heart. That hope sustained Job through unbelievable misery and despondency.

I recall one attempted suicide in the Bible that was thwarted: *And when the jailer had been roused out of sleep and had seen the prison doors opened, he drew his sword and was about to kill himself, supposing that the prisoners had escaped.*[1]

Do you remember what happened? Paul urged him to do no harm to himself since all prisoners were present. Paul shared a truth with the jailer and that truth brought hope and saved a life. Then Paul shared the truth of the gospel and the man's soul was saved.

When we cross paths with a friend or stranger, we usually don't know the depths of despair that may be in that life. Regardless, a word of hope and encouragement is always appropriate. When possible, let's share the eternal hope of the gospel – a soul may be saved.

[1]Acts 16:27

1. List all the reasons for discouragement that were experienced by Elijah and Asaph. Do you have an area of discouragement in your life these days? If yes, write below the Biblical view you should have toward that circumstance.

2. Do you know anyone who seems depressed and discouraged? Pray for an opportunity to say a word of encouragement to them this week. Share a testimony with them about how God has given you hope in the midst of your discouragement.

Prayer Starter: Lord Jesus, the Psalmist said "I had fainted unless I had believed to see the goodness of the Lord in the land of the living." (Psalm 27:13) Help me to draw close to you when I lose hope. As I think about those in my sphere of influence that are discouraged, I pray for...

For this cause a man shall leave his father and mother, and shall cleave to his wife; and the two shall become one flesh. This mystery is great; but I am speaking with reference to Christ and the church.
Ephesians 5:31-32

Paul relates the Genesis account of the marriage of the man to his wife to that of Christ and His Bride, the Church. Thus the man's marriage to his wife is one of many foreshadows in the Old Testament of the coming Messiah. As such, it becomes instructive as to what God intended marriage to be like since we have witnessed Christ's union with the Church.

Note that Christ is only joined with Christians. A Biblical marriage is between a man and a woman, both of whom are followers of Jesus. Hence, Paul's admonition: *Do not be bound together with unbelievers.*[1] Missionary dating is unwise. Don't rationalize dating or marrying an unbeliever for the purpose of winning them to Christ. Don't presume that God's grace will accompany an act of disobedience.

Consider Christ's act of sacrificial love for the Church. He left His Father and the splendor of heaven to seek and to wed His Beloved, the Church. He extends His offer of marriage to all mankind but only some accepted. Christ asks His Bride to submit their bodies as living sacrifices which are acceptable to the Father, just as He did.[2] If husband and wife submit themselves to God and love each other as Christ has loved the Church, the marriage cannot fail. Selfishness can doom a marriage.

The declaration that the two shall become one flesh is a reference to sexual intimacy between the man and woman. When wed to Christ, the Holy Spirit of God comes to abide with us. The soul and the Spirit reside in one flesh. The presence of this Spirit can also empower us in our marriage, and cause our marriages to glorify God and honor Christ.

[1]II Corinthians 6:14a   [2]Romans 12:1

Where no oxen are, the manger is clean, but much increase comes by
the strength of the ox.   Proverbs 14:4
Behold, children are a gift of the Lord; the fruit of the womb is a
reward.   Psalm 127:3

When I first memorized the proverb, I titled it "cost-benefit
analysis". I understood that anything in life has its pros and cons.
After marriage, Patricia and I would visit couples with small
children. Upon leaving their home, we would look at each other and
say "not this year". For us as a newly married couple, the
disadvantages of having children seemed to greatly outweigh the
advantages.

After three years we began to warm up to the idea. We
believed that the psalm was true and that children were a gift and a
reward from God. Shortly after, God blessed us with fraternal twins,
a boy and a girl. Sure enough, the manger was seldom clean. But
today, Paul is serving in the Air Force and Lindsay is a nurse who is
married and living in Scotland. Both love Jesus and are productive
members of society. The manger is clean again.

A manger is a feeding trough. In addition to feeding them,
you also have to clothe, educate, entertain, and strive to grow them
up in the nurture and admonition of the Lord. All that attention takes
time and money which are resources that you are not spending on
yourself. The reward and strength that comes from children may be
developing a selfless attitude in the parent just as much as the impact
the children have in society and in the kingdom of God.

The psalmist goes on to liken children to arrows in the hand
of the warrior and wishes for a quiver full of them. Our quiver only
held two arrows but they are truly a blessing from the Lord.

Hear, O sons, the instruction of a father, and give attention that you may gain understanding. When I was a son to my father, ... he taught me and said to me, "Let your heart hold fast my words; keep my commandments and live."   *Proverbs 4:1, 3a, 4*

Part of the strength and wisdom in the family unit is the responsibility and privilege the parents have to pass on spiritual truth to their children. We see this at work here as Solomon prepares to share wisdom with his sons and reflects on how his father David instructed him.

Notice that David shared God's commandments with Solomon in spite of his past moral failures dealing with Bathsheba. Parents have a responsibility to share God's word with their children regardless of their past shortcomings. In fact, when parents are transparent about their sins with their children, that openness provides the children with an example of how to deal with their own sin.

We can pass on spiritual truth to our children or others within our sphere of influence in both formal and informal ways. Formal ways include church attendance, a devotional thought before a meal or a scheduled family Bible study time. Although these methods are great for systematically exposing your children to the Word of God, don't miss the power behind informal instruction of spiritual principles.

Informal opportunities occur as life happens. The newscaster describes a crime and you relate it to sin and sin's consequences. You share what spoke to you from Sundays' sermon as you drive home in the car with the family. During a family outing at a restaurant, you ask the server if there is something you can pray about for him or her. You share a thought from where you have been reading or studying. The opportunities are endless. However, we do have to be walking in the Spirit and constantly on the lookout for teachable moments. They are there; we just have to seize them!

David and Solomon were good examples to us in passing on spiritual truth. As we pass truth on to our sons and daughters, let's pray that they catch the same vision and pass it on also.

*But I want you to understand that Christ is the head of every man,
and the man is the head of a woman, and God is the head of Christ.*
I Corinthians 11:3
*Wives, be subject to your own husbands, as to the Lord. Husbands,
love your wives, just as Christ also loved the church and gave
Himself up for her.*   *Ephesians 5:22, 25*

The Biblical command for the wife to submit to the husband
has been maligned by many outside the Christian faith and
misunderstood by many inside the faith. We readily recognize the
need and benefit of leadership positions in government, business,
and the military. So why do some take exception with God directing
the man to be the leader or head of the family unit?

We know from Scripture that Jesus is the beloved Son of
God. The Apostle Paul tells us that God is the head of Christ. When
mankind was made in the image of God, perhaps this Lover-
Submitter relationship in the Godhead was transferred to the
husband-wife relationship. We know that the Father and the Son are
equal in importance and personhood, but they serve different roles.
Likewise, the husband and the wife are of equal importance in God's
sight but each is given a different function.

Jesus is our example in all matters pertaining to life. The
husband is to love the wife as Jesus loved the church. If a man
selflessly cares for his wife up to and including giving his life for
her, she will have no problem submitting to that kind of love and
leadership. A Christ-like man will always value the opinions of his
spouse, but the decisions in the household fall on his shoulders. As
such, God will hold him accountable for his leadership and hold the
wife accountable for her submission to him.

When Mary was pregnant with Jesus, an angel revealed to
Mary and Joseph separately that the conception originated from God.
However, when the family needed to move to Egypt for their safety,
the angel spoke only to Joseph, the head of the family. Similarly, the
angel communicated to Joseph when it was time to return home. If
each spouse fulfills their Biblical role in marriage, the home can be
heaven on earth.

But when David returned to bless his household, Michal, the daughter of Saul came out to meet David and said, "How the king of Israel distinguished himself today! He uncovered himself today in the eyes of his servants' maids as one of the foolish ones shamelessly uncovers himself!"   II Samuel 6:20

It was a day of celebration in Israel. The Ark of the Covenant was being brought into Jerusalem. King David joined in the festivities by leaping and dancing before the Lord. Michal, one of David's wives, grew up in a king's household and was disgusted by the perceived shameless behavior of her husband. She told him so. David responded.

In his marriage book <u>Love and Respect</u>, Dr. Eggerichs calls similar scenarios the start of the Crazy Cycle. The husband withholds love from his wife while the wife withholds respect from her husband. Eggerich views the wife's greatest need as love and the husband's as respect, so the situation worsens as each withholds what the other needs.

In our story Michal is clearly disrespecting her husband. David has returned home to bless his household and Michal throws some hurtful, denigrating barbs at him. David justifies his actions to her but we don't know what happens after that. Regardless, this is the classic start of the Crazy Cycle.

In our day of the God-ordained one man and one woman marriage, it is imperative that we maintain a healthy marriage relationship by being sensitive to each other's needs. Christ-like love demands that we meet the need of our mate whether our need is met or not. The stakes are too high to ignore an unhealthy marriage and let the Crazy Cycle continue. Did this incident between David and Michal and the fallout that occurred have any bearing on David's great sin with Bathsheba? We don't know, but it is safe to say that if the Crazy Cycle keeps spinning faster and faster, the marriage will be destroyed.

Nevertheless, let each individual among you also love his own wife even as himself; and let the wife see to it that she respect her husband.[1]

[1]Ephesians 5:33

1. If you are married, would you say you and your spouse are both growing together in Christ? If yes, then praise the Lord and keep pressing forward! If no, would you say that you and your spouse are in a Crazy Cycle that is spinning out of control? If so, prayer and patience are needed. Professional counseling might also be required. Husband, what is one way you can show love to your wife today? Wife, what is one way you can show respect to your husband today?

2. If you are not married, but want to be, prayer and patience are also needed. Don't get ahead of God in this area of your life. Your best preparation for a godly marriage, if God wills it, is for you to focus on growing in Christ-likeness. A needy man marrying a needy woman seldom has a good outcome. However, if both spouses are mature in their faith, they will be able to deal with the challenges of marriage in a godly manner and thrive.

Prayer Starter: As a bride to the perfect husband Jesus, I come to You for wisdom and encouragement in my marriage, or my desire to be married. Help me to see my situation through Your eyes. Show me what I need to do to...

I came that they might have life and might have it abundantly. I am
the good shepherd; the good shepherd lays down His life for the
sheep.   *John 10:10b-11*

What does an abundant life look like? Some might equate it
to a month-long vacation on the Riviera. Others might say that the
manifest presence of the fruit of the Spirit in our lives results in a life
of abundance. We know for certain that Jesus is the best example
we have of what an abundant life should look like. What was there
about Jesus' life that set Him apart from all others? I believe the
primary element that characterized Jesus' life was His willingness to
lay down His life for the sheep. He poured out His life in and for
others. In return He experienced abundant life and modeled that life
for us.

Abundant refers to a plentiful supply. Our world system
teaches that abundance comes from receiving. Jesus said it was
more blessed to give than to receive. Jesus gave a great description
of abundance in this context of giving: *Give, and it will be given to*
you; good measure, pressed down, shaken together, running over,
they will pour into your lap; For by your standard of measure, it will
be measured to you in return.[1] In God's economy, the one who loses
his life for God's sake is the one who finds life. [2] And that life is
found in abundance.

Would you say Paul experienced abundant life? His life was
hard, but it was abundant. He said to the members of the Corinthian
church: *And I will most gladly spend and be expended for your*
souls.[3] Paul invested his resources and time in people, as did Jesus.
When Jesus entrusted us with the Great Commission, He blessed us
with the key to discovering abundant life on earth.

[1]Luke 6:38   [2]Matthew 10:39   [3]II Corinthians 12:15a

And He gave some as apostles, and some as prophets, and some as evangelists, and some as pastors and teachers, for the equipping of the saints for the work of service, to the building up of the body of Christ ... to a mature man ...   *Ephesians 4:11-13*

Paul here addresses the church at Ephesus concerning its role as disciple makers. The primary thrust of the Great Commission is to make disciples, so the Ephesian believers needed that focus. Paul pictures the church as the local body of Christ with each member performing its specialized function. The pastoral and lay leadership exist to equip the believers for the work of ministry. But the overall goal is that each person in the body grows to become a mature disciple.

Successful churches offer all the instruction and training needed for a new believer to become a disciple. A new member's class will acquaint the convert with the basic doctrines and disciplines of the faith. Bible study classes will be offered on Sunday or during the week to provide Bible-based life application and to encourage the believer through fellowship. A witnessing class is offered in which you learn and practice a gospel presentation. All the disciple building blocks are in place but how many new believers have the discipline and desire to actively engage in the program?

Something is still missing. What I haven't stressed is that *the proper working of each individual part causes the growth of the body for the building up of itself in love.*[1] The church is only as effective as the individuals that make up the body. Programs aren't enough. We must discuss the role of the individual to fully understand the model.

[1]Ephesians 4:16b

*And the things which you have heard from me in the presence of
many witnesses, these entrust to faithful men, who will be able to
teach others also.*   *II Timothy 2:2*

   Here Paul is writing an individual pastor, not a church. Paul
has spent years pouring into Timothy's life. He said of Timothy: *But
you followed my teaching, conduct, purpose, faith, patience, love,
perseverance, persecutions, and sufferings.*[1] Timothy learned and
followed these things because Paul taught and lived out godliness in
his presence. This process is often referred to as one-to-one
discipleship.
   Paul reminds Timothy that the end goal is not just to become
a disciple, but to share what you learned with others so they also will
be disciples. As he shared Biblical content and life skills with
Timothy, Paul was also modeling how Timothy could share these
truths with others.
   Now Timothy was to instill in his "faithful men" that they in
turn must invest in the lives of "others also". This process is often
referred to as multiplication.
   The benefits of a godly mentor in a new believer's life cannot
be overstated. Anyone will be more likely to share troubling hurts,
habits and hang-ups with a concerned individual before he or she
shares with strangers in a classroom setting. Many aspects of the
Christian life are more effectively caught from a mentor than taught
by a teacher. A church's discipleship program is more likely to
positively impact the growth of a babe in Christ if a mature believer
is concurrently walking alongside the new Christian.
   Ideally, a new believer is connected to a mentor in the
church. They should work through a study together dealing with the
basic doctrines and disciplines of the Christian life. The new
believer should also be introduced to a group Bible study and any
discipleship classes available so he or she can benefit from other
individual members in the body. The mentor is responsible for the
discipleship process but the church body co-labors with the mentor.
   Where do you fit in this model? Are you actively involved?

[1]II Timothy 3:10-11a

For I am confident of this very thing, that he who began a good work in you will perfect it until the day of Christ Jesus. For it is only right for me to feel this way about you all, because I have you in my heart, since both in my imprisonment and in the defense and confirmation of the gospel, you all are partakers of grace with me.

Philippians 1:6-7

Paul is well known for his evangelistic efforts during his three missionary journeys. However, a lesser recognized strength is his consistent follow-up with the new believers. In fact, the stated intent of his second missionary journey was *to visit the brethren in every city in which we proclaimed the word of the Lord, and see how they are.*[1] Only after he and his companions visited the new churches did the Spirit lead him into Macedonia to proclaim the gospel. The first city in which he shared the gospel was Philippi.

About ten years after his initial trip to Philippi, Paul wrote his letter to the Philippian church from a prison in Rome. Paul's confidence that the Christians in Philippi had continued to mature was based on the Holy Spirit's presence in their lives and God using Paul's efforts to disciple them. Several times in the letter's introduction he mentioned that they were often in his thoughts and prayers.

Paul was able to keep in touch with them through the many messengers they sent to Paul with gifts during his missionary journeys and his imprisonment in Rome. In fact, one of the purposes of this letter was to acknowledge and thank them for the recent gift he had received from Epaphroditus.[2] He also wrote that he intended to send Timothy to them and that he hoped to visit them soon as well.[3]

Why did Paul work so hard at follow-up? When a believer becomes grounded in his faith he learns to accept his responsibility in the Lord to disciple others. He partners with brothers like Paul and the result is the furtherance of the gospel. We need to ask ourselves where we are in this process and work toward being an approved workman who labors with God in His harvest. A first step might be to surrender to God in this matter through prayer.

[1]Acts 15:36   [2]Philippians 4:15, 18   [3]Philippians 2:23-24

*I am writing to you, little children, because your sins are forgiven
you for His name's sake. I am writing to you, fathers, because you
know Him who has been from the beginning, I am writing to you,
young men, because you have overcome the evil one. I have written
to you, children, because you know the Father.   I John 2:12-13*

The phrase "little children" literally means "born ones" and
refers to all believers. The second reference to "children" uses a
different Greek word which represents an immature Christian. Both
of these uses of "children" have a spiritual connotation. Notice that
John uses the term father, not men. Father excludes all single men
and married men without children. John has in mind spiritual
fathers, those who have spiritual children. He is referring to three
different levels of spiritual maturity: children (new believers), young
men (disciples), and fathers (disciple-makers).

One goal of the Christian life is to grow to fatherhood. Paul
states that the purpose of the Church is to grow believers to *a mature
man, to the measure of the stature which belongs to the fullness of
Christ*.[1] The fullness of Christ certainly involves leading people to
Christ and discipling them. Jesus said *follow Me and I will make you
fishers of men*.[2]

Another way men become fathers is by adoption. Paul
referred to Timothy as his son in the faith, but he did not lead
Timothy to Christ. When Paul met Timothy on his second
missionary journey he was already a disciple. Paul recruited
Timothy to accompany him and over time trained him to be a
disciple-maker.

If you are a follower of Christ, you fall in one of these three
categories. Which one is it? You can share the gospel and lead
someone to Christ at any stage of maturity. But if you are to fulfill
the Great Commission (make disciples) you should ensure the
spiritual newborn matures, as any good father would.

[1]Ephesians 4:11-13   [2]Matthew 4:19

1. Does your church have a discipleship program? If so, list the various classes that your church offers. Do you feel led to assist or attend any of these classes? Why?

2. Have your thoughts on what Jesus meant by an "abundant life" changed this week? In your own words, write below what you think the Biblical meaning of abundant life is. Would you say you are experiencing abundant life? Why or why not?

Prayer Starter: Father God, I am thankful for the offer of an abundant life available through Jesus, Your Son. Help me to experience that spiritual abundance on a daily basis as I seek to be a disciple and make disciples. I pray that You would lead me to…

For whatever is born of God overcomes the world; and this is the victory that has overcome the world – our faith.   I John 5:4

If you are a follower of Christ, do you see yourself as someone who has overcome the world? Many believers would say they have been overcome by Satan's world system, rather than being victors over the world. When we trusted in Jesus we received much more than just forgiveness and a home in heaven. We also received the power to say no to sin and yes to righteousness.

Knowing this, that our old self was crucified with Him, that our body of sin might be done away with, that we should no longer be slaves to sin.[1] Paul is communicating doctrine, or truth, in this statement. In the Garden of Eden, man was given one commandment so that he could choose to love and obey God. Our old self has been crucified with Christ, but we can give it permission to influence our lives. Having the Holy Spirit in our lives does not compel us to obey; obedience is still a choice so we can demonstrate our love for God.

Do you not know that when you present yourselves to someone as slaves for obedience, you are slaves of the one whom you obey?[2] More doctrine. It is our responsibility to go on the offensive and *present our members as instruments of righteousness to God.*[3] Are your eyes reading the Bible daily? Are your feet taking you places where you can fellowship with other believers? Is your mouth praying regularly to God and sharing the gospel with others? Are your hands serving the Lord? Are your ears hearing what is godly and wholesome?

Rely on God's grace and the power of the Holy Spirit within you to make right choices. Choose obedience and appropriate all that Jesus bought for you on the cross. Be an overcomer!

[1]Romans 6:6   [2]Romans 6:16a   [3]Romans 6:13

But put on the Lord Jesus Christ and make no provision for the flesh to fulfill its lusts.
                                                    Romans 13:14

Many times in Scripture when we are commanded to put on Christ, we are also challenged to put off the flesh. The verses may contrast putting on the new man and putting off the old man[1] or submitting to God and resisting the devil[2], but both thoughts are present. Both actions are needed.

The believer who has his daily time with the Lord in prayer and the Word but knowingly has left the door open for some fleshly appetite is insincere and headed for trouble. Similarly, Christians who through shear willpower crucify the flesh and its lusts without an abiding reliance on Christ's presence will eventually fall.

Paul states that the flesh and the Spirit are in opposition to each other[3]. Every believer is engaged in battle. Victory demands that we submit to the Spirit's power and presence in our lives while minimizing opportunities for the flesh to rise up.

During the course of a day, temptations will present themselves as an unavoidable fact of life. If we are walking in the Spirit, we will find God's escape route[4] and not sin. If however, we allow ourselves to see, hear and touch the unclean day after day, then we arouse the flesh, while subduing the Spirit, to our peril.

[1]Ephesians 4:22-24   [2]James 4:7   [3]Galatians 5:17
[4]I Corinthians 10:13

But thanks be to God that though you were slaves of sin, you became obedient from the heart to that form of teaching to which you were committed, and having been freed from sin, you became slaves of righteousness.   Romans 6:17-18

Frank Sinatra popularized the song with the refrain "I did it my way". Many people today ascribe to that notion. Biblically, a more accurate statement is either: "I did it God's way" or "I did it Satan's way". While on Earth, we are slaves of God or slaves of Satan. We serve The God or the god of this world. We obey righteousness or sin. We have no other choices. We are not autonomous. Rather, we are involved, knowingly or unwittingly, in a battle for the souls of humanity. We align in the battle with God or Satan.

Jesus said: *No one can serve two masters; for either he will hate the one and love the other, or he will hold to one and despise the other. You cannot serve God and mammon.*[1] Mammon is riches, one of the carrots that Satan uses to ensnare and enslave us. None of us should deceive ourselves into thinking we are serving God while we dabble with sin. We must choose to serve God. If we straddle the morality fence, our default setting is to Satan's side. Our sin nature will tip the balance toward Satan if given the chance.

As obedient children, do not be conformed to the former lusts which were yours in your ignorance, but like the Holy One who called you, be holy yourselves also in all your behavior.[2] Life involves a choice: God or Satan. Resist being conformed to your former lusts. Submit to God and the result will be holy behavior.

[1]Matthew 6:24   [2]I Peter 1:14-15

Give me neither poverty nor riches; feed me with the food that is my portion, lest I be full and deny Thee and say, "Who is the Lord?" or lest I be in want and steal, and profane the name of my God.

Proverbs 30:8b-9

This request is part of a prayer to God from Agur. Even though nothing is known about him, I appreciate his prayer. It reminds me of a part of the Lord's model prayer: *And do not lead us into temptation, but deliver us from evil.*[1] For Agur the temptation would be having too little or too much materially. With too much he fears independence with no perceived need for God. With too little he fears dishonoring God by relying on his sinful nature to meet his needs rather than depending on God.

Throughout the Bible we encounter godly people with too much and with too little. The apostle Paul said: *in any and every circumstance I have learned the secret of being filled and going hungry, both of having abundance and suffering need.*[2] Paul's secret was to totally depend on Christ in all situations. And I am sure Agur would have also depended on God if he found himself at either extreme of the materialism scale. What is admirable about Agur is his recognition of a weakness and his desire to overcome that weakness and walk with his God. He pled with God to not allow him in situations that might tempt him to turn his back on God.

Earlier in the book of Proverbs, Solomon warns: *Watch over your heart with all diligence, for from it flow the springs of life.*[3] Agur had identified a vulnerable area of his heart and was proactively dealing with it. May we do likewise!

[1]Matthew 6:13   [2]Philippians 4:12b   [3]Proverbs 4:23

For My people have committed two evils: They have forsaken Me,
the fountain of living waters, to hew for themselves cisterns, broken
cisterns, that can hold no water.   *Jeremiah 2:13*

Everyone wants a full cistern. We all have an emptiness that needs to be filled. We are aware of the void and thus seek to fill it. Life's biggest question is: What are you doing to fill your cistern?

In Biblical days cisterns were dug out of the earth or hewn out of rock to collect water during the rainy season. Empty cisterns were sometimes used as prisons, as with Joseph when his brothers threw him in the pit which had no water.

The Lord has the only cistern that really works with the only water, the Holy Spirit, Who really satisfies. When Israel rejected God as their cistern, they had to turn elsewhere to meet that need. The evil associated with forsaking God will always lead to a second evil of pursuing other avenues to get a full cistern.

Today, as then, a popular broken cistern is sexual immorality. Solomon advised his sons to *drink water from your own cistern.*[1] God has provided the marriage bed to legitimately satisfy one's sexual needs. When we look outside of marriage to meet that need, we err.

Another broken cistern today, as then, is alcohol and drugs. Paul said: *do not get drunk with wine ... but be filled with the Spirit.*[2] Regardless how much alcohol you pour into your cistern today, tomorrow you will still feel the emptiness. However, as we walk in obedience to Christ, His Spirit fills us with a fulfillment and satisfaction beyond comparison.

Many temptations simply involve the urge to build your own cistern. Since worldly broken cisterns hold no water, they always end up serving instead as a prison in which we are enslaved to our evil desires. Seek a Spirit-filled life and avoid an empty enslavement to sin.

[1]Proverbs 5:15   [2]Ephesians 5:18

1. In week 1 you were asked to identify an area in your life where the "old man" reigned. Have you made any progress in putting off the old man? Can you think of positive actions you can take to put on the new man to help with the struggle? One suggestion would be to find Bible verses that address that topic and memorize them.

2. Which illustration best depicts your struggle: a broken cistern or enslavement? Why?

Prayer Starter: Father God, I praise You for Your righteousness today. Thank you that You want me to grow in Christ-likeness. Help me to spend more time in your Word this week as I seek to feed the new man and starve the old man. By Your grace, I plan to …

And He said to them, "Go into all the world and preach the gospel
to all creation.   Mark 16:15
Teaching them to observe all that I commanded you...
                                                    Matthew 28:20a

    The Great Commission encompasses several actions: preaching the gospel, baptizing new believers, and teaching the believers. Preaching communicates the gospel to unbelievers, whereas teaching instructs believers in the Word. We tend to think of preaching and teaching as occurring to groups of people. We attend a church service and the preacher shares a sermon. We visit a Bible study class and the teacher shares a Bible lesson. However, the Great Commission is given to individual Christians who happen to be part of a local fellowship of believers in a church where preaching and teaching occur.

    Any mature follower of Christ will be able to preach and teach, not necessarily to a group, but to another individual. Remember, preaching is just sharing the gospel message and teaching is just expounding the truths of the Scriptures. The Matthew account of the Great Commission says: *Go therefore and make disciples.* In order to make a disciple you have to be a disciple. You cannot teach someone to be a plumber if you are not a plumber. So, to make a disciple you have to know how to share the gospel and then teach that new believer the basic truths of the Bible so spiritual growth occurs.

    Paul exhorted Timothy: *Be diligent to present yourself approved to God as a workman who does not need to be ashamed, handling accurately the word of truth.*[1] A lack of knowledge and experience with the word of God results in an ashamed worker who will one day give account of his life to God. Let's be diligent students of the Bible so God can use us to fulfill the Great Commission.

[1]II Timothy 2:15

"Arise, go to Nineveh the great city, and cry against it, for their wickedness has come up before Me." But Jonah rose up to flee to Tarshish from the presence of the Lord. Jonah 1:2-3a

When God created mankind in His own image, one characteristic man inherited was free will. God allows us to choose, just as He chooses. He gives mankind numerous commandments but He doesn't force obedience. A sovereign king in medieval times would require instant obedience from his subjects. God is not that way. God desires our obedience. He exercises His sovereignty and omnipotence to encourage obedience, but does not coerce obedience during our lives on Earth.

We see this truth played out in the story of Jonah. God commanded Jonah to go to Nineveh but Jonah disobeyed and went elsewhere. God then commanded the wind to foment a great storm, a great fish to swallow Jonah, a plant to grow and shade Jonah, and a worm to attack the plant. The only disobedient element from creation in this story was Jonah.

All of God's creation is hard-wired to obey God except man and angels. When Satan and his band of angels rebelled against God they were cast out of heaven.[1] The angels have chosen sides and now the battle for the hearts of mankind rages.

Mankind exercises free will toward God on two levels. The first level involves the initial decision to accept Jesus Christ as Savior and Lord which leads to salvation. The second level involves the believer's moment by moment decision to be obedient to the Holy Spirit which leads to sanctification and spiritual growth. The Ninevites' decision to repent was similar to a first-level decision today, whereas Jonah's decision to disobey was a second-level decision.

The presence of the Holy Spirit in the believer's life enables the believer to be heart-wired to God. The challenge for us is to keep our hearts soft toward God. Let's exercise our free will by remaining responsive to God while sharing the gospel with those who need to make that first-level commitment to Jesus.

[1]Revelation 12:9

It was revealed to them (prophets) *that they were not serving themselves, but you, in these things which now have been announced to you through those who preached the gospel to you by the Holy Spirit sent from heaven – things into which angels long to look.*
I Peter 1:12

Angels are amazed at the grace of God expressed through the gospel message. Peter reminds us in his second letter that *God did not spare angels when they sinned, but cast them into hell.*[1] The angels who rebelled and were cast out of heaven received judgment, not grace. Given the amount of revelation they had concerning God, that sentence shouldn't surprise us.

God uses angels in some ways to advance the gospel but the primary responsibility falls on human followers of Christ. *Therefore, we are ambassadors for Christ, as though God were entreating through us; we beg you on behalf of Christ, be reconciled to God.*[2] The angels have never experienced God's grace to the degree the human race has. In His wisdom, God chose human-to-human communication as the primary method of propagating the gospel.

An angel announced to the shepherds the birth of a Savior, who is Christ the Lord. An angel dispatched Philip to a rendezvous with an Ethiopian eunuch so the gospel could be shared. An angel freed Peter from prison so he could continue to preach the gospel. An angel struck Herod with death and *the word of the Lord continued to grow and be multiplied.*[3] Finally, *there is joy in the presence of the angels of God over one sinner who repents.*[4]

Angels are on the periphery of evangelism but we have no record of an angel ever presenting the gospel to anyone. They are excluded; we are included. The most important task in the universe, the Great Commission, has been given to Christians, not angels. Angels are standing by to help. How often are they called into action on your behalf?

[1]II Peter 2:4a   [2]II Corinthians 5:20   [3]Acts 12:24   [4]Luke 15:10

Son of man, I have appointed you a watchman to the house of Israel; whenever you hear a word from My mouth, warn them from Me. When I say to the wicked, "You shall surely die"; and you do not warn him or speak out to warn the wicked from his wicked way that he may live, that wicked man shall die in his iniquity, but his blood I will require at your hand.   *Ezekiel 3:17-18*

God conveyed consequences for Ezekiel if he didn't relay God's warnings to the intended audience. As watchmen in New Testament times, we followers of Christ should see impending eternal doom for each nonbeliever in our sphere of influence. We have God's sin warning and His solution to the sin problem. Jesus has commissioned His disciples to share His gospel with the world. That charge should weigh heavy on our hearts as we rub elbows with lost humanity.

Paul spoke this to the Ephesian elders: *Therefore I testify to you this day, that I am innocent of the blood of all men. For I did not shrink from declaring to you the whole purpose of God.*[1] I suspect Paul was referring to Ezekiel's watchman role when he said he was innocent of the blood of all men. I have shunned too many Spirit-prompted witnessing opportunities to make that claim. But whenever Paul was led by the Spirit to speak God's word, he spoke, as did Ezekiel.

God will require an accounting of our lives at the Judgment Seat of Christ.[2] Based on the Great Commission, all believers have been designated as watchmen. We will receive a reward or we will suffer loss depending on how faithful we have been to what God has called each of us to do.[3] Let's ask God to give us His heart for the souls of men and women. Let's be obedient watchmen.

[1]Acts 20:26-27   [2]II Corinthians 5:10   [3]I Corinthians 3:14-15

You are the salt of the earth; but if the salt has become tasteless,
how will it be made salty again? ... Nor do men light a lamp, and put
it under the peck-measure, but on the lampstand.
                                                    Matthew 5:13a, 15a

When a person understands and responds to the gospel of Jesus Christ, life suddenly involves a relationship with the Creator, rather than just interaction with His creation. This new perspective should cause the believer to become salt and light in the world. A newly found meaning in life adds zest and enlightens the mind and heart.

The follower of Christ moves from darkness to light, from a life controlled by Satan to a life submitted to the Holy Spirit living within. However, the evil one's desire is to thwart the believer's obedience and spiritual growth. When Satan is successful, the believer retakes control of his or her life and turns a deaf ear to the Spirit's leading. Over time, the thoughts and habits observed during the pre-Christ era re-emerge and no discernible lifestyle difference exists between this Christian and any non-Christian. The salt has become tasteless.

Other believers recognize the benefits of remaining separate from the world's system of thinking and acting, and resist Satan's worldly temptations. *If we walk in the light as He Himself is in the light, we have fellowship with one another.*[1] They regularly enjoy time in the Word, prayer, and fellowship with other Christians. Soon, they seldom associate with unbelievers and are never deliberate in sharing the gospel with non-Christians. Rather than putting their light on a lampstand, they hide it within the church walls.

For salt and light to be effective, the salt must retain its saltiness and be spread while the light must shine in the darkness. Paul refers to the gospel as *the power of God for salvation to everyone who believes.*[2] Before the gospel can be believed, it must be heard – telling is the job of those whom Jesus has called to be salt and light.

[1] I John 1:7a   [2] Romans 1:16b

1. On a scale of 1 to 5 (highest), how prepared are you to share the gospel? You can always start by becoming familiar with a gospel tract like "The Four Spiritual Laws" or "Steps to Peace with God". Carry a tract on your person and ask God for an opportunity to read through its contents with someone.

2. All believers will one day give an account of our lives to God. Since Jesus died to offer salvation to the world and then made us His ambassadors, expect that our execution of that ambassadorship will be the primary criteria for our evaluation. It is never too late to start giving, praying and witnessing to fulfill our roles as ambassadors. What do you need to start doing to make you a better ambassador of the gospel?

Prayer Starter: Lord God, I acknowledge that you have made me your ambassador and your watchman to share the Gospel of Jesus Christ. Instill in me Your heart for souls. Help me over the next few days to better equip myself to share the gospel by…

Since I know, O my God, that Thou triest the heart and delightest in uprightness, I, in the integrity of my heart, have willingly offered all these things; so now with joy I have seen Thy people, who are present here, make their offerings willingly to Thee.
I Chronicles 29:17

Although God didn't allow David to build the temple because of bloodshed in his past, David was allowed to gather the construction materials that Solomon would need for the project. David gave from the king's treasury and the people also gave from what they had. Their example provides an excellent model of the attitudes God is looking for in our giving today.

David gave with integrity. His motives were pure. He wasn't trying to impress others with the largess of his contributions to the temple construction. David sincerely loved God and wanted to be a part of something that would glorify God long after his death.

David and the people gave willingly. David initiated the project and the people wholeheartedly followed his lead. No one felt forced to give. There are some churches and organizations that employ coercion tactics or guilt trips to elicit finances. Here, the project was worthy and the response was genuine.

Those who gave exuded joy. David and the Israelites could have reasoned that giving was the right thing to do, and thus their offering would have been willing. But the presence of joy involves the heart and not just the mind. David observed in his prayer that God is concerned with the heart. Paul noted that *God loves a cheerful giver.*[1] Willingness is an important attribute of a giver, but joy is the goal.

[1]II Corinthians 9:7b

Beware of practicing your righteousness before men to be noticed by them; otherwise you have no reward with your Father who is in heaven.
                                                                Matthew 6:1

If Ananias and Sapphira had applied this teaching of Jesus to their financial gift to the church, they would probably have been alive at the end of Acts 5. You recall that they sold a piece of property, gave part of the proceeds to the church, but portrayed that the amount given was the full selling price.[1] They highly valued the praise of men and the security of riches; it cost them their lives.

Jesus encourages us to give, pray and fast but warns us to do these righteous acts secretly. Man sees what is done openly; God sees what is done secretly. The problem is that we often care more about what man sees than what God sees. We enjoy the applause of man. We value being recognized by our peers and superiors. Praise strokes our ego and it feels good. We are impressed with ourselves and want others to be also.

A corollary of Jesus' maxim above is: *Humble yourself in the presence of the Lord, and He will exalt you.*[2] One way to humble yourself is not to mention to others a gift of generosity, or a season of prayer, or a period of fasting. Jesus also said: *Let your light shine before men in such a way that they may see your good works, and glorify your Father who is in heaven.*[3] The key to determining whether to share an act of righteousness with others is answering the question: Who is going to get the glory?

Barnabas also sold land and publicly laid the proceeds at the apostles' feet.[4] God was obviously glorified through his actions. However, since Ananias and Sapphira were clearly struggling over the gift, they would have been better served to have given their gift anonymously. Anonymity keeps pride in check.

[1]Acts 5:8   [2]James 4:10   [3]Matthew 5:16   [4]Acts 4:36-37

*Beloved, I pray that in all respects you may prosper and be in good
health, just as your soul prospers.*   *III John 2*

     This is one of only two verses in the New Testament where
"prosper" is used. I have recently started using this verse when I
write a personal note on a "get well" card. I like it because it is a
prayer for prosperity and good health but it balances that wish with
the more important desire that the person's soul prospers.

     When you think of Jesus and the disciples you certainly don't
think of financial prosperity. They had all walked away from their
jobs. They probably depended primarily on the generosity of others
for their basic needs. They were focused on Kingdom work and
gave no thought to material prosperity.

     Whenever Jesus talked about the rich, his theme was "*It is
hard for a rich man to enter the kingdom of heaven.*"[1] When Paul
addressed rich Christians, he instructed them "*not to be conceited or
to fix their hope on the uncertainty of riches.*"[2] Paul gave his attitude
toward prosperity when he said "*If we have food and covering, with
these we shall be content.*"[3] Prosperity was seen as a potential
stumbling block for both the saved and the unsaved.

     Today a certain level of prosperity is needed just to provide
for a family. However, if Paul were to visit us today and see our
standard of living, I suspect he would categorize us as rich. Jesus
said "*...And from everyone who has been given much shall much be
required.*"[4]

     The only other New Testament verse using prosperity is this:
"*On the first day of every week let each one of you put aside and
save, as he may prosper, that no collections be made when I come.*"[5]
Paul was encouraging them to set aside a portion of their financial
prosperity to be used in Kingdom work. He would say the same to
us today.

[1]Matthew 19:23   [2] I Timothy 6:17   [3]I Timothy 6:8   [4]Luke 12:48
[5] I Corinthians 16:2

For where your treasure is, there will your heart be also.
$\qquad\qquad\qquad\qquad\qquad\qquad$ *Matthew 6:21*

     Jesus shared this spiritual principle as part of the Sermon on the Mount. Earlier in the sermon He refers to five Old Testament laws and enlarges the scope of each, giving a more spiritual perspective. As an example, *"You have heard that the ancients were told, 'You shall not commit murder ... ' but I say to you that everyone who is angry with his brother shall be guilty before the court."* [1] Jesus always moves from the letter of the law to the spirit of the law. If Jesus had addressed the tithe, the statement may have read: You have heard that it was said, *Bring the whole tithe into the storehouse,*[2] but I say to you ... How would you finish this statement?

     In Matthew 6, Jesus gave additional warnings and encouragements regarding giving. He warned us not to give so we will be noticed by other people. Rather, we should give secretly, knowing that God sees in secret and will reward us. Jesus also stated that we cannot serve both God and riches at the same time. We must seek God first in everything, depending on Him to meet our basic needs in life, rather than riches. Finally, He encouraged us to lay up treasures in heaven, rather than on earth. We will be rewarded for that action in heaven, but more importantly, giving to God will help us focus our hearts on eternal matters while on earth.

     Jesus ended His clarification of the five laws with this statement: *Therefore you are to be perfect, as your heavenly Father is perfect.*[3] The goal of sanctification is that we become like Christ. Perhaps a possible ending to the hypothetical statement could be..., but I say to you, give, as I have given to you.

[1] Matthew 5:21-22a   [2] Malachi 3:10a   [3] Matthew 5:48

And He saw a certain poor widow putting in two small copper coins. And He said, "Truly I say to you, this poor widow put in more than all of them; for they all out of their surplus put into the offering, but she out of her poverty put in all that she had to live on."

Luke 21:2-4

In God's economy, our monetary offerings to Him have their value based on our heart, not the size of the gift. After all, God has unlimited resources available to meet any need in His church. When the widow gave all that she had to live on, she was placing her life in God's hands and trusting Him to meet her needs. Her heart was surrendered to God. In eternity we will discover how Jesus met her need.

When Jesus encountered the rich young ruler who said he had kept the law, Jesus asked him to sell all his possessions and give it to the poor to receive eternal life.[1] The issue once again was the young man's heart. He put his trust in his wealth and he wouldn't release his grip on money to accept Jesus' offer.

Finally, consider Zaccheus. After an encounter with Jesus, the tax collector decided to give half of his possessions to the poor. In response, Jesus said to him: *"Today salvation has come to this house."*[2] A changed heart caused Zaccheus to see his possessions in a different way. His goal changed from accumulating wealth to using his wealth to bless others since he had been blessed by God.

The monetary value of our gifts to God doesn't impress Him. However as our heart commitment to Him grows, we look for ways to increase our giving in response to His love for us. Whether you are poor or rich, look for ways to invest financially in God's Kingdom. You won't regret anything given with a good heart.

[1]Luke 18:22   [2]Luke 19:9a

1. If you gave to a charitable cause, the recipients wouldn't care about your motive for the gift. Why do you think God is so concerned about our heart and attitudes in giving?

2. Is God leading you to increase your giving to Kingdom causes? If so, please annotate below what action you will take.

Prayer Starter: Lord, I acknowledge that You are the owner of all I have and I am your steward. Thank you for entrusting me with all that I have. I pray that the Holy Spirit will confirm to my heart as I consider giving …

"But regarding the fact that the dead rise again, have you not read in the book of Moses, in the passage about the burning bush, how God spoke to him, saying, 'I am the God of Abraham, and the God of Isaac, and the God of Jacob'? He is not the God of the dead, but of the living; you are greatly mistaken."   Mark 12:26-27

God did not say that He **was** the God of Abraham or that He will be the God of Abraham. Rather, I am the God of Abraham – present tense. Since the Sadducees had not grasped the subtlety of the verb tense in Scripture, Jesus pronounced them greatly mistaken. It is proper to consider God as existing in the past, present, and future: *"I am the Alpha and the Omega", says the Lord God, "who is and who was and who is to come, the Almighty."*[1] However, to live the victorious Christian life, we should strive to view God primarily with us in the present.

Many events tie us to the past. Failures, disappointments, hurts, successes, good times, and hard times from the past all work to draw our minds into yesteryear. Perhaps we blame God for painful memories or wish that God had permitted a good experience to last. The Apostle Paul had a lot of baggage from his pre-Christ life. But his goal was to forget what lay behind and always press forward.[2] He lived with Jesus in the present, accepted His forgiveness for the past, and trusted His sovereignty over his life.

Others exclude God from their present life but have plans to include Him in the future. Some think that once they are married and have a family then they will put God first in their life. Truthfully, the best way to prepare for marriage is to mature in Christ now so that you can be a godly husband or wife in the future.

Jesus wants to be your Lord in the here and now. You should be able to speak of His work in and through your life in the present tense, not relying on a relationship in the past or looking forward to a connection with Him in the future. Without a focus on Christ in the present, you are greatly mistaken.

[1]Revelation 1:8   [2]Philippians 3:13-14

I am the vine, you are the branches; he who abides in Me, and I in him, he bears much fruit; for apart from Me you can do nothing.

John 15:5

In response to the polio epidemic in the 1950s, 800-pound machines known as iron lungs were invented. Individuals were laid in the iron lung from the neck down and negative air pressure passively moved air into and out of lungs stricken by the polio virus. Tragically, some died over the years when the iron lung lost power and stopped working.

Jesus is the iron lung for the believer in a spiritual sense. We access His enabling strength by abiding in Him just like the iron lung functions properly by being plugged into an electrical outlet. Abiding in Christ occurs when we spend meaningful time with Him reading and studying the Bible. We abide in Him when we offer prayers of praise and petitions. Private and corporate worship allow us to connect with Jesus in a significant way. Jesus says that we will accomplish nothing for the Kingdom of God without abiding in Him.

The responsibility to exercise the spiritual disciplines to abide in Christ is on our shoulders. As we abide in Him, Jesus will lead us into a life of service and ministry which will bear fruit. But any fruit from our lives comes directly from the Spirit of God working through us and thus God receives the glory. Our job is to abide; the Spirit's job is to produce fruit.

"But he answered and said to his father, 'Look! For so many years I have been serving you, and I have never neglected a command of yours; and yet you have never given me a kid, that I might be merry with my friends; but when this son of yours came, who has devoured your wealth with harlots, you killed the fattened calf for him.'"

Luke 15:29-30

Jesus warned that the entrance to heaven is through a narrow gate. As a believer enters the gate of salvation, he or she finds a narrow path to discipleship as well. Jesus' parable of the prodigal son shows God, the loving father, interacting with his two sons. The younger son was drawn off the path into self-indulgence and the older son has strayed into self-righteousness. Both left the pathway of true discipleship.

The younger son lost sight of all the riches available to him in his father's house and was drawn to the distractions and enticements of the world. He pursued pleasure and forgot the love, joy, peace, and meaningful life that his father offered. Many believers are captivated by materialism and worldly lusts, failing to wholeheartedly pursue all that Christ has purchased for them through His blood.

The older son was doing all the right things but with the wrong motive. Perhaps he was filled with pride because he had been able to keep his father's commands. Whatever the reason, the older son did not have the father's heart. While the father rejoiced to see the younger son repent, the older son was angered.

The father ran to meet the wayward son and left the celebration to reason with the embittered son. God desires that all followers of Jesus remain on the pathway leading to Christ-likeness and will pursue us to that end. The key to avoiding both divergent paths is to stay focused on Jesus who made eternal life and a godly life possible. If we maintain a fresh walk with Jesus the lure of the world will be seen for what it is – shallow and temporary. A vibrant fellowship with Christ will also remind us that whatever good comes from us originates from Him alone. Do you have a daily encounter with Jesus?

For the one who has entered His rest has himself also rested from his works, as God did from His. Let us therefore be diligent to enter that rest, lest anyone fall through following the same example of disobedience.
                                                                Hebrews 4:10-11

A popular farewell remark is "Take it easy." With stories of stress and burnout abounding, we wish rest for our friends and family. The rest spoken of in Hebrews is primarily a resting of the soul in Jesus – relying on Him for strength, direction, and comfort. A word picture Jesus uses is how a branch "abides" in the vine to produce fruit in its time.[1] The vine-branch relationship represents an idyllic rest, in which all the needs of the branch are met by the vine.

Jesus gave this invitation: *Come to Me, all who are weary and heavy-laden, and I will give you rest. Take My yoke upon you, and learn from Me, for I am gentle and humble in heart; and you shall find rest for your souls. For My yoke is easy, and My load is light.*[2] A yoke is used to harness two work animals together. The invitation is to share His yoke, meaning that we agree to go where He is going. As we travel together, He does the heavy lifting, but we are co-laboring with Him. Work is required on our part, but it is an investment in eternal matters that yields a restful soul.

I have a friend that ends his emails with "Keep charging." I prefer that to the more lax farewell. We are challenged to diligently enter into that rest with Christ because there are many false sources of rest drawing us nigh. Put on Christ's yoke today and rest in Him!

[1]John 15:1-5   [2]Matthew 11:28-30

*My well-beloved had a vineyard on a fertile hill. And He dug it all
around, removed its stones, and planted it with the choicest vine.
And he built a tower in the middle of it, and hewed out a wine vat in
it; then He expected it to produce good grapes, but it produced only
worthless ones.*   Isaiah 5:1b, 2

    Our Bible is subdivided into the Old and New Testaments.
The two names imply that the covenant between God and man has
changed. The change is beautifully portrayed by comparing the vine
in the Old Testament with the vine in the New Testament.
    The Psalmist declared that God removed a vine (Israel) from
Egypt, drove out the nations before it, and planted it[1]. Isaiah
expands on the parable and expresses how God was disappointed
that His vine produced bloodshed and distress rather than justice and
righteousness.
    When God gave Israel the Ten Commandments, the covenant
that came with it was that if they obeyed, God would bless[2]. Israel
failed to obey the law, broke their part of the agreement, and thereby
received God's judgment against sin time and time again. Paul
describes the law as our tutor which taught us that we would never
be able to please God because we cannot keep the law[3]. The vine
was never going to be able to produce good fruit based on its own
power and ability. Israel needed a new covenant.
    Jesus describes Himself as the true vine and we are the
branches.[4] If we have admitted our sinfulness, trusted in Jesus to pay
the penalty for our sin, and made Him Lord of our lives, then we
have been engrafted to the Vine. Our strength now flows through
Him, not ourselves. We are living under a new covenant with God,
one based on faith, not works.
    *As you have therefore received Christ Jesus the Lord, so
walk in Him.*[5] We received Christ by faith and we are to grow to
maturity by faith. Let's be careful not to revert back to the old
covenant and live life by our own strength. Instead, let's abide in the
Vine on a daily, moment-by-moment basis and rely on Jesus for
strength and guidance.

[1]Psalm 80:8   [2]Deuteronomy 4:40   [3]Galatians 3:24   [4]John 15:5
[5]Colossians 2:6

1. On a scale of 1 to 5 (highest), how would you rate your perceived dependence on Jesus in your daily life? If you answered a five then you probably agree with Jesus that without Him you can do nothing. Would you agree that the more you abide in Jesus, the greater the perceived dependence number would be? Why or why not?

2. List the spiritual disciplines you currently employ to help you abide in Christ. Do you need to add any disciplines to your current practices? If so, what?

Prayer Starter: Lord Jesus, I want my life with You to be like the branch with the vine. I want to visualize myself as being yoked with You as I go through each day. Show me if there is any spiritual discipline I should add to help me abide more in you? ...

Moreover, by them thy servant is warned; In keeping them there is great reward. Who can discern his errors? Acquit me of hidden faults. Also keep back Thy servant from presumptuous sins; Let them not rule over me.   Psalm 19:11-13a

In Psalm 19 David praises God's revelation to man through His creation and His Word. David also mentions two types of sin that plague mankind: hidden faults and presumptuous sins.

Hidden faults are those sins that the individual is committing but he or she is not aware that they are sins. Saul's persecution of Christians was likely a hidden fault. Jesus revealed his sin to him on the road to Damascus. Prior to that revelation, Saul believed that he was pleasing God by imprisoning Christians. For many Christians, it may be some time before they learn that Christ commanded us not to worry because it shows we are not trusting the Father to meet our needs. Until God reveals these hidden faults as sins, they are lurking incognito.

Presumptuous sins are generally those committed with knowledge, deliberation, and repetition. They are willful. Ananias and his wife Sapphira planned to deceive the apostles by giving only part of the proceeds from the sale of their property to the needy while claiming that it was the full selling price.[1] We know that if we follow through with a thought or action it will be sin but we do it anyway.

The remedy for both types of sin is the word of God. We will more quickly discern our errors if we are regularly in the Word and open to its message. The Word warns us of sin's consequences and reminds us of the reward that comes from obedience. The carrot and the stick are both present in God's word. A daily intake of God's word is vital for every Christian if he or she is to live in victory over sin.

For the word of God is living and active and sharper than any two-edged sword, and piercing as far as the division of soul and spirit, of both joints and marrow, and able to judge the thoughts and intentions of the heart.[2]

[1]Acts 5:1-4   [2]Hebrews 4:12

Thy word have I hid in my heart that I might not sin against Thee.
Psalm 119:11 (KJV)

But He answered and said, "It is written, 'Man shall not live by bread alone, but on every word that proceeds out of the mouth of God.'"
Matthew 4:4

What does it mean to hide God's word in your heart? If the verse said to hide God's word in your mind, we could probably agree that involves memorizing Scripture. Of course, the best reason for memorizing Scripture would be the desire that through meditation and obedience, God's word would take root in the heart and transform us. Thus scripture memory could be viewed as one possible step in the process of hiding God's word in our heart.

The Gospels record over thirty times when Jesus quoted Old Testament Scriptures in His discussions with people. Since Jesus is both man and God, did He invoke His omniscience or had He memorized them just as you or I would. Paul says that when Jesus came to earth, *He emptied Himself and was made in the likeness of men*[1]. Luke reports that *Jesus increased in wisdom and stature and in favor with God and men*[2]. So, perhaps as God's perfect example to man, Jesus went through the process of memorizing scripture just as we would.

Have you ever been to a gathering where children recited verses that they had memorized? Jesus probably took part in such an event as a child. However, He chose not to let the memory verses lapse. He kept them current and probably added to them through His adult years. He valued His Father's words.

Dawson Trotman, founder of The Navigators, said "I know of no form of intake of the Word which pays greater dividends for the time invested that Scripture memory." How do you hide God's word in your heart?

[1]Philippians 2:7   [2]Luke 2:52

*For on the first of the first month he began to go up from Babylon;
and on the first of the fifth month he came to Jerusalem, because the
good hand of his God was upon him. For Ezra had set his heart to
study the law of the Lord, and to practice it, and to teach His statutes
and ordinances in Israel.*   *Ezra 7:9-10*

Ezra was commissioned by Persian King Artaxerxes to lead a
second expedition of Jews back from Babylonian exile into Palestine
about 459 B.C.   Ezra's life provides an example of three ingredients
to spiritual growth and usefulness in Kingdom work.

The first step for us as believers is to immerse ourselves in
the word of God. Ezra committed to studying the Word. In Ezra's
day, the law of the Lord just consisted of the Pentateuch, the first
five books of the Old Testament.   Today we are blessed to have 66
God-inspired books on which we can hear, read, study, memorize
and meditate. Paul challenged Timothy: *Study to show yourself
approved unto God, a workman that needs not to be ashamed,
rightly dividing the word of truth.*[1] Our intake of the Bible needs to
be intentional, not haphazard.

As we maximize our exposure to the Bible, we must ensure
that we respond with a heart of obedience. Ezra practiced what he
read and studied. Jesus levied his most harsh criticism on the
Pharisees who studied the Word but didn't apply it to their lives.
James writes: *But prove yourselves doers of the word, and not
merely hearers who delude themselves.*[2]

Finally, as we consistently and thoughtfully receive the word
of God in our lives, God will lead us to an area of ministry where we
can be a positive, spiritual influence in the lives of others. Ezra used
his knowledge and giftedness to teach. At the end of life, when we
reflect on our relationship with Jesus and the way He has used us, we
will be grateful that the good hand of our God was upon us, as it was
with Ezra.

[1]II Timothy 2:15 (KJV)   [2]James 1:22

All Scripture is inspired by God and profitable for teaching, for reproof, for correction, for training in righteousness; that the man of God may be adequate, equipped for every good work.

II Timothy 3:16-17

Scripture is indispensible in our growth toward maturity in Christ. Paul reminds Timothy that Scripture is useful in four areas. Teaching has been likened to the pathway on which Christians walk. When we veer off the pathway, reproof is needed to alert us and correction is needed to guide us back to the path. Training in righteousness is needed to keep us on the path.

As an example, let's look at Romans 12:18-21 to see how these elements work together to keep us on the straight and narrow path toward Christian maturity. The teaching or doctrine that the passage is based on is "Vengeance is mine, I will repay". Paul is quoting Deuteronomy 32:35. In Romans 13, Paul discusses how God has established government to be one arm of His vengeance on earth.

Any reader who has a grudge and is plotting payback would be reproved when Paul says: *Never take your own revenge.* The authority for that reproof is the stated doctrine. Unfortunately, it is part of human nature to strike back when we are hurt. However, as Christians we are to forgive the offender and leave any retribution to God, the just Judge.

Then Paul provides correction by quoting from Proverbs 25:21. *But if your enemy is hungry, feed him, and if he is thirsty, give him a drink.* In other words, Paul encourages the one offended to respond by repaying good for evil to allow God an opportunity to work in both the one offended and the one who offended.

Instruction in righteousness is found in verse 18: *If possible, as far as it depends on you, be at peace with all men.* Verse 21 declares: *Do not be overcome by evil, but overcome evil with good.* If we ask God to instill these two attitudes in our lives, we will be heading in the right direction on the path of life.

God uses Scripture to mold our lives. Let's commit to a daily, meaningful exposure to the word of God so we can be the man or woman that God desires us to be.

*And these words, which I am commanding you today, shall be on
your heart; and you shall teach them diligently to your sons and
shall talk of them when you sit in your house and when you walk by
the way, and when you lie down and when you rise up.*
                                              Deuteronomy 6:6-7

These verses are an excerpt from a passage known as the
Shema which is Hebrew for "hear". The first phrase of this passage
is "Hear, O Israel!" Orthodox Jews consider the Shema to be the
most important part of the prayer service in Judaism. This portion of
the Shema deals with the importance of teaching God's word to the
children in a Jewish family.

Jesus grew up in an orthodox Jewish family so His parents
taught the Scriptures to Jesus. As His ministry begins, He is led by
the Spirit into the wilderness to be tempted by Satan.[1] Three times
Jesus is tempted and three times He responds with "It is written."
Each of the verses comes from this section of Deuteronomy. It is as
though Jesus was modeling how to use Scripture to overcome
temptation by using verses that accompanied the Shema.

When Satan offered the world if Jesus would worship him,
Jesus quoted 6:13 which commands to worship and serve only God.
When tempted to jump from the temple and let angels catch Him,
Jesus quoted 6:16 which commands not to test God. After fasting 40
days, the temptation to change stones to bread was very real but
Jesus quoted 8:3 stating that man doesn't live by bread alone but by
God's word.

In each of these three temptations Jesus applies Scripture to a
life situation. This ability requires more than just rote memorization.
Jesus, or anyone, would need to give in-depth thought to how a verse
or passage of Scripture applies to a life that is lived for God. It
requires talking and thinking about God's word as you sit in your
house and walk by the way and reliance on the Spirit to bring the
appropriate verse to your mind. The Psalmist describes the blessed
person as one whose *delight is in the law of the Lord, and in His law
he meditates day and night.*[2] Meditation is a skill that comes from
practice. May each of us be that blessed person!

[1]Matthew 4:1-11   [2]Psalm 1:2

1. How can the word of God be used for both offensive and defensive purposes in your life? Do you tend to use it more for defense than offense? Why or why not?

2. The four primary methods of getting the Word into our lives are hearing, reading, studying and memorizing. As each of these methods is coupled with meditation, spiritual growth occurs. Is God prompting you to increase your intake and meditation of the Word? If so, how? If interested in Scripture memory, I recommend using the Navigator's "Topical Memory System" and asking a friend or family member to do it with you for increased accountability.

Prayer Starter: Jesus, you are the living Word. I acknowledge my daily need for the written Word in my life to help me abide in You. Supply me with the discipline I need to …

...the king planned to appoint him over the entire kingdom. Then the commissioners and satraps began trying to find a ground of accusation against Daniel in regard to government affairs; but they could find no ground of accusation or evidence of corruption, inasmuch as he was faithful, and no negligence or corruption was to be found in him.   *Daniel 6:3b-4*

King Nebuchadnezzar made Daniel ruler over Babylon after he discerned and interpreted the king's dream.[1] In Chapter 6 the Persians have conquered Babylon. King Darius selected Daniel as one of three commissioners to oversee 120 satraps (province governors) to ensure they didn't defraud the king. Government officials then and now are known to skim money from collections and Darius was trying to stop this thievery. A possible implication of Darius wanting Daniel as the only commissioner is that the other two were either incompetent or also thieves.

Today people are fired from their jobs for either incompetence or corruption, and the same was true in Daniel's day. Since the commissioners and satraps saw the writing on the wall regarding Darius' impending organizational shake-up, they sought some means to discredit Daniel. His workplace reputation was impeccable, so they decided to use his devotion to God as the avenue to his dismissal by death. When God delivered Daniel from the lions, Darius decreed *that in all the dominion of my kingdom men are to fear and tremble before the God of Daniel.*[2]

Christians in the workplace should have two objectives: to be the best employee or employer possible and to ensure that all know that you are a follower of Jesus Christ. If you have a great reputation and others don't know you are a Christian, then you get the credit. If both objectives are met then God is glorified and others will be more open to the gospel.

[1]Daniel 2:48   [2]Daniel 6:26a

Now when Daniel knew the document had been signed, he entered his house (now in his roof chamber he had windows open toward Jerusalem); and he continued kneeling on his knees three times a day, praying and giving thanks before his God, as he had been doing previously.

Daniel 6:10

Daniel's workplace enemies convinced King Darius to sign a law in which no one could pray to any god or man other than the king for 30 days. They were convinced the king's pride would lead him to sign and Daniel's devotion would lead him to disobey. They were right on both counts.

In Solomon's prayer of dedication for the temple, he prayed specifically about a future situation in which Israel would be taken captive due to their sin. He asked God to hear and forgive them if they repented as they prayed toward the temple in Jerusalem.[1] I suspect that part of the reason for praying three times daily toward Jerusalem was in response to Solomon's prayer.

I am not aware of any command in the Old Testament requiring Israelites to pray a certain number of times daily. So Daniel's prayer time was based on conviction, not command. When Daniel objected to eating the king's food and his three friends refused to bow to the golden image, they were obeying God's command and God proved faithful. Daniel has now grown spiritually and is ready to trust God by adhering to a godly conviction in the face of death.

How easy it would have been for him to set aside his prayer routine for 30 days and avoid the hassle of the lion's den. Obviously, Daniel was convicted by God to continue praying as he had been doing previously. Do we treat our spiritual convictions as seriously as Daniel did?

[1]II Chronicles 6:36-39

Whatever you do, do your work heartily, as for the Lord rather than for men; knowing that from the Lord you will receive the reward of the inheritance. It is the Lord Christ whom you serve... Masters, grant to your slaves justice and fairness, knowing that you too have a Master in heaven.   *Colossians 3:23-24; 4:1*

The believer in Christ often focuses on the horizontal relationships in the workplace and forgets the vertical relationship that Paul reminds us of above. Christ-followers have a two-fold allegiance to God: He created us and He purchased us with the blood of His Son. Our primary obligation in the workforce, as employee or employer, is to God.

In the movie Courageous, a Christian was offered a promotion with the stipulation that he be willing to falsify inventories from time to time. Even though he desperately needed the raise to support his family, he declined since his ultimate boss, Jesus, would not approve. Fortunately, his employers had devised this stipulation as a test to ensure they hired a man of integrity – he got the job. In real life, Christian employees should always act with integrity and be the best employee that the company has. After all, it is God that issues the final paycheck, not the employer.

Christian employers will also one day give account to God regarding their integrity and how they treated their employees. A great proverb that applies to all, but especially employers is: *Do not withhold good from those to whom it is due, when it is in your power to do it.*[1] Are you just and fair in your dealings with all of your employees?

A significant portion of many Christians' lives is spent in the workplace. Let your light shine before your coworkers in such a way that they may see your good works, and glorify your Employer in heaven.

[1]Proverbs 3:27

And seeing them straining at the oars, for the wind was against them, at about the fourth watch of the night, He came to them, walking on the sea; and He intended to pass by them.   Mark 6:48

Jesus did not come to Earth to address the physical curse of sin but rather the spiritual curse of sin. Because of Adam's sin, the ground was cursed and now we all suffer: *By the sweat of your face you shall eat bread.*[1] When Adam was expelled from the garden, he could no longer walk into his back yard to get his next meal. Toil was now required as a constant reminder that sin has its consequences.

So when Jesus saw His disciples straining at the oars because nature was working against them, he was unmoved and intended to pass by them. After all, as a son of Adam, He had labored in a carpenter's shop, sweating to earn a living so He could support His brothers, sisters, and mother, assuming His father had passed away. And now He was working hard in His Father's ministry: *For there were many people coming and going, and they did not even have time to eat.*[2] Jesus willingly submitted Himself to sin's consequences on our behalf even though He was sinless.

Don't seek to avoid hard work unless your motivation is for spiritual reasons. God uses hard work in our lives to build character, to increase our reliance on Him, and to financially support our families. As we seek God's kingdom first in our work, we will view hard work as a blessing, not a curse.

[1]Genesis 3:19a   [2]Mark 6:31b

But when they saw Him walking on the sea, they supposed that it was a ghost, and cried out; for they all saw Him and were frightened. But immediately He spoke with them and said to them, "Take courage; it is I, do not be afraid."   Mark 6:49-50

Jesus responds to our spiritual needs. Although Jesus was unmoved by their straining at the oars, He did respond when they became fearful, thinking they had seen a ghost. When Jesus got into the boat with them, the wind stopped. Jesus was not willing to stop the wind to make it physically easier, but the wind ceased blowing as He dealt with their fear, a spiritual issue.

Hard work can easily turn from a routine physical issue to a spiritual issue. Usually, the transition occurs when excessive time is spent in work. We all will experience seasons of time where the workload increases and more hours are required. However, if the increase appears unending and family and personal life are being impacted, then there is a spiritual problem which needs to be addressed. In those situations, we should be asking God for relief. Jesus will intervene to lessen our hard work if it is impacting our spiritual life.

Another situation in which we can ask for God's intervention in our work is when our job is one that doesn't bring glory to God. *Seek first the kingdom of God and His righteousness.*[1] There are many jobs that involve unrighteousness or lead to unrighteousness. If you have one of those jobs, ask Jesus to provide a job that will honor Him and still meet your needs.

[1]Matthew 6:33a

1. Would your boss and fellow employees say that you are one of the best workers in your workplace? How many of your peers in the workplace know you are a follower of Christ? Are you comfortable with your answers? Why or why not?

2. Is the amount of time you spend at work negatively impacting your family time at home? Does your occupation bring dishonor to God? If the answer is yes to either then ask God to show you an alternative plan that will meet your financial and spiritual needs.

Prayer Starter: Master in heaven, I realize that ultimately I work for You and it is my job to honor You. Help me to be a better employee/employer of Yours by …

But now Christ has been raised from the dead, the first fruits of
those who are asleep.   *I Corinthians 15:20*

The Feast of Firstfruits[1] was observed at the beginning of barley harvest since it was the first grain to come in. The priest would wave the first sheaf of the new crop before the Lord on the day after the Passover Sabbath. By doing so, Israel acknowledged that their crops came from God and belonged to Him. The first fruits were also a sample of what they could look forward to for the remainder of the harvest.

When Christ rose from the dead the day after the Passover Sabbath, He became the first fruits of all dead believers who will one day receive glorified bodies. Jesus was not the first to be raised from the dead, but He was the first to be resurrected and never die again. The resurrection demonstrated that Jesus belonged to the Father and thus all followers of Jesus belong to the Father and will be resurrected.

Paul's personal preference was *to be absent from the body and to be at home with the Lord.*[2] He recognized that when he dies, his spirit goes to be with Jesus while his body remains on Earth. But he also knew *the Lord Himself will descend from heaven with a shout, with the voice of the archangel, and with the trumpet of God; and the dead in Christ shall rise first.*[3] Since Paul has died, his spirit will be reunited with his glorified body at the rapture.

When Jesus rose from the dead and walked among the people for forty days, He was displaying a glorified body. That first fruit will one day house the spirit of each believer. When you celebrate Easter, rejoice in that living hope.

[1]Leviticus 23:9-14   [2]II Corinthians 5:8b   [3]I Thessalonians 4:16

I am the door; if anyone enters through Me, he shall be saved, and shall go in and out, and find pasture. I am the good shepherd; the good shepherd lays down His life for the sheep. John 10:9, 11

Here we have two of the seven "I am" statements Jesus made in the Gospel of John. They are connected. When Jesus died on the cross and paid the penalty for our sins, He became the door through which we must enter to be saved. The door exists because of Jesus' substitutionary death. But it had to be the death of a good shepherd.

The Bible uses "good" in two ways when referring to people. Barnabas is described as a "good man"[1] which simply means he was honorable and had traits of goodness in him. However, when the rich young ruler called Jesus "good Teacher", Jesus responded that "No one is good except God alone."[2] From a human perspective Barnabas was good, but from God's perspective no person, other than Jesus, is good. Jesus presented Himself as the unspotted lamb for the final blood sacrifice of all times. Thus the shepherd that laid down His life had to be perfectly good to satisfy God's requirement.

When is the last time you heard of an actual shepherd dying for a sheep in his care? I suspect that is a fairly rare event given the value we place on humans above animals. How would you compare the value of the Son of God to a human? Yet Jesus, the good shepherd, died for humans to allow our justification before a Holy God. Let's live our life today in thankfulness and obedience with that thought in mind!

[1]Acts 11:24   [2]Mark 10:17-18

*Now the God of peace, who brought up from the dead the great
Shepherd of the sheep through the blood of the eternal covenant,
even Jesus our Lord, equip you in every good thing to do His will,
working in us that which is pleasing in His sight, through Jesus
Christ.*   *Hebrews 13:20-21*

Jesus is the great Shepherd because of the power displayed in
the resurrection and the empowerment provided to His sheep.
Notice that God equips us and works in us through Jesus. Jesus
ascended into heaven after His resurrection so that our Helper, the
Holy Spirit, could come.   Two ways the Holy Spirit empowers us
are through spiritual gifts and the fruit of the Spirit.

One method God uses to equip us is providing us with one or
more spiritual gifts. While discussing spiritual gifts, Paul says: *But
to each one is given the manifestation of the Spirit for the common
good.*[1] The great Shepherd is concerned for the sheep, individually
and collectively. Giftedness endows purpose to the believer since he
or she has a unique role in building up the body of Christ.

The Spirit's indwelling presence gives us access to the fruit
of the Spirit[2], thereby working in us that which is pleasing in His
sight. Whereas gifts equip us outwardly, the fruit of the Spirit
changes us inwardly. In essence, as we surrender more and more to
the Spirit's control, those fruits become more evident in our lives
and we become more Christ-like. The individual believer benefits
from this spiritual transformation and the church does also.

Sanctification in the believer's life involves maturing in both
the inward change and the outward involvement in ministry. The
great Shepherd lives today to empower us to manifest the fruit and
gifts of the Spirit. Let's cooperate today with His efforts in our
lives!

[1] I Corinthians 12:7   [2] Galatians 5:22-23

Shepherd the flock of God among you, exercising oversight not under compulsion, but voluntarily, according to the will of God; and not for sordid gain, but with eagerness. And when the Chief Shepherd appears, you will receive the unfading crown of glory.

I Peter 5:2, 4

Here Peter is exhorting fellow elders to properly shepherd the flock that God has entrusted to each of them. His exhortation is given with an eye to the future when Jesus, the Chief Shepherd, returns. If the elders shepherd their flock as Jesus would, then Peter is confident they will be rewarded with a crown of glory. Peter doesn't address what will happen if elders shepherd for the wrong reasons but we know the Chief Shepherd will hold them accountable.

Not all believers are called to be elders but all believers are gifted in some way and will be rewarded on how they employed their giftedness. The chief is the leader or the person of highest authority. Thus all sheep will one day report to the Chief Shepherd and give an account. Speaking to believers, Paul said: *For we must all appear before the judgment seat of Christ, that each one may be recompensed for his deeds, according to what he has done, whether good or bad.*[1]

The death of the Good Shepherd justifies those who trust in His sacrifice for salvation. The resurrection of the Great Shepherd demonstrated Christ's power to sanctify those who walk daily in the Spirit's power. The return of the Chief Shepherd initiates the rewards process and the glorification of the saints. Our Shepherd leads His sheep to invest our lives in the same way He invested His: the justifying, sanctifying, and glorifying of lost sheep. May we follow His lead, as sheep follow the shepherd.

[1] II Corinthians 5:10

Do not think that I came to abolish the law or the Prophets; I did not come to abolish, but to fulfill.   Matthew 5:17
For the law was given through Moses; grace and truth were realized through Jesus Christ.   John 1:17

The Law of Moses can be subdivided into three parts. The moral law was expressed largely in the Ten Commandments. The ceremonial law described how Israel was to atone for their sins through various sacrifices. The social law governed how society was to deal with conflicts arising between individuals. Jesus fulfilled these three aspects of the law through His life and death.

Jesus fulfilled the moral law by living a sinless life. The Ten Commandments represent a superficial view of God's holiness requirements. Jesus expounded on these commandments in the Sermon on the Mount when He said, as an example, *everyone who looks on a woman to lust after her has committed adultery with her already in his heart.*[1] God is concerned with our hearts, not just our outward actions. Jesus' heart and actions were perfect toward God.

When John the Baptist referred to Jesus as *the Lamb of God who takes away the sin of the world,*[2] he alluded to Jesus' fulfillment of the ceremonial law. The killing of the unblemished lamb to atone for Israel's sins was simply a picture of the lamb that God would one day provide in His Son. *Without shedding of blood, there is no forgiveness.*[3]

The social law could be summarized by "love your neighbor as yourself". Jesus expanded that thought when he said "love your enemies and pray for those who persecute you."[4] Jesus' love for His enemies kept Him on the cross until the debt was paid. In His relationship with people, Jesus only did good, never evil.

Jesus became the very fullness of God's amazing grace. We access this marvelous grace when with grateful hearts toward God, we simply embrace it as ours.

[1]Matthew 5:28   [2]John 1:29   [3]Hebrews 9:22b   [4]Matthew 5:44

1. As we enter the Easter season, we think of Jesus in His role as the good Shepherd who laid down His life for the sheep. But we can rejoice that His death opened the door to our sanctification on earth and glorification in heaven. Thank Jesus now for His role in each of these three areas.

2. *Blessed be the God and Father of our Lord Jesus Christ, who according to His great mercy has caused us to be born again to a living hope through the resurrection of Jesus Christ from the dead.* (I Peter 1:3) The crucifixion temporarily killed the hope Peter had in Jesus as Messiah. The resurrection brought that hope alive again. Do you have a "living hope" today?   Why or why not?

Prayer Starter: Jesus, my Shepherd, thank you for this Easter season when I celebrate Your death, burial and resurrection. I am Your sheep and I thank You for my justification, I ask for Your help in my sanctification, as I look forward to my glorification. In particular, help me with …

And just as they did not see fit to acknowledge God any longer, God gave them over to a depraved mind, to do those things which are not proper, ..., slanderers, haters of God, insolent, arrogant, boastful, inventors of evil, disobedient to parents.   Romans 1:28, 30

In the New Testament "pride" is conveyed by three Greek words, the translations of which all appear in verse 30 above. Pride caused the fall of Satan and is ever present with us today. We shouldn't be surprised it appears in multiple forms in Paul's listing of sins.

Arrogant translates a Greek word that means "appearing above others". Paul warns against empty conceit and encourages all to have humility of mind so that each one *regards one another as more important than himself.*[1] Arrogance has the opposite view: I am more important than others.

Jesus taught that *the mouth speaks out of that which fills the heart.*[2] If pride and arrogance are in the heart, then boasting is on the lips. The Apostle John used the second Greek word, translated boastful, when listing the three evils of the world system: *the lust of the flesh and the lust of the eyes and the boastful pride of life.*[3]

Finally, insolent is translated from the Greek word hubris which appears in the English dictionary as a transliteration. In English, hubris is defined as wanton insolence or arrogance resulting from excessive pride or passion. Here, pride is manifested not just in words, but also in despiteful actions.

Pride, as with other sins, starts in the heart but eventually manifests itself outwardly in words and actions. Humility is possible if we maintain a daily, abiding walk with Jesus and recognize that anything good we accomplish is through His power and grace.

[1]Philippians 2:3   [2]Matthew 12:34b   [3]I John 2:16

The king reflected and said, "Is this not Babylon the great, which I myself have built as a royal residence by the might of my power and for the glory of my majesty?" While the word was in the king's mouth, a voice came from heaven, saying, "King Nebuchadnezzar, to you it is declared: sovereignty has been removed from you."
Daniel 4:30-31

We all deal with self-pride, but I suspect those with power and riches struggle with it the most. Since God resists the proud[1], we should not be surprised to see situations where God deals with Biblical kings over this issue. God used Daniel to confront King Nebuchadnezzar and his son, King Belshazzar, about their pride.

Daniel chapter 4 is King Nebuchadnezzar's personal testimony of how God humbled him. God removed his sovereignty by removing his sanity and causing him to live in the wild eating grass like an animal for seven years. You cannot reign without your mental faculties.

Daniel had interpreted a dream for the king which warned him of this impending judgment but he didn't heed the warning. One year after the dream, the king uttered the boastful words above which triggered God's judgment.

Notice the pride oozing from his bravado. The king views himself as the sole reason for his accomplishments. Pride focuses on the importance of self with little or no acknowledgement of God in the life. Pride also seeks to glorify self as the king did. Amassing glory for self instead of glorifying God for His part in any accomplishment invites God's judgment. Let's commit afresh to glorifying God in our thoughts and actions rather than self.

[1]James 4:6

But when his heart was lifted up and his spirit became so proud that he behaved arrogantly, he was deposed from his royal throne, and his glory was taken away from him. Yet you, his son, Belshazzar, have not humbled your heart, even though you knew all this.
Daniel 5:20, 22

      Here Daniel reminds King Belshazzar how God dealt with King Nebuchadnezzar's pride but notes that he did not learn from his father's mistakes. Prior to this reminder, Belshazzar had defied God by drinking wine from the holy vessels taken from the temple in Jerusalem by his father. His blasphemous actions prompted "the writing on the wall" in his palace which Daniel interpreted as an announcement of impending doom. His kingdom and his life were taken that night by King Darius the Mede.

      Now I Nebuchadnezzar praise, exalt, and honor the King of heaven, for all His works are true and His ways just, and He is able to humble those who walk in pride.[1] This is the last statement of the king's testimony regarding how God worked in his life. What a shame that his son could not have learned from his father's experience and example. How do we communicate the dangers of pride and the proper response to pride to our children?

      The most powerful communication is through your example. When you are prideful, admit your sin to your children and explain why it was pride and why it offended God. Share how you asked for and received forgiveness. Also take opportunity to discuss Biblical or headline examples of pride with them. Children will exercise their own free will in issues related to pride, but as parents we are responsible to bring them up in the nurture and admonition of the Lord. Let's do our part and pray that our children will respond appropriately when they are tempted to be prideful.

[1]Daniel 4:37

The arrogance of your heart has deceived you, you who live in the clefts of the rock, in the loftiness of your dwelling place, who say in your heart, 'Who will bring me down to earth?'   *Obadiah 3*

      Obadiah is prophesying against Edom, the nation that descended from Esau, the son of Isaac and brother of Jacob. The capital of Edom was present day Petra, Jordan, the filming site for the temple that contained the Grail in <u>Indiana Jones and the Last Crusade</u>. The Edomites lived in a mountainous region with accesses that were easily defended. (Remember the narrow, rose-colored passage Jones rode through to get to the temple?) They were surrounded by fertile land and were located on several of the main trade routes of the ancient world. As a result they were prosperous, safe, and self-sufficient. This feeling of superiority and independence led to pride and arrogance.

      An attitude of self-sufficiency is very deceptive. With power, position, and wealth, one thinks that he is in control. He is the master of his fate. He is accountable to no one. He does what he pleases. He forgets that he has little control over his health, economic downturns, and even his lifespan. Even if he does live to be one hundred, what happens then?

      Paul urges us to not be deceived because in the end, God is not mocked.[1] If a man is self-indulgent and sows only for himself then he will eventually reap from that misdirected life. God has the final say.

      We all have a tendency to be proud and self-sufficient, regardless of our wealth or position. God has given to all of us various strengths and talents. If we use these gifts for selfish ambition rather than for God's glory we are travelling down a road of deception. We walk wisely if we constantly evaluate our motives and ensure our heart is right before God.

[1]Galatians 6:7

Let another man praise you, and not your own mouth; a stranger,
and not your own lips.   *Proverbs 27:2*

     It is often noted that the middle letter of "sin" is "I". The sinful nature of mankind has an unhealthy focus on self. Hence, Scripture warns us about purposefully drawing attention to ourselves.

     The focus on self is prominently displayed through our words and our actions. However, the same set of words and actions can be self praise for one individual and an act of ministry for another. It is all dependent on motive. If I share a Bible memory verse with someone, I may be trying to impress with my Bible knowledge or I may be seeking to minister through the power of God's word. God knows the motive of my heart and He will reward accordingly.

     The Apostle Paul gives us some advice for this perplexing problem. He commands us to do nothing from selfishness or conceit but to view everyone as more important than ourselves. Since actions are many times easier to accomplish than controlling thoughts, Paul gives further advice and tells us to look out for the interest of others. If we focus on serving others, the time spent focusing on self will be reduced.   The joy of serving will replace the inward focus. We will become more like Jesus who left heaven to be a servant to mankind[1].

     If we insist on elevating self rather than serving God and others, God says that we have our reward. If we are looking for men's admiration we will surely find it. But in the end it will be empty and useless. We do well to remember that God opposes the proud but gives grace to the humble[2]. Let's strive to be a recipient of God's grace by focusing on others and Him.

[1]Philipians 2:3-8   [2]James 4:6

1. Some have speculated that pride is the source of the majority of the sins with which we struggle. Make a list of sins below that could have pride as their root cause.

2. Do you struggle with being boastful, arrogant or insolent? Have you ever confessed a display of pride to your wife, children or others? How could Proverbs 28:13 help someone dealing with pride? *He who conceals his transgressions will not prosper, but he who confesses and forsakes them will find compassion.*

Prayer Starter: Father God, since You resist the proud, I pray that You would give me a desire to be humble in my spirit and in my actions. Help me to focus more on others, and less on myself. I confess that …

Now I make known to you, brethren, the gospel which I preached to you, which also you received, in which also you stand, ... For I delivered to you as of first importance what I also received, that Christ died for our sins according to the Scriptures.

I Corinthians 15:1, 3

Gospel means "good news". Here is the gospel message in five words: **Christ died for our sins**. Let's consider each word.

Paul uses **Christ**, Greek for Messiah, instead of Jesus to connect his readers with Old Testament prophesies (according to the Scriptures). Only the death of the Messiah, the spotless Lamb of God, could make the gospel work as intended. *For the life of the flesh is in the blood, and I have given it to you on the altar to make atonement for your souls.*[1] God instituted animal sacrifices as a temporary means to forgive Israel's sin. The permanent method for atonement rested on Messiah. Thus **died** is the verb of necessity to allow the gospel transaction to be completed.

Christ's death on the cross should be thought of as substitutionary, hence **for**. Jesus was sinless and thus didn't deserve death. Rather, Jesus submitted Himself to death as part of an exchange. He took on the penalty of our sin, while we received His righteousness. Paul expressed it this way: *He made Him who knew no sin to be sin on our behalf, that we might become the righteousness of God in Him.*[2]

For God so loved the world, that He gave His only begotten Son...[3] **Our** represents everyone in the world. Jesus died for the sins of all mankind. **Sins** originated when Adam and Eve disobeyed God and ate the forbidden fruit. Our sins are what separate us from a holy God.

Through the gift of Jesus' death we have access to God. But each person must receive the gift by faith to receive the forgiveness of sin and be reconnected to God. Have you responded to this good news?

[1]Leviticus 17:11a   [2]II Corinthians 5:21   [3]John 3:16

Then He will also say to those on His left, 'Depart from Me, accursed ones, into the eternal fire which has been prepared for the devil and his angels.   Matthew 25:41

Jesus had more to say about hell than heaven. Here Jesus is describing what Revelation refers to as the great white throne judgment.[1] At the end of time, everyone stands before God and is judged according to their deeds. Since *all have sinned and come short of the glory of God,*[2] all deserve eternal separation from a holy God. However, those who have personally trusted in the sacrifice of Christ on the cross, have their sins forgiven and their names written in the book of life. Hell was created in response to the rebellion of the devil and his angels, but God has determined that rebellious mankind will suffer the same fate. Mankind was offered a way of escape; Satan and his angels have no options.

The degree of punishment in hell will be proportional to the amount of revelation of God one received. Jesus said, *Woe to you, Chorazin! Woe to you, Bethsaida! For if the miracles had occurred in Tyre and Sidon which occurred in you, they would have repented long ago in sackcloth and ashes. Nevertheless I say to you, it shall be more tolerable for Tyre and Sidon in the day of judgment, than for you.*[3] There is no appeal process before a just and holy God.

I believe that the Spirit of God reveals Himself to every soul through creation, or conscience, or the Bible, or the witness of a Christian, or all of these. Jesus said concerning the Holy Spirit, *And He, when He comes, will convict the world concerning sin, and righteousness, and judgment.*[4] The most important question everyone will one day have to answer is: How did you respond to God's revelation to you?

[1]Revelation 20:11-15   [2]Romans 3:23   [3]Matthew 11:21-22
[4]John 16:8

And opening his mouth, Peter said: "I most certainly understand now that God is not one to show partiality, but in every nation the man who fears Him and does what is right, is welcome to Him."
                                                            Acts 10:34-35

Life is not fair! One doesn't study for a test and makes an A; the other studies hard and earns a C. One is considered beautiful or handsome; the other is thought to be homely. One is born into a wealthy family; the other grows up in poverty. One benefits from years of undetected crime, the other is caught after the first infraction. We can observe daily that all people don't get the same treatment, opportunities, and justice. So we correctly conclude that life is not fair.

At the end of time when each of us stands before our Creator and gives an account of our life, only one question of fairness will matter. Did everyone have an opportunity to know God and receive forgiveness for their sins on earth? Peter came to understand that the answer to that question is yes. God used his providential encounter with the Gentile centurion Cornelius to reveal this fact to Peter.

The Bible describes Cornelius as *a devout man, and one who feared God with all his household, and gave many alms to the Jewish people, and prayed to God continually.*[1] Cornelius had responded positively to whatever revelation he had received about God. God in turn sent Peter with the gospel message to Cornelius who believed and was saved.

Since God chose Abraham, and the Jews were called the children of God, Peter had assumed that Jews were forever favored above all others. Now Peter realized that Israel was simply the instrument God used to bless the world with the gospel through the Lord Jesus Christ. *For "Whoever will call upon the name of the Lord will be saved."*[2]

[1]Acts 10:2   [2]Romans 10:13

For He Himself is our peace, who made both groups into one, and broke down the barrier of the dividing wall, by abolishing in His flesh the enmity, which is the Law of commandments ...and might reconcile them both in one body to God through the cross, by it having put to death the enmity.   *Ephesians 2:14-16*

Shortly after delivering Israel from Egyptian bondage, God gave Israel the Law to separate them from the other nations they would encounter. Israel was to be a holy nation so a moral wall was needed to block the unholy influence from other nations. The Law guided their moral and social conduct, restricted their diet, required circumcision of all males, established festivals and prescribed a sacrificial system. If Israel followed the Law, it would safeguard them from the evil influences of the world around them.

But walls also create enmity. Because of the Law, Jews felt superior to Gentiles. During Jesus' time, Jews were not allowed to eat with Gentiles because that would make them unclean. Similarly, Gentiles viewed Jews with disdain.

Although the vertical wall of the Law separated Jew and Gentile, they did have something in common: both were sinners. Israel had failed to keep the Law and the Gentiles had failed to keep the law dictated by their conscience. A horizontal wall of sin separated both groups from a holy God.

Paul later refers to a mystery that was revealed to him concerning the Gentiles[1]. It was not a mystery that all nations would one day be blessed by the descendents of Abraham[2]. The tabernacle and temple even had a court of the Gentiles to accommodate those who had become "Jewish". The question was "What would this blessing look like?" Paul declares that Gentiles are in fact *fellow heirs and fellow members of the body, and fellow partakers of the promise in Christ Jesus*. The vertical and horizontal walls have been torn down and all mankind has equal access to God.

In a sense, the cross symbolized the vertical wall of the Law and the horizontal wall of sin. Both the Law and sin's payment were satisfied through Jesus' death on the cross. Jews and Gentiles alike now have full, equal access to God through the gospel. Praise God!

[1]Ephesians 3:1-6   [2]Genesis 12:3

For now salvation is nearer to us than when we believed.
Romans 13:11b

Have you ever asked someone how long they have been a Christian and the response was: "I have always believed." They may say that because they trusted in Christ as a young child. But they may have simply been religious their whole life and there is no date because there has never been a conversion. The New Testament always speaks in term of "when we believed", referring to a specific time in history. A date exists for when you were physically born; so also for when you were spiritually born.

Saul the Pharisee would point to a time when he was travelling to Damascus when he encountered Jesus as Lord, resulting in a name changed to Paul the Apostle. The Philippian jailer would recall the night of the earthquake when he and his family heard the gospel and were saved. The Ethiopian eunuch would cite that day in the chariot when he was reading Isaiah and Philip explained who Jesus was. Lydia would remember that Sabbath day by the riverside when Paul told her the gospel message and she believed. The thief on the cross would tell of his last day on earth when he trusted Jesus to take him to heaven that very day. They all knew when.

If you or a friend cannot remember a time when you admitted your sinfulness and asked Jesus to forgive your sin and enter your life as your boss, then please do that now. When people grow up in a religious environment, they can easily focus on religion and miss the relationship with Jesus, through Whom eternal life is offered. *Behold, now is "the acceptable time", behold, now is "the day of salvation".*[1]

[1] II Corinthians 6:2

1. God used many Old Testament prophets to discuss the gospel ahead of time to help validate the message once the Messiah arrived on scene. In Isaiah 53:6 we read: *All of us like sheep have gone astray, each of us has turned to his own way; but the Lord has caused the iniquity of us all to fall on Him.* Translation: We are all sinners, separated from God. When Jesus died on the cross, God placed the penalty for our sins on Jesus. Through belief in the atoning work of Jesus' sacrifice, we can reconnect with God with our sins forgiven and with the righteousness of Christ. Have you ever acknowledged belief in the gospel message? If not, are you ready to trust Jesus as the Lord of your life and Savior of your soul?

2. The Apostle Paul said this about decision day in Romans 10:9. *If you confess with your mouth Jesus as Lord, and believe in your heart that God raised Him from the dead, you shall be saved.* "Saved" means that Jesus will rescue you from sin's penalty which is eternal separation from God, or hell. Since God is just, He has to judge sin. But you can accept God's gift of eternal life since Jesus paid sin's penalty on your behalf. I urge you to sincerely pray the below prayer.

Prayer Starter: Dear God, I admit that I am a sinner and deserve eternal separation from Your presence. I thank You that Jesus died in my place on the cross. I accept the forgiveness of sins and the gift of eternal life that You offer through Jesus' death. I ask you to come into my life and take control. Help me to grow in my faith in the days and weeks ahead. ...

Consider it all joy, my brethren, when you encounter various trials.
James 1:2
But each one is tempted when he is carried away and enticed by his
own lust.   *James 1:14*

The words "trials" and "tempted" above originate from the same Greek word which means to prove by an experiment of good or evil. Every trial in our lives comes through the sovereign hand of God for the purpose of making us stronger. However, Satan can take that same trial and turn it into a temptation in an effort to make us weaker. God intends trials for good; Satan uses temptations for evil.

As an example, the tree of the knowledge of good and evil was placed in the Garden of Eden by God as a test or a trial. The only way Adam and Eve had to demonstrate obedience to God was by not eating from this tree. The presence of the tree tested their obedience. Satan questioned what God had said and enticed Eve by appealing to her pride and lusts of taste and sight. The test from God became a temptation from Satan. They failed the test and gave in to the temptation.

However, trials do not have to end in sin like the first one did. After Job lost his children, possessions and health, his wife urged him to curse God and die. Job responded: *"Shall we indeed accept good from God and not accept adversity?"* The Scripture says: *In all this Job did not sin with his lips.*[1] As a result of the trial, there was a temptation to blame and curse God for his misfortune but Job accepted the trial knowing that God would use it in his life for good.

When we see a trial morphing into a temptation, James advises us to: *Resist the devil and he will flee from you. Draw near to God and he will draw near to you.*[2] Half the battle is recognizing what is happening. The other half is running toward God.

[1]Job 2:10b   [2]James 4:7b-8a

Remember, O Lord, on David's behalf, all his affliction.

Psalm 132:1

David wrote about half of the 150 Psalms. Of those that he wrote, over half deal with affliction. So, if you were to randomly select a Psalm to read, you would have at least a one in four chance that the subject of the Psalm would be affliction.

Afflictions can be divided into two categories: those that we bring on ourselves because of some sin in our lives and those that just happen to us through no fault of our own. David experienced both and so do we.

As a result of David's adultery with Bathsheba and subsequent murder of her husband, Uriah, God told David through His prophet: *Now therefore, the sword shall never depart from your house*[1]. David repented of his sin, God forgave the sin, but consequences remained. After all, *God is not mocked; for whatever a man sows, this he will also reap.*[2] This spiritual law is just as valid as any physical law that God has set in His universe.

However, David endured much affliction at the hand of King Saul that David did nothing to deserve. In fact, David was above reproach when it came to his reaction to Saul's attempts to kill him. On two occasions David had the opportunity to kill Saul. Both times he reacted with *The Lord forbid that I should stretch out my hand against the Lord's anointed.*[3] David recognized that God was sovereign and allowed this affliction and that in God's timing He would rectify the situation. God had a purpose in the affliction and David accepted that purpose even though he didn't fully understand it.

When faced with affliction, we must first determine the source as best we can. If there is sin in our lives, we must immediately confess and forsake it. If we are not aware of any unconfessed sin, then we ask God for the faith and patience to endure it, knowing that God has our best interest at heart and will grow us spiritually.

[1] II Samuel 12:10a   [2] Galatians 6:7   [3] I Samuel 26:11a

Then they cried out to the Lord in their trouble; He delivered them out of their distresses. Let them give thanks to the Lord for His lovingkindness, and for His wonders to the sons of men!
                                                                Psalm 107:6, 8

The Psalmist repeats these two verses four times in this psalm. Therefore the theme of the psalm is that we should thank God when He delivers us out of trouble. This first pair of verses follows the description of wanderers without a home who are hungry and thirsty. When these individuals reached their extremities they cried out to God and he delivered them.

Mankind has an adverse reaction to trouble. We avoid it when possible. Prior to the fall, the Garden of Eden was a place void of trouble --- it was Paradise. One of sin's consequences was that the ground was cursed and bore thorns and thistles --- that's trouble. And we have had trouble ever since.

But trouble is actually more of a blessing than a curse. Perhaps you have noticed that during times of peace and prosperity it is easy for Christians to put God and godly activities on the back burner. However, if we are in trouble, we are seeking God and His direction for our lives on a moment by moment basis.

Trouble is also a blessing for the unbeliever. When circumstances are going well, non-Christians feel independent with no need for God in their lives. But bring those same people to the end of their rope and they may call on God for help. This perspective is the reason we Christians should view relationships with unbelievers as a long term commitment. We are friends with them in the good times in the hope that during the bad times they will ask us for a reason of the hope that is in us.[1]

So with joy let's thank God for the trouble in our lives and in the lives of our unbelieving friends, anticipating deliverance, both temporal and eternal.

[1] I Peter 3:15

Now it came about when Pharaoh had let the people go, that God did not lead them by the way of the land of the Philistines, even though it was near; for God said, "Lest the people change their minds when they see war, and they return to Egypt."   Exodus 13:17

After living in Egypt's protective custody for over four hundred years, Israel left that safety with no experience in warfare. They headed for Canaan, the Promised Land, but God lead them in a very indirect route. God knew that if they had to battle the Philistines along the direct route to Canaan, Israel would become discouraged and want to return to Egypt.   Warfare would be too difficult for them at this stage of their experience with God.

Perhaps the way God dealt with Israel at this time in their history is an example of what Christ meant when He taught us to pray: *And do not lead us into temptation, but deliver us from evil."*[1] God alone knows the many times He has protected us from temptation and sin to the praise of His glory.

We know that God allows some trials and temptations into our lives to mature us as we depend on Him. Paul reminds us that: *"No temptation has overtaken you but such as is common to man; and God is faithful, who will not allow you to be tempted beyond what you are able, but with the temptation will provide the way of escape also, that you may be able to endure it."*[2]

Whenever temptations are allowed to enter our lives, we can claim God's promise that there is a way of escape so that we do not have to sin. Comedian Flip Wilson's popular use of "the devil made me do it" became a national expression in the 1970s but it has no Biblical basis. When we sin, it is because we chose not to seek the escape route that God provided.

God desires us to be holy, as He is holy.[3] To that end, on one hand He removes unbearable temptations from our path, but on the other hand He offers grace to be victorious over temptations we must experience. Our desire to be holy will motivate us to seek the protective path if possible and to seek God's way of escape when we are tempted. Lord, give us your desire for holiness.

[1]Matthew 6:13   [2]I Corinthians 10:13   [3]I Peter 1:16

Behold, I go forward but He is not there, And backward, but I cannot perceive Him;
When He acts on the left, I cannot behold Him; He turns on the right, I cannot see Him.
But He knows the way I take; When He has tried me, I shall come forth as gold.   *Job 23:8-10*

God was bragging to Satan about His servant Job. To prove that Job was a blameless and upright man who feared God and turned away from evil, He first gave Satan permission to take away all Job had, leaving Job's body untouched. Later, God allowed Satan to afflict Job's body but not to the point of taking his life.

Other than Jesus' agony on the cross, it is hard to imagine that any other person has ever experienced such a devastating loss while enduring such physical discomfort. This was a trial for the record books. In the midst of this trial, Job is looking for God but cannot find Him. Job doesn't doubt that God is there but he senses God is hiding from him.

However, Job takes consolation in two facts. He knows God is there, watching him. He also knows the trial will one day end and the time spent in trial will have added value to his life, like gold.

If we understand that God is there even if we do not feel Him, we also know His love, care and sovereignty are still operational. We are trusting in His heart since we cannot see His hand.

Even 4,000 years ago Job knew that all things work together for good to those who love God.[1] God had a purpose for this time of testing. He would one day, here or in heaven, understand the reason and benefit from the time of pain. Since there was a future hope and a loving God who knew his pain, he could endure. If we learn from Job's example, we can also endure whatever trials come our way.

[1]Romans 8:28

1. Think of an affliction you experienced that was directly caused by some wrongdoing in your life. Now think of a trial that seemed to have no connection to anything you did wrong. What did you gain from each experience?

2. Can you think of an unsaved friend who is going through a trial now? Show him or her concern over the trial and ask God for a way to minister and share your hope in Jesus.

Prayer Starter: Lord, help me to live a holy life before You so that I can grow from trials You send and avoid tribulation that I might cause. As I think of my friend, I pray that …

Brethren, my heart's desire and my prayer to God for them is for
their salvation.   *Romans 10:1*

Have you seen the Seinfeld episode in which Elaine discovers accidentally that her boyfriend is religious? She confronts him and asks if it is a problem that she doesn't believe in God. He replies that it doesn't bother him because she is the one going to hell, not him. Elaine is then disturbed that her boyfriend shows so little concern for her eternal destiny.

I often think that scene is a fair portrait of how the unbelieving world views many Christians. My friend, the Christian, believes in the existence of hell and yet my friend has never expressed any concern that I am going to hell. Two possible conclusions from this situation are that either my friend doesn't care about my eternal destiny or he/she doesn't really believe in hell after all.

No one who knew Paul would ever consider either of those two possibilities. Paul's statement above referred to his Jewish countrymen but it could be said of anyone Paul encountered. In the first chapter of Romans he said: *For I am not ashamed of the gospel, for it is the power of God for salvation to everyone who believes, to the Jew first and also to the Greek.*

Perhaps a good indicator of our concern for lost friends and family members is how often we talk about them to God. If we truly are burdened for the souls of those around us, we will pray for them. Not only will we pray for their salvation, but we will also ask God how we can influence their decision for Jesus.

Lord, give us a burden for those around us! Help us to see them as You see them, lost and in need of a Savior to keep them from a devil's hell.

The woman said to Him, "Sir, give me this water, so I will not be
thirsty, nor come all the way here to draw." He said to her, "Go,
call your husband, and come here."   *John 4:15-16*

When Jesus asked about the husband of the Samaritan
woman He met at the well, He touched the most spiritually sensitive
area in her life. The reason she was a social outcast alone at the well
at noon was because she had had five husbands and the man she
currently lived with was not her husband. Jesus had earlier initiated
a spiritual discussion about living water with her and she showed an
interest in knowing more by requesting the water. Before
proceeding with the conversation Jesus indirectly uncovered her
need for repentance.

There is no true salvation without sincere repentance. I help
teach a Systematic Theology class to inmates in a nearby prison. All
of these students can tell of a time when they experienced heartfelt
sorrow for their crimes against humanity and God. Some of these
men are incarcerated for murder, but that doesn't disqualify them
from God's saving grace as long as they are repentant. Jesus eagerly
engaged this immoral woman in conversation because He loved her.
In fact, He came into the world to die for all mankind, from the self-
righteous to the self-condemning.

As you share the Gospel story with those around you, never
omit the listener's need for repentance. Otherwise, you are sharing
an incomplete gospel, and therefore a false gospel. During Jesus'
time on earth after His resurrection, He said: *Thus it is written, that*
the Christ should suffer and rise again from the dead the third day;
and that repentance for forgiveness of sins should be proclaimed in
His name to all the nations, beginning from Jerusalem.[1] Salvation is
more a response from the heart, than a response with the mouth.

[1]Luke 24:46-47

The Lord is good, a stronghold in the day of trouble, and He knows those who take refuge in Him. But with an overflowing flood He will make a complete end of its (Ninevah) *site, and will pursue His enemies into darkness.*   *Nahum 1:7-8*

Nahum is the sequel to the Book of Jonah. It relates bad news and good news. About one century has passed since Ninevah repented due to the preaching of Jonah and was forgiven by God. However, the succeeding generations returned to the wicked ways of the past and now God is bringing judgment on them. That was bad news for Ninevah. Since Ninevah, the capital of the Assyrian Empire, had been an enemy of Judah, its destruction was good news for Judah.

One lesson from Nahum is that at the end of life everyone finds themselves either an enemy of God or someone who has taken refuge in God. People discover that they are God's enemy because *the Lord will by no means leave the guilty unpunished.*[1] They have sinned and are accountable for that sin to God. However, there are others who recognize they are sinners and have taken refuge in God.

Nahum proclaims: *Behold on the mountains the feet of him who brings good news, who announces peace!*[2] The good news here was that Judah would no longer have to fear the wicked Assyrians. Since "good news" in the New Testament is known as the gospel, Paul uses this verse in Romans to emphasize the point that preachers of the gospel have to put feet to the message and be sent[3]. The New Testament clarifies what is required for one to take refuge in God. The Lord was good when He sent His Son to die on the cross for our sins. By trusting in the substitutionary death of Christ to pay the penalty of our sin, we take refuge in God's provision.

As followers of Christ we have received the good news because someone took the time to ensure that we heard the gospel. Now we need to use our feet to ensure others hear as well.

[1]Nahum 1:3   [2]Nahum 1:15a   [3]Romans 10:15

Greet Epaenetus, my beloved, who is the first convert to Christ from Asia.
                                                        Romans 16:5b
You know the household of Stephanas, that they were the first fruits of Achaia, and that they have devoted themselves for ministry to the saints.
                                                    I Corinthians 16:15b

    As the gospel traveled from Jerusalem to Judea to Samaria and to the uttermost part of the earth, there were obviously people in each region of the world that could be referred to as the first convert of that region. Sometimes the first convert was an individual; sometimes a family. Paul emphasized the significance of the first fruits by baptizing Stephanus' family even though he normally let others baptize.[1] It was an exciting time.

    Today, missionaries and Bible translators in remote villages are probably the only ones to experience the excitement of leading that first person in a region to Christ. However, each believer can experience the joy of the first fruits when God uses us to lead our first person to Christ. You might be thinking: If I had the conversion experience and knowledge of the Apostle Paul, then I would be sharing my faith also. Listen to what Paul says about his approach to witnessing: *And when I came to you, brethren, I did not come with superiority of speech or of wisdom, proclaiming to you the testimony of God. For I determined to know nothing among you except Jesus Christ, and Him crucified.*[2]

    Paul goes on to explain that he didn't want their conversion to be based on his wisdom, but rather on the power of God. The power for salvation is in the gospel, not us. God has chosen us to be the messengers so that we can experience the thrill of the harvest with Him. Don't miss out on the opportunity to partner with the God of the universe in transforming lives through the power of the gospel of Jesus Christ!

[1] I Corinthians 1:16-17   [2] I Corinthians 2:1-2

*And as Moses lifted up the serpent in the wilderness, even so must
the Son of Man be lifted up; that whoever believes may in Him have
eternal life.*   John 3:14-15
*For since in the wisdom of God the world through its wisdom did not
come to know God, God was well-pleased through the foolishness of
the message preached to save those who believe.*   I Corinthians 1:21

The Old Testament contains types or foreshadows of the
Messiah's coming. The historical account of the foreshadow Jesus
refers to above can be found in Numbers 21. Israel sinned once
more against the Lord and He sent serpents into their midst. Since
Israelites were dying from the snake bites, they confessed their sin
and asked Moses to intercede with God. God instructed Moses to
make a bronze snake and put it on a pole. Anyone who was bitten
could simply look at the snake on the pole and they would be healed.

God answered the Israelites' request for salvation but not in
the way they expected. They wanted the snakes to be removed; God
provided a miraculous method of healing based on simply obeying
His instructions. Any snake-bitten individual who viewed the
remedy as ridiculous and didn't comply died.

The correlation of this incident with belief in Jesus' death on
the cross is striking. Mankind was essentially snake-bitten in the
Garden of Eden and the resultant sin led to physical and spiritual
death. Looking to the atoning work of Jesus on the cross saves us
from the spiritual death we deserve due to our sin. We must simply
follow the remedy God has offered.

The Apostle Paul recognized that many would consider the
gospel message foolishness. Theologically, the gospel makes perfect
sense. However, since no human would ever have devised such a
solution to the sin problem, many dismiss it without further thought.
While Paul was sharing the gospel message with Festus, the Roman
governor, Festus interrupted and told Paul that he was out of his
mind.[1] We can expect the same reaction from some with whom we
share the gospel. But we must not let the indignation of others deter
us from sharing. Part of suffering on Christ's behalf is being
considered a fool.

[1]Acts 26:24

1. Who are you praying for to be saved? Is it possible that some of your friends and neighbors view you the same way Elaine viewed her boyfriend? List below any additional people for whom you need to be praying.

2. Why do some consider the gospel foolishness? Did you at one point think that way? If you are now a follower of Christ, you can share that the "foolishness of the message preached" radically changed your life. Look for an opportunity this week to share the Good News with someone.

Prayer Starter: Lord Jesus, burden my heart for those You died for that are in my circle of influence. Open my eyes to opportunities to share the gospel with ...

For it seemed good to the Holy Spirit, and to us, to lay upon you no greater burden than these necessary things: Acts 15:28

This statement was given by the Jerusalem Council after they concluded that circumcision would not be a requirement for salvation in Christ. In Genesis God uses strong language to establish circumcision as the sign of the covenant between Him and Abraham.[1] Circumcision was also a requirement for any foreign servant Abraham might have.

In the gospels there is no record of Jesus addressing the issue of circumcision as it relates to belief in Him for salvation. It never came up since He was primarily preaching and ministering to Jews who had already been circumcised. Given the Pharisees' strict adherence to the law and Old Testament scriptures, it is no wonder that some of those Pharisees who became believers thought that circumcision should be part of the salvation process for the Gentiles.

However, God allowed Peter to witness the conversion of Cornelius, a Gentile, in which the Spirit was given without the requirement of circumcision. Paul also had similar experiences as he shared with the Gentile world. Therefore when Peter and Paul made their case for excluding circumcision as a requirement for salvation, the church leaders conferred with each other and concurred.

There will be important questions and issues in our lives that are not directly addressed in print from God. Like the Jerusalem Council we must discover the answers through the Holy Spirit. The Holy Spirit can use circumstances and an abiding sense of His peace in our lives, as He did with Peter and Paul. Collaboration with other believers may also be helpful in discerning God's will since in the abundance of counselors there is victory.[2] God promises to direct our paths as we trust and acknowledge Him.[3] As we look to His Word, consider circumstances, are sensitive to His peace, and get counsel from godly friends, He will show us the way.

[1]Genesis 17:9-14   [2]Proverbs 11:14   [3]Proverbs 3:5, 6

And the tempter came and said to Him, "If you are the Son of God, command that these stones become bread." ... Then the devil took Him into the holy city; and he had Him stand on the pinnacle of the temple, and said to Him, "If You are the Son of God throw Yourself down..."
                                                                Matthew 4:3, 5, 6a

Two of the three temptations posed by Satan to Jesus in the wilderness required Jesus to use miracles. The question was not whether Jesus could perform the miracles but whether it was God's will for the miracles to be accomplished. The same is true in our lives today. We know God can perform miracles in our lives, but is it His will to do so?

Jesus had not eaten for forty days so the idea of miraculously turning the many stones to bread had to be appealing. But the fast He was currently involved in was directed by His Father, and God's will was that He finish what He started. Even though the miracle met a legitimate need of hunger, it did not fit into God's purpose for Him at that time. Thus Jesus said *"Man shall not live by bread alone..."* There are times when God is glorified by not meeting our physical needs.

When Satan took Jesus to the top of the Jerusalem temple, he suggested the ultimate public relations stunt. Jesus gets everyone's attention, jumps, and then angels miraculously appear to catch him and safely transport Him to ground level. What a great way to establish the fact that you are the Son of God. However His Father's plan was for Jesus to go town by town and person by person revealing Himself through miracles that met people's needs one at a time. He was to take no shortcut for the three-year ministry plan which ended in crucifixion. At times we may pray for God to act miraculously in certain ways because it seems logical and reasonable to us. However, God has another plan and thus says no to our request.

Imagine having the power to work miracles, but abstaining because it was not your Father's will. It is proper for us to continue to ask God for miracles, but we should not be despondent if He says no – He has a greater good in mind.

And there arose such a sharp disagreement that they separated from one another, and Barnabas took Mark with him and sailed away to Cyprus. But Paul chose Silas and departed, being committed by the brethren to the grace of the Lord.   Acts 15:39-40

Disagreements are inevitable, even in ministry. Paul wanted to visit every city where they shared the gospel during their first missionary journey. Barnabas wanted to take Mark along as a helper. No reason is given in Scripture as to why Mark left Paul and Barnabas shortly after the first missionary journey began, but it is clear that Paul didn't consider the reason valid.

Both Paul and Barnabas were godly men sensitive to the Holy Spirit's leading in their lives, yet they disagreed. Paul, a hard-charging evangelist, had no time for quitters since the destiny of men's souls hung in the balance. "Barnabas" was a nickname which meant "Son of Encouragement".[1] We should not be surprised that he would want to give Mark a second chance, especially since Mark was a cousin.[2] Since the matter could not be resolved, they agreed to disagree and each went their separate ways.

In our generation, disagreements among godly people persist. One movement among some Christians today is to get more involved in politics to make our laws more pro-Christian. An opposing viewpoint held by others argues that Christians need to be focused on sharing the gospel only. Both sides have godly supporters and yet they cannot agree.

Disagreements can produce harmful results. Most Christians have either been involved in or heard of church splits caused by disagreements and, as with Paul and Barnabas, separation is usually the best solution. Except in the case of blatant sin, we should trust that our brothers and sisters in Christ are walking by faith to the best of their ability. When we accept their decisions with love and understanding rather than assuming they are wrong, harm to the body of Christ is minimized.

[1] Acts 4:36   [2] Colossians 4:10   [3] II Timothy 4:11

But the Lord answered and said to her, "Martha, Martha, you are worried and bothered about so many things; but only a few things are necessary, really only one, for Mary has chosen the good part, which shall not be taken away from her."   Luke 10:41-42

Jesus had come to the home of Martha and Mary for a visit. While Martha was busy with preparations Mary was seated at Jesus' feet listening to him. When Martha suggested to Jesus that Mary help her, Jesus defended Mary's inactivity and said that she had chosen the one necessary thing. Fellowship with Jesus trumps all else.

David expressed this priority when he said: *One thing I have asked from the Lord, that I shall seek: that I may dwell in the house of the Lord all the days of my life, to behold the beauty of the Lord, and to meditate in His temple.*[1] David realized the most needful thing in his life was to experience the abiding presence of the Lord. One of the best ways to do this is to set aside a daily time to meditate on His Word and talk to Him in prayer.

As we consistently and meaningfully meet with God, we discover that we can echo the blind man who reported: *One thing I do know, that, whereas I was blind, now I see.*[2] The blind man knew that Jesus had healed him because there had been a physical transformation in his life. So also, we who abide daily with Jesus over time will notice a spiritual transformation has taken place. We know without a doubt it is true because we have experienced it. As we pursue the one thing we desire it leads to the one thing we know.

[1]Psalm 27:4   [2]John 9:25

Brethren, I do not regard myself as having laid hold of it yet; but one thing I do: forgetting what lies behind and reaching forward to what lies ahead, I press on toward the goal for the prize of the upward call of God in Christ Jesus.   *Philippians 3:13-14*

As we mature in our faith in Christ Jesus, we should be able to say with the apostle Paul that there is one thing we do. Time with God will grow us in our faith and motivate us to be active for the Kingdom of God. As we understand what Jesus has done for us and see His heart for others, we are challenged to invest in Kingdom work that will last for eternity.

Whether we are at work, or walking through the neighborhood, or attending a little league game, we should see ourselves on mission for God – that is the one thing we do. We are continually praying that God will use us in whatever situation we find ourselves. We have a one track spiritual mind. Past successes and failures are history; we press on, longing to one day hear: *Well done, good and faithful slave, you were faithful with a few things, I will put you in charge of many things; enter into the joy of your master.*[1]

When we have a singular focus on knowing Jesus, growth occurs. Spiritual growth confirms our salvation because we see God's transforming power in our lives. We see and experience God's call on our lives as He sends us as laborers into His field. The one thing becomes many things.

[1]Matthew 25:23

1. Have you ever been mad at God because His will differed from what you thought was best? How were you able to work through it?

2. God's will for every person is that they make His Son their Lord and Savior, that they grow in Christ-likeness and that they share Jesus with others. Are you in the center of God's will today? If not, what area do you need to confess?

Prayer Starter: Lord Jesus, I want to be in the center of Your will. Show me any attitude or action that is not pleasing to You. Help me to …

And everyone who competes in the games exercises self-control in all things. They then do it to receive a perishable wreath, but we an imperishable. Therefore I run in such a way, as not without aim; I box in such a way, as not beating the air.   I Corinthians 9:25-26

      Paul uses sports metaphors here to encourage us to be disciplined followers of Christ. He challenges us with logic. If athletes discipline their lives to gain something that perishes with time, shouldn't we discipline our lives in view of eternal rewards? I suspect the self-control Paul exercised in his pursuit of Christ and the spread of the gospel exceeded that of any athlete in his day. Paul walked in the Spirit and one fruit of the Spirit is self-control.

      Paul says he ran with a purpose. He knew that Jesus had called him to share the good news with Jew and Gentile, and he was focused on that goal. Beatings didn't dissuade him; discouragement didn't slow him; and abandonment didn't redirect him. Paul said: *I press on toward the goal for the prize of the upward call of God in Christ Jesus.*[1]

      He fought with a purpose. Shadowboxing warms up the muscles and maintains a fighter's rhythm in preparation for the actual fight. Paul had a time of preparation in Arabia but then stepped into the ring and never got out. How many followers of Jesus spend their entire lives preparing to fight but never engage the enemy? A disciplined, focused life will move us through the training and into the fight.

      Paul provided good input for his obituary: *The time of my departure is at hand. I have fought the good fight, I have finished the course, I have kept the faith.*[2] God has placed before each of us a race to run and an enemy to fight. If we have embraced the revelation of Jesus Christ to us, then we need to embrace that daily discipline of Christ in us.

[1]Philippians 3:14   [2]II Timothy 4:6b-7

Wine is a mocker, strong drink a brawler, and whoever is intoxicated by it is not wise.

Proverbs 20:1

And do not get drunk with wine, for that is dissipation, but be filled with the Spirit.

Ephesians 5:18

The Bible cautions us about the potential dangers of alcoholic beverages. There are several Biblical examples of individuals who totally abstained from drinking alcohol. Anyone who took the vow of a Nazirite was dedicating himself or herself to the Lord. One of the prohibitions they agreed to was to abstain from wine and strong drink.[1] Samson was a Nazirite. Daniel refused wine during his Babylonian captivity and drank water. An angel stated that John the Baptist would drink no wine or liquor. No evidence exists that Jesus abstained from alcohol.

Living the Christian life is both simple and complicated. It is simple because all we have to do is walk in the Spirit and thus be led by the Spirit. However our flesh opposes being led by the Spirit and that makes it complicated. The issue with drinking alcoholic beverages is that at some point in the consumption process we are led by the alcohol's influence and not the Spirit's. The challenge is to stop drinking before reaching the intoxication stage, but that is easier said than done.

Jesus is our example of One who was controlled by the Spirit one hundred percent of the time. Perhaps that explains why drinking wine was not an issue for Him. However, Christians today who recognize their weakness in the flesh may take the Nazirite approach and abstain from alcohol. Other Christians set limits on what they drink so as not to approach intoxication levels. The admonition of Scripture is to be wise and be led by the Spirit in whatever we decide. Wisdom involves having some boundaries previously established, whether abstinence or limits, to protect us from our fleshly appetites. So, be wise!

[1]Numbers 6:2-3

Discipline yourself for the purpose of godliness; for bodily discipline is only of little profit, but godliness is profitable for all things, since it holds promise for the present life and also for the life to come.
                                                                I Timothy 4:7b-8

The believer's primary life goal should be to become more and more Christ-like, to increase in godliness. One of the first lessons we learn about goal setting is that we must have a plan to reach the goal. We must connect some activity with the goal if we expect to move forward toward that goal. So what is the Biblical plan for increasing in godliness? There are many Christian disciplines that God uses to grow us in godliness, but one of the primary ones is immersion in the Bible, the word of God.

Paul states in his second letter to Timothy that Scripture is profitable for several things including training in righteousness so *the man of God may be adequate, equipped for every good work.*[1] Peter echoes this thought when he says *like newborn babes, long for the pure milk of the word, that by it you may grow in respect to salvation.*[2] The Word of God is the primary sustenance the believer needs to grow in Christ-likeness.

Four activities we can use to get the Word in our lives are hearing, reading, studying and memorizing. Each one of these activities should be linked with meditation where we seek to apply Scripture to our lives. Many Christians rely on hearing in church and on Christian radio as their primary intake of the Word. Some augment hearing with a daily Bible reading plan. Still others will hear and read, but also set aside a few hours a week for an in-depth study of a Biblical passage or topic. Finally, some will memorize Scripture on a regular basis while maintaining the other disciplines.

All believers have to start with some action to get the Word into our lives. Any spiritual activity requires discipline but God will empower us if we ask. Spiritual growth comes over time as we immerse ourselves in the Bible in as many ways as possible with a heart of obedience. Christians should give greater priority to spiritual fitness compared to physical fitness given what we know about the present life and the life to come.

[1]II Timothy 3:16-17   [2]I Peter 2:2

...but I buffet my body and make it my slave, ...   I Corinthians 9:27a

Walking in the Spirit occurs as we walk in our body. We engage in spiritual warfare while in a physical body. Although the spiritual is more important than the physical, it doesn't mean that the physical should be ignored. Paul encouraged Christians to exercise self-control in all things, the spiritual and the physical. He sought to make his body a slave of the Holy Spirit within him so he could complete the work God had given him to do. The more physically fit the body is, the more energy and stamina is available to devote to the Lord's work. Also, statistically speaking, increased longevity affords more time to invest in Kingdom work.

Paul also reminded us: *your body is a temple of the Holy Spirit who is in you...therefore, glorify God in your body.*[1] In the context, he referred to avoiding actions in the body such as immorality which dishonors God. The appearance of our body can also honor or dishonor God. Except for uncontrollable medical conditions, the body's health can be attributed to healthy eating habits, and regular, appropriate exercise. One of the fruits of the Spirit is self-control and a disciple of Christ should be disciplined to do what is good and avoid what is bad.

The Center for Disease Control reports that approximately one-third of adults in America are obese (body mass index greater than 30). In the time of Christ, most likely, that statistic would have been a single-digit percentage. The Industrial and Technology Revolutions have empowered us in many ways to be more productive than ever before. But they have also created sedentary workplaces and leisure times for many that have taken a physical toll. As Christians, we have been challenged to exercise self-control and to buffet our bodies for the glory of God.

A properly cared for temporal body will help us to finish strong spiritually for eternity's sake.

[1] I Corinthians 6:19-20

These are matters which have, to be sure, the appearance of wisdom in self-made religion and self-abasement and severe treatment of the body, but are of no value against fleshly indulgence.

Colossians 2:23

Here Paul is addressing the religious practice of asceticism in which one exercises severe self-discipline and avoids all forms of indulgences. Religions recognize that the sin nature needs to be tamed, thus self-effort is invoked to manage the problem. Although that appears to be a wise approach, as Paul states, it is not the solution because sin originates from the heart. Attempting to control outward actions does not change the heart – we need a new heart.

Asceticism is similar to what Jesus was chastising the scribes and Pharisees for when He said: *For you clean the outside of the cup and of the dish, but inside they are full of robbery and sel-indulgence.*[1] These religious leaders were disciplined in their fasting, tithing, and public praying but their heart was far from God. Externally they looked spiritual but internally there was no connection to God.

A common theme of the Bible is that followers of Christ must exercise discipline so that we are not conformed to the world and its ways. However, Christians have the Holy Spirit indwelling them which provides a new heart and the power to resist the lusts of the flesh. An example of Paul challenging us in this regard is: *But put on the Lord Jesus Christ, and make no provision for the flesh in regard to its lusts.*[2] Notice that his admonition to rely on Jesus precedes his command to reign in the flesh.

"Self-made religions" offer a commendable goal, but don't provide the means to attain it. As a result they will always fall short in God's sight. Jesus Christ lived and died to make available to us the ability to live a life pleasing to God. Are you living a disciplined life empowered by the Spirit?

[1]Matthew 23:25   [2]Romans 13:14

1. On a scale of 1 to 5 (highest), how disciplined are you in exercising your body? In controlling your appetites and desires? Is there some action you should take? If so, ask someone to hold you accountable.

2. Read Romans 13:14 again. Ask God to help you find meaningful ways to "put on" Jesus and list them below. By abiding in the Vine, you will find strength for self-discipline.

Prayer Starter: Father, I want to be more disciplined in my life so I can accomplish all that You have me to do. Show me what areas I should focus on first. Give me a plan to deal with ...

Greater love has no one than this, that one lay down his life for his friends.   *John 15:13*

Three people in Scripture were willing to do more than lay down their lives for others – they were willing to offer their souls in exchange for the souls of others. They wanted God to judge them instead of judging others that they dearly loved. They were willing to go to hell so others could go to heaven.

After the nation of Israel left Egypt, they sinned by creating and worshipping a golden calf while Moses was on Mount Sinai with God. Moses approached God on their behalf and said: *But now, if Thou wilt, forgive their sin – and if not, please blot me out from Thy book which Thou hast written.*[1] God refused his offer, saying that whoever sinned would be blotted out.

The Apostle Paul said: *For I could wish that I myself were accursed, separated from Christ for the sake of my brethren.*[2] Paul referred to his desire as a wish because he knew it could not happen. He knew that his own righteousness was as filthy rags before God. He was guilty of his own sins and could not take on the sins of others. Paul was a spiritual pauper himself and had nothing with which to pay the sin debts of those he loved.

The third person was Jesus. *He (God) made Him (Jesus) who knew no sin to be sin on our behalf, that we might become the righteousness of God in Him.*[3] When Jesus was made sin for us, He experienced hell on our behalf. Jesus was the God-man. Moses and Paul were just men.

So among mortal men and women, Jesus statement above is true: the greatest demonstration of love is to die for someone else. But we must always remember that Jesus did more than that. He willingly laid down His life and exposed His soul to the tortures of hell because of His love for us. How can we repay so great a love?

[1]Exodus 32:32   [2]Romans 9:3   [3]II Corinthians 5:21

You have heard that it was said, 'An eye for an eye, and a tooth for a tooth.' But I say to you, do not resist him who is evil; but whoever slaps you on your right cheek, turn to him the other also.
Matthew 5:38-39

Old Covenant laws sought justice with the punishment proportional to the crime. The punishment was also intended to strike fear into everyone to inhibit future evil.[1] When Jesus ushered in the New Covenant, He changed the rules as they applied to His followers. The context seems to imply that Jesus is referring to situations when believers are being persecuted for their faith.[2] In the Church Age, the Holy Spirit is present in the believer's life, allowing him or her to respond to persecution with supernatural love.

Jesus asks His followers to treat persecutors in the same way the Father treats those who hate Him: *for He causes His sun to rise on the evil and the good, and sends rain on the righteous and the unrighteous.*[3] Without the Spirit of God in our lives, it would be impossible to respond to enemies in loving ways. With the Spirit, all things are possible.

The fear of retribution was never sufficient to erase evil. We pursue sin knowing that disastrous consequences ensue. We need a change of heart. When a believer doesn't seek retribution when persecuted for the sake of Christ, the lack of retaliation demonstrates a changed heart to the perpetrator. The power of the gospel is on display and sinners are drawn to the possibility of a changed life through Christ.

If possible, so far as it depends on you, be at peace with all men.[4] We cannot control how others treat us. But we are in total control of how we treat others if we rely on the Spirit's power to react as Jesus would. We must allow our responses to persecution to draw others to Jesus, not push them away.

[1]Deuteronomy 19:20-21   [2]Matthew 5:10-12   [3]Matthew 5:45
[4]Romans 12:18

Peter said to Him, "Lord, why can I not follow You right now? I will lay down my life for You."   *John 13:37*

So when they had finished breakfast, Jesus said to Simon Peter, "Simon, son of John, do you love (Greek: agapao) *Me more than these?" He said to Him, "Yes, Lord; You know that I love* (Greek: phileo) *You." He said to him, "Tend My lambs."*   *John 21:15*

As Jesus and Peter walked along the shore of the Sea of Galilee after Jesus' resurrection, Jesus asked Peter the same question three times – Do you love Me? In the first two questions Jesus used the word which means a God-like love, and Peter responded with a word representing a friend-like love. Immediately prior to Jesus' crucifixion, Peter said he would die for Jesus – clearly a God-like love. But a few hours later Peter denied His Lord three times and realized he did not love Jesus in a God-like fashion. These denials are fresh on his mind as he responds to Jesus using the friend-like love.

When the question comes the third time, Jesus asks Peter if he has a friend-like love for Him. Jesus met Peter where he was. He is the same with us. Jesus meets us where we are, but leads us to where we need to be. Peter needed to be focused on tending Jesus' lambs, and so do we. In a short time Peter and the other disciples would be empowered with the Holy Spirit at Pentecost and the world would never be the same.

Later, Peter exhorted all church elders to shepherd the flock of God among you.[1] He had embraced Jesus' charge to him and was in turn ensuring that others did the same. Laymen and laywomen today are not necessarily responsible for a flock, but the Great Commission does charge us to evangelize and disciple one sheep at a time. We may not be doing that now, but if we continue to follow Jesus, He will lead us to be disciple-makers.

Church tradition says that Peter was martyred for his faith. He ended his life with a demonstration of a God-like love for the Lord Jesus. May we do the same!

[1] I Peter 5:2

For now we see in a mirror dimly, but then face to face; now I know in part, but then I shall know fully just as I also have been fully known. But now abide faith, hope, love, these three; but the greatest of these is love.   *I Corinthians 13:12-13*

Love is greater than faith and hope because love will exist throughout eternity. The author of Hebrews says that "faith is the substance of things hoped for, the conviction of things not seen."[1] Faith and hope are linked because they are both tied to a belief in an as yet unseen future event. Once we have seen Jesus Christ face to face, faith and hope cease to exist. They are no longer required.

Love will exist forever because God is love.[2] Love will also exist as the basis for all the good works for which we are rewarded. At the beginning of this chapter extolling love, Paul notes that any speaking in tongues, any gifts of prophecy, any acts of faith, and any gifts to the poor will have no eternal value if the motive for the acts was not love.

Earlier in this letter Paul specifies two types of building materials used on earth to construct a building that will be tested by fire in heaven. The materials are gold, silver, precious stones and wood, hay and stubble.[3] The precious metals and stones will obviously survive the fire and thus must have been motivated by love. Rewards will be allocated to believers based on what survives the testing by fire.

In this life we walk by faith, not by sight, hoping for a future in heaven with Jesus Christ, our Lord and Savior. While here our goal is to love God and our neighbors as ourselves so that all our acts of Kingdom service come from that motive of love. When one day faith and hope become sight, we will be eternally grateful for every act of love done for Jesus' sake during our short stay on planet Earth.

[1]Hebrews 11:1   [2]I John 4:8   [3]I Corinthians 3:12

I know your deeds and your toil and perseverance, and that you cannot endure evil men, and you put to the test those who call themselves apostles, and they are not, and you found them to be false; and you have perseverance and have endured for My name's sake, and have not grown weary. But I have this against you, that you have left your first love. Revelation 2:2-4

     It is possible to do the right things for the wrong reasons. Jesus found fault with the church at Ephesus for that very reason. This church was able to discern false prophets among them and deal with them appropriately. They worked hard for the Lord and persevered in the midst of difficulty for Jesus' sake. Yet, Jesus noted that their motivation for their labors was not their love for Him.

     How do we lose our love motivation? One possibility may relate to our goal-oriented focus in life. We pour our lives into a ministry of service or discipleship. We see God use our efforts for His Kingdom. We relish the satisfaction and fulfillment that comes from a life serving God. As we dedicate more time to ministry there seems to be less time for sitting at the feet of Jesus as Mary did.

     Have you recently been around a new Christian? He or she was probably visibly excited about a new life in Christ. We are reminded of the honeymoon phase of marriage but in this case the individual is married to Christ. A fervent excitement about following the Lord is palpable. As we mature, we never want to lose that vitality with Jesus.

     Busyness is an enemy of the soul. The Psalmist said: *Be still and know that I am God.*[1] Jesus said: *I am the vine, you are the branches*; *he who abides in Me, and I in him, he bears much fruit; for apart from Me you can do nothing.*[2] We must nurture a love relationship with Jesus if we expect to bear fruit for the long haul. Without Him, we can do nothing.

[1]Psalm 46:10a (KJV)   [2]John 15:5

1. Never underestimate the love Jesus showed on the cross for sinful man. When Jesus instituted the Lord's Supper, He was asking us to remember His sacrifice – *this do in remembrance of Me.* Pause now and thank Jesus for His ultimate expression of love – don't let your love for God grow cold.

2. Do you work or live around someone who is tough to love? Consider that God loves them 24/7 and you have His Spirit in you. What act of kindness can you do this week for someone who is unlovable?

Prayer Starter: Lord Jesus, I want to love You more each day. I thank You for Your sacrifice of love on the cross for me. Help me as I show Your love this week to …

But I am hard-pressed from both directions, having the desire to depart and be with Christ, for that is very much better; yet to remain on in the flesh is more necessary for your sake. Philippians 1:23-24

If we were to devise a linear scale labeled "new believer" on the left-end section and "full maturity" on the right-end section, how would you know when someone had reached the full maturity range? Anyone that can honestly claim Paul's attitude above as his or her own is likely in the full maturity range. Full maturity is not 100% Christ-likeness because no one achieves that on Earth. However, if we had such a scale, most people would place the Apostle Paul at the time of this writing in the full maturity range of the scale.

In this section of Paul's letter to the church at Philippi, he is thinking out loud about whether he would choose life or death if given the choice. Paul's rationale involves two considerations. First, he has a deep, abiding fellowship with Jesus in his life that is of primary importance to him. Paul later says: *I count all things to be loss in view of the surpassing value of knowing Christ Jesus my Lord.*[1] So, Paul longs to see his Savior face-to-face and death is attractive to him because it would make that reunion a reality.

But there is another consideration impacting his decision: ministry. If he is in the presence of Jesus in heaven, he is not available to minister to people on Earth. Jesus called Paul on the road to Damascus to be the apostle to the Gentiles and he was fulfilling that calling. He led some Philippians to Christ during his second missionary journey and established a church at Philippi. Paul taught them in person and is now continuing their discipleship through this letter. He is investing his time and energy into their spiritual growth and thus is reluctant to wish for his earthly departure, as desirable as that would be.

Paul summarized his philosophy of life with: *For to me, to live is Christ, and to die is gain.*[2] A follower of Christ has reached full maturity when he or she is absorbed in making disciples and has an intimate walk with Jesus which makes death more welcome than fearful.

[1]Philippians 3:8a   [2]Philippians 1:21

Whom I wished to keep with me, that in your behalf he might
minister to me in my imprisonment for the gospel; but without your
consent I did not want to do anything, that your goodness should not
be as it were by compulsion, but of your own free will.

Philemon 13-14

Growing in Christ-likeness means that as we mature we learn
to think more and more like God thinks. We develop the mind of
Christ.

Although the Old and New Testaments are filled with
commands, God desires willing obedience. His commands are not
supposed to be burdensome. Even when it came to building the
tabernacle, God only wanted offerings that were given willingly.[1]
Paul echoed this principle when he urged each man to give
cheerfully, not grudgingly or under compulsion.[2]

Paul incorporated this desire for willing offerings in his
relationship with others. He concluded that if God desires willing
offerings from me, then he should act the same way toward others.

While Paul was imprisoned in Rome he led Onesimus, a
runaway slave, to Christ. Paul happened to know Philemon, the
slave's master. Onesimus ministered to Paul in prison and grew as a
new believer. At some point Paul acknowledged that he was
benefiting from the services of Philemon's slave without Philemon's
expressed approval. To rectify the matter, he sent Onesimus back to
his master in Colossae with the letter that now bears Philemon's
name.

Much ministry for the Kingdom of God is done through
volunteers. For volunteers it is important to maintain a willing spirit
in your service. For those who coordinate and supervise volunteers,
it is important to not become overbearing, but to express thanks
often for the volunteers' labor of love. Have the mind of Christ!

[1]Exodus 25:1-2   [2]II Corinthians 9:7

Again the Lord spoke to Moses, saying, "Speak the sons of Israel, and say to them, 'When a man or woman makes a special vow, the vow of a Nazirite, to dedicate himself to the Lord, he shall abstain from wine and strong drink; ... All the days of his separation he is holy to the Lord.'"   *Numbers 6:1-3a, 8*

God divided the sons of Israel into two groups that we would today call the clergy and the laity. The priests and the Levites were set apart to offer sacrifices for the sins of the people and to set up, break down, and maintain the tabernacle. As clergy, they fulfilled the religious duties that God assigned them. The remainder of the Israelites composed the vast majority and had secular jobs that provided the food needed by the priests and Levites to live.

God established the vow of the Nazirite to allow any man or woman in Israel to set himself or herself apart as holy to the Lord for a time period of his or her choosing. If the opportunity for the Nazirite vow didn't exist, I wonder if the laity would view the clergy as having a special relationship with God that they could never attain. The presence of the Nazirite vow offers every Israelite the opportunity to be set apart as holy to the Lord.

In the New Testament, Paul urges all believers to present themselves as living and holy sacrifices to the Lord.[1] James proclaims: *Draw near to God and He will draw near to you.*[2] God, the Father, took the first step in establishing a relationship with us when He offered His Son upon the cross of Calvary. When we respond in faith to His act of love and appropriate the forgiveness and restoration Jesus' blood provides, we are adopted into the family of God.

Implicit in making Jesus the Lord and Savior of our lives is a vow to offer ourselves as holy sacrifices to God. If every believer would fulfill that vow, it would be very difficult to distinguish the clergy from the laity apart from vocation.

[1]Romans 12:1   [2]James 4:8a

And he will be like a tree firmly planted by streams of water which yields its fruit in its season and its leaf does not wither; and in whatever he does, he prospers.
Psalm 1:3

Blessed be the God and Father of our Lord Jesus Christ, who has blessed us with every spiritual blessing in the heavenly places in Christ.
Ephesians 1:3

How would you describe a person who is blessed by God? Do you think your description would differ from that of a believer who lives in a third world country? The Psalmist likens the person blessed by God to a fruitful tree. Aside from bearing children, a fruitful person always has a spiritual connotation in the New Testament.

The blessed person produces spiritual fruit both internally and externally. Internal fruit can be thought of as the fruit of the Spirit manifested in the believer: love, joy, peace, patience, kindness, goodness, faithfulness, gentleness, and self-control.[1] External fruit is anything produced through a believer by the Spirit which results in the advancement of God's kingdom.

However, fruitful trees undergo pruning so being fruitful is not always pleasant. James encourages us to *consider it all joy, my brethren, when you encounter various trials, knowing that the testing of your faith produces endurance.*[2] So God typically grows the fruit of patience through trials. The apostle Paul was very fruitful in winning souls to Christ but fruit was produced in the midst of much bodily persecution.

God does bless His children with material blessings. However, compared to the spiritual blessings available, material blessings are secondary. Let's thank God daily for the physical blessings of life. But let's recommit to giving our primary attention to pursuing spiritual blessings even though they may not initially feel as good as material blessings.

[1]Galatians 5:22-23   [2]James 1:2-3

"And he called ten of his slaves, and gave them ten minas, and said to them, 'Do business with this until I come back.' But his citizens hated him, and sent a delegation after him, saying, 'We do not want this man to reign over us.'"   *Luke 19:13-14*

Paul places all people in one of three categories: natural, spiritual, or carnal.[1] When Jesus shares this parable, the cast of characters includes Him and these same three categories. Let's examine how Jesus, the nobleman receiving a kingdom, interacts with each group.

The natural person is the citizen who doesn't want Jesus reigning over him or her. This individual wants autonomy from God. Jesus is a benevolent, loving ruler but the citizen cannot or will not accept that fact. In verse 27 of the parable, Jesus refers to them as His enemies and they are slain in His presence. Anyone on Judgment Day who has not accepted Jesus' atonement for their sins will spend eternity separated from God.

The spiritual and carnal people are both considered slaves in that they have at a point in time surrendered their lives to Jesus as Lord and Savior. All slaves have been entrusted with the Holy Spirit and the accompanying spiritual gifts. The distinction between the two categories relates to what they have done with the gifts given them. The spiritual used what was given to advance the kingdom of God; the carnal was self-absorbed and did not. In the afterlife the spiritual will be rewarded and the carnal will suffer loss.[2]

The mission of the spiritual is to lovingly restore the carnal and share the gospel with the natural, all under the power of the Holy Spirit. We all need to be spiritual. Where are you?

[1]I Corinthians 2:14-3:1   [2]I Corinthians 3:14-15

1. Which people category are you in today: natural, spiritual, or carnal? Only the spiritual person is on the road to maturity. No other road is worth travelling because Satan is directing traffic for the natural and the carnal. Repentance puts you on the spiritual road. Do you need to repent?

2. Do you think every Christian today should view himself or herself as a Nazarite? Why or why not?

Prayer Starter: Lord Jesus, I want to walk as a spiritual person day by day. I desire to be on the road to full maturity in Christ and I ask for strength to stay focused on You. When asked if I was natural, spiritual or carnal, I said I was _____ because …

So the king consulted, and made two golden calves, and he said to them, "It is too much for you to go up to Jerusalem; behold your gods, O Israel, that brought you up from the land of Egypt."
I Kings 12:28

This verse describes the creation of a new religion. After Solomon's death, his kingdom was divided into the Northern Kingdom of Israel ruled by Jeroboam and the Southern Kingdom of Judah ruled by Rehoboam. Jeroboam was concerned that when his constituents went to the temple in Jerusalem (Judah) to offer sacrifices, their hearts over time would be drawn to the king of Judah. His solution was to create two golden calves and locate them at two new worship sites in Israel. His invention was convenient and had all the trappings of religiosity. Soon all of Israel abandoned the God of Israel and worshipped the golden calves.

How many times over the millennia has this type situation occurred? Someone has instituted a new religion or cult to satisfy a perceived personal need. Satan was undoubtedly involved in the deception which found fertile soil in the heart of the perpetrator.

Most religions and cults today are modifications of previously existing religions, as Jeroboam's creation was with Judaism. Buddhism modified aspects of Hinduism. Cults such as Mormonism and Jehovah's Witness have altered many mainline Christian doctrines. But what about the argument that Christianity modified Judaism to create a new religion?

In fact, Christianity replaced Judaism. The prophet Jeremiah said: *Behold, days are coming, declares the Lord, when I will make a new covenant with the house of Israel and with the house of Judah.*[1] The author of Hebrews expanded on this thought: *When He said, "A new covenant", He has made the first obsolete. But whatever is becoming obsolete and growing old is ready to disappear.*[2] The Bible is boldly divided into two sections: the Old Testament (covenant) and the New Testament. If you view Jesus as the Jewish Messiah, you recognize the new covenant is in place.

Christianity is not a religion, it is the way, the truth, and the life – no one comes to the Father except through Jesus.[3]

[1]Jeremiah 31:31   [2]Hebrews 8:13   [3]John 14:6

If anyone advocates a different doctrine, and does not agree with sound words, those of our Lord Jesus Christ, and with the doctrine conforming to godliness, he is conceited and understands nothing ..., who suppose that godliness is a means of gain. I Timothy 6:3-4a, 5b

In the days immediately following the crucifixion of Christ, believers were disturbed and perplexed. They expected the Messiah would be a conquering king to deliver them from Roman rule. Instead they got the suffering Savior to deliver them from sin's rule. Based on their perceived need they focused on the wrong prophetic scriptures and were thus disappointed.

Today many believers have a perceived need of health and wealth, and unfortunately there is a prosperity gospel in the market that fits the bill. Prosperity theology claims the Bible teaches that God has promised believers financial and physical well-being. God's blessing is obtained through faith and positive confession.

Jesus said: *If anyone wishes to come after Me, let him deny himself, and take up his cross daily, and follow Me.*[1] When I read about the lives of Jesus and the early disciples, I don't see lives that are awash in financial prosperity. I do see men who are living sacrificial lives so that others can receive an abundant spiritual life and eternity with Jesus in heaven.

After reading this devotional, please read the remainder of I Timothy 6. I will give you a jump start by sharing verse 6 here: *But godliness actually is a means of great gain, when accompanied by contentment.* Paul was content. Through the power of Christ in him, he had learned to be content whether he had nothing or much.[2] Financial prosperity was never a focus in his life. He accepted whatever God gave him with gratitude and used what he had to reach the world with the gospel. May we focus on a gospel that puts others first and our own prosperity last.

[1]Luke 9:23   [2]Philippians 4:11-13

For I bear them witness that they have a zeal for God, but not in accordance with knowledge. For not knowing about God's righteousness, and seeking to establish their own, they did not subject themselves to the righteousness of God. Romans 10:2-3

Although Paul's comments above refer to his fellow Jews, they also apply to any of the major religions in the world today. God's righteousness was made available to all mankind through Jesus' substitutionary death on the cross as payment for our sin's penalty. Since most Jews rejected Jesus as Messiah, they decided to observe the law as their means of pleasing God and getting to heaven.

Mankind has always been zealous in its attempts to reach and please God. Since we are aware of God's holiness and our unrighteousness, we surmise that the key to knowing God must be through being a better person. Mohammed taught that one earns salvation by observing the five pillars of Islam: making a statement of belief, saying daily prayers, giving alms, observing Ramadan and completing a pilgrimage to Mecca. Hindus believe that man is justified through devotion, meditation, good works and self control which through reincarnation eventually lead to Nirvana. Gautama instituted Buddhism by modifying Hinduism to include the Eightfold Path of right living to reach Nirvana. Each of these major religions involves a list of things to do to reach heaven. They have each established their own version of what righteousness is.

The irony of religion is that the premise of religion is correct: we do have to be better people to reach heaven. Unfortunately, God's standard is perfection and the Bible declares that *all have sinned and come short of the glory of God.*[1] The "perfection clause" in salvation is what necessitated God's offer of his own sinless Son as the payment for our shortcomings. When religions interpret what they think will satisfy God's righteousness, they in effect reject the true righteousness that God has provided through Jesus.

Take a moment right now and thank God for providing His righteousness so that through faith in Christ we can spend eternity with Him.

[1]Romans 3:23

I hate, I reject your festivals, nor do I delight in your solemn assemblies.
                                                                    Amos 5:21
But let a man examine himself, and so let him eat of the bread and drink of the cup.
                                                            I Corinthians 11:28

A ritual is a formal, solemn act, observance, or procedure in accordance with a prescribed rule or custom. God instituted festivals as a ritual to ensure His people would periodically remember His past faithfulness to them. As an example, the Passover was a yearly ritual that commemorated God's deliverance of the Hebrew nation from slavery in Egypt. By sacrificing a lamb and staining the doorposts with its blood, the death angel "passed over" the house and the Israelites lives were spared.

A potential problem with a rite is that it can become rote. A ceremony ceases to be meaningful when it becomes mechanical. In the passage above, the prophet Amos spoke to the northern kingdom of Israel in the 8th century BC. The people celebrated festivals with sacrifices, songs, and music but their lives displeased the God they sought to worship and thank. Words and actions during the festivals were incongruent with their heart and actions in day-to-day life.

The New Testament counterpart of the Passover is the Lord's Supper or Holy Communion. Paul alludes to this when he declares "Christ our Passover also has been sacrificed"[1]. Jesus established the Lord's Supper so His followers would remember His blood was spilled and His body was broken for their sins on the cross. However, when the Corinthian church came together for the ritual, some believers quarreled and others gorged themselves on the food. The intent of the ceremony had been lost.

Paul's admonition for the Corinthians to examine themselves is good advice for us today. For many of us activities such as church attendance, daily devotional time, and the Lord's Supper can easily develop into habits that can lose their meaning over time. A time of self-evaluation as we examine our motives and rededicate our activities to the Lord is essential to prevent these rituals from becoming routine and less meaningful.

[1] I Corinthians 5:7

Therefore let no one act as your judge in regard to food or drink or in respect to a festival or a new moon or a Sabbath day – things which are a mere shadow of what is to come; but the substance belongs to Christ.   Colossians 2:16-17

God instituted various dietary restrictions, festivals, and days as signs or foreshadows of the coming of Christ. If you see a restaurant sign, you don't go to the sign to get food. Instead you follow the sign's direction to the restaurant. Once Jesus arrived on scene, the foreshadowing was no longer needed. As an example, when Peter refused to eat unclean animals he had seen in a vision, God spoke to him: *What God has cleansed, no longer consider unholy.*[1] Because of Jesus' atoning death, all people have the opportunity to be clean before God.

However, a Jewish group of converts wanted to cling to the ceremonial law of the past – they were grasping the shadows instead of the substance – and were coercing others to do the same. Paul was combating this form of legalism and wanted the Colossians to be free to walk in the Spirit.

Today we still deal with shadows but we call them traditions. Traditions are found in every mass or worship service and include liturgy spoken, songs sung, prayers prayed, instruments played, furnishings used, and the order of service. Traditions were developed to aid us in our worship of God. Most traditions are more like shadows than substance, but the laity usually revolt when church leadership tries to deviate from the norm. Just as there were reasons for the original traditions, so there are reasons for change. View tradition as more of a shadow than substance and it will be easier to embrace change in the non-essentials of the Christian faith.

Don't be trapped in the shadows.

[1]Acts 10:15b

1. What traditions and rituals are you following today that are more of a hindrance than a help to your obedience and worship of God?

2. How would you respond if someone asked you: "Are you religious?" or "What is your religion?" Write a sentence or two below that makes a distinction between religion and a Christ follower.

Prayer Starter: Father God, open my eyes to see whether any of my religious practices are just rote traditions and rituals. Help me to worship you in Spirit and truth. Make the following practices more meaningful: …

May the Lord reward your work, and your wages be full from the Lord, the God of Israel, under whose wings you have come to seek refuge.   Ruth 2:12

Have you ever prayed a prayer only to realize later that you are the answer to that prayer? That was Boaz's experience after he prayed this prayer over Ruth. Ruth was a Moabite and the daughter-in-law of Naomi, an Israelite. Both ladies were widowed while living in Moab and were now returning to Bethlehem, Naomi's home. Without a man in the house, Ruth provided food for them by gleaning wheat and barley in nearby fields. Providence brought Ruth to the field owned by Boaz who happened to be related to Naomi. Based on a Jewish law known as the Kinsman-Redeemer, Boaz married Ruth and thus became the answer to his prayer.

Jesus said to his disciples: *The harvest is plentiful, but the workers are few. Therefore beseech the Lord of the harvest to send out workers into His harvest.*[1] After Jesus' death, these same disciples became the answer to the prayer as they carried the gospel throughout the known world. They were sharing the good news that a Kinsman-Redeemer had come to earth as a man and had redeemed their souls.

Providentially, Boaz and Ruth were the great grandparents of King David and thus in the lineage of Jesus who was also born in Bethlehem. The progeny of a human Kinsman-Redeemer was a divine Kinsman-Redeemer who asks us to pray that God will send workers into His harvest. Let's pray for workers and be ready to respond when God leads us to answer our prayer.

[1]Matthew 9:37-38

Remember me for this, O my God, and do not blot out my loyal deeds which I have performed for the house of my God and its services.

Nehemiah 13:14

Three times in the above chapter Nehemiah asks God to remember him for actions that he has taken for the sake of God's kingdom. I like the prayer "remember me" and want to use it more. It accomplishes several purposes for me.

First of all, it means that I am in a running dialog with God. When I do something that is Kingdom related I ask God to remember me. I acknowledge that He is watching what I do and say. Anything that makes me aware of His presence is worth doing.

Secondly, this prayer encourages me to seek God's approval and not man's approval. Each of Nehemiah's actions was unpopular with a particular segment of the Jerusalem population. As an example, he reprimanded the nobles who encouraged working, buying and selling on the Sabbath, a violation of the Fourth Commandment. If he had been concerned with pleasing man he would never have taken the actions he did. My goal in life should not be to impress or please men but God. This prayer reminds me of that elusive purpose.

Finally, the frequency with which I say "remember me" is a gauge of how successful I am investing my time, talent and treasure in God's kingdom. If it becomes an infrequent prayer, then I need to reevaluate how I am responding to the daily opportunities God gives me to serve Him.

This prayer is only recorded once in the New Testament. The dying thief on the cross said: *"Jesus, remember me when You come in Your kingdom!"*[1] How appropriate that the only reference is the most important reference. God can never remember my actions until He has remembered and granted my request for salvation from my sins. Prior to saving faith in Christ, all my good intentions are just filthy rags.

Therefore, my beloved brethren, be steadfast, immovable, always abounding in the work of the Lord, knowing that your toil is not in vain in the Lord.[2]

[1]Luke 23:42   [2]I Corinthians 15:58

And all things you ask in prayer, believing, you shall receive.
                                                    Matthew 21:22

　　　Have you noticed that things tend to be more complicated than they seem at face value? This promise from Jesus hinges on the word "believing". So, what is meant by "believe"? James informed us that belief is more than mental assent when he stated: *the demons also believe, and shudder.*[1] The best commentary on the above verse would be other verses from the Bible that also relate to prayer. Let's investigate three other verses on prayer to clarify what Jesus meant.

　　　The Apostle John said: *and whatever we ask we receive from Him, because we keep His commandments.*[2] John goes on to say that one of God's commands is that we believe on the name of Jesus. So belief and obedience are connected. If I am in a state of disobedience to God when I pray, then I should not expect to receive. In fact, David said: *If I regard wickedness in my heart, the Lord will not hear.*[3]

　　　Later in the same book, John noted this: *if we ask anything according to His will, He hears us. And if we know that He hears us in whatever we ask, we know that we have the requests which we have asked from Him*[4] God will not grant something we ask for if it is against His will. The Biblical idea of believing is tied to asking according to God's will. Jesus ended His prayer in the Garden of Gethsemane with *Thy will be done.*

　　　Finally, James offered this admonition: *You ask and don't receive, because you ask with wrong motives, so that you may spend it on your pleasure.*[5] We can ask for something that is according to God's will, but if our motives are wrong, God may not answer. Ultimately, God answers our prayers so that He will be glorified, not us.

　　　As obedient children, let's keep praying to our Father in faith, seeking His will and His glory, expecting Him to answer.

[1]James 2:19b　　[2]I John 3:22a　　[3]Psalm 66:18　　[4]I John 5:14b-15
[5]James 4:3

Is anyone among you suffering? Let him pray. Is anyone cheerful?
Let him sing praises.
                                                                James 5:13

  At any time during the day we find ourselves somewhere on this continuum between suffering and cheerfulness. The proper response to both extremes and anywhere in the middle is the same: communication with God. Paul was echoing the same thought when he said *pray without ceasing.*[1]

  It seems today that almost everyone has a cell phone. We can be in instantaneous contact with those we know and love anytime, anywhere. The "anytime" assumes the cell phone is properly charged. The "anywhere" assumes we are not operating in a dead zone. Prayer is our cell phone to God. If we are walking in the Spirit we are charged and ready to talk. If we avoid living in the dead zones of sin, we have open access to the Father. [2]

  When life seems unfair and we are hurting, the natural reaction is to complain. We seem to quickly forget that most of our growth comes during adversity. That notion caused Paul to say, I glory in my infirmities. James admonishes us to pray during these tough times. Ask for deliverance; pray for guidance.

  When we are running smoothly on all eight cylinders, we tend to forget about God. James encourages us to sing praises to remind ourselves of the source of the current blessing. Praise is a form of prayer as we speak to God of His goodness and greatness.

  As Christians, we are hardwired for communication with God through the presence of the Holy Spirit in our lives. We must take advantage of our prayer connection with Him in the good and tough times of life.

[1] I Thessalonians 5:17 [2] Psalm 66:18

Moreover, as for me, far be it from me that I should sin against the Lord by ceasing to pray for you; but I will instruct you in the good and right way.   *I Samuel 12:23*

This verse convicts me. Samuel spoke these words to the children of Israel. He was God's prophet to the people but they had recently asked for and received a king, Saul. However, Samuel was still their spiritual leader and thus we read his commitment to pray for them and teach them truth.

My conviction comes from Samuel's assertion that a lack of prayer for people under his leadership and influence was a sin against God. I have been a Bible teacher for over forty years and I take that responsibility very seriously. I understand the importance of accurately teaching the truth of God's Word and living my life as an example to others. I further understand that I would be in sin if I taught from wrong motives or tried to intentionally mislead someone. But Samuel included prayerlessness as a sin also. Why?

Ministry is not something we do for God, but with God. Paul described himself as laboring together with God.[1] Jesus portrayed Himself as the vine and us as the branches.[2] The branches bear fruit only as they remain attached to the vine, receiving the nourishment they need to grow. Prayer is a significant means of abiding in the vine.

Prayer invites God into the moment. Prayer acknowledges that without God at work in and through us, our labors are in vain. Prayer connects the supernatural with the natural. Prayer empowers the efforts of mankind in kingdom work. Unfortunately, I often treat it as secondary to the preparation and presentation of a Bible lesson.

Samuel was committed to his teaching ministry and he saw prayer for the people under his teaching as equally important. He taught the people the word of God and spoke words to God on their behalf. Lord, enable us to include prayer for people in our ministry to people.

[1] I Corinthians 3:9   [2] John 15:4-5

1. Do you spend more time praying for yourself or others? Does your ministry to others include prayer for others? Do you need to change your prayer life in any way? What?

2. What do you think Paul meant when he commanded the Thessalonians to pray without ceasing?

Prayer Starter: Jesus, give me Your heart for people. I want to be an intercessor for others, not always focused on myself. I pray now for these people who are on my heart: …

Now concerning the things about which you wrote, it is good for a
man not to touch a woman. But because of immoralities, let each
man have his own wife, and let each woman have her own husband.
I Corinthians 7:1-2

     Sexual sins can be placed in three categories. Firstly, sexual
intimacy with someone other than your spouse is forbidden. This
category would include adultery, fornication and homosexuality.
Secondly, imagining a sexual relationship with someone other than
your spouse is sin since Jesus said that *everyone who looks on a*
woman to lust for her has committed adultery with her already in his
heart.[1] This sin has increased exponentially over the years through
the evil of pornography. Finally, withholding sex from your spouse
creates more vulnerability to the first two categories and is therefore
wrong.[2]

     When God created Adam and Eve, the first married couple,
the only way they could sin was to eat the forbidden fruit from the
tree of the knowledge of good and evil. None of the three categories
of sexual sins was even available to them because they were alone.
However, once the human race populated, sexual sins became
rampant. Many lives and marriages are destroyed daily by sexual
immorality.

     God created sex for procreation, intimacy, and pleasure. God
commands that we wait until marriage before we enjoy sex to protect
us, not punish us. Today that notion is considered old fashioned and
passé, but the consequences of violating the command are
nevertheless very real. The spiritual law stating that you reap what
you sow[3] is just as valid as any physical law.

     Since the fall, it is as though every tree in the garden has fruit
which tempts us sexually. God has provided the marriage tree from
which to freely eat. If single, trust God to provide that tree in His
timing. If married, look only to your tree to satisfy your sexual
needs. Sexually speaking, live a life with no regrets.

[1]Matthew 5:28   [2]I Corinthians 7:5   [3]Galatians 6:7-8

I have made a covenant with my eyes; how then could I gaze at a virgin?
                                                                        Job 31:1

And if your right eye makes you stumble, tear it out, and throw it from you.
                                                            Matthew 5:29a

Job was being practical; Jesus was using hyperbole. Job reasoned that if he didn't take that second look, he could stem thoughts of sexual impurity. Jesus argued that since eternal consequences far outweigh temporal considerations, it would be better to remove your eye than have it negatively impact your eternal state. Both were extolling the need for self-control.

Self-control is a fruit of the Spirit given to us when we become followers of Christ. Paul notes that the flesh and the Spirit *are in opposition to one another, so that you cannot do the things that you would.*[1] The struggle with the flesh will always be there, but because you have the mind of Christ you can make decisions that honor the Spirit. Part of the battle is simply recognizing that there is a battle for our thoughts and actions. Many Christians are living defeated lives spiritually because they don't put on the armor of God each day and prepare for battle.[2]

God has given us minds with which we can reason and make decisions. He has further given believers the Holy Spirit and His Word to guide our minds in the right direction. If we make decisions based on emotions or knee-jerk reactions, they will likely be wrong. In determining how we invest our time, let's be prayerful and thoughtful, submitting to the Spirit, not the flesh.

[1]Galatians 5:17b   [2]Ephesians 6:10-18

Now flee from youthful lusts, and pursue righteousness…
II Timothy 2:22a

Whenever one runs from something, he or she is running toward something else. Sin and righteousness are polar opposites. Paul encourages Timothy to run from lustful sin and run toward righteousness. God wants the same for us and provided us with examples of men in the Bible that ran opposite ways so we can learn from each of them.

Joseph was sold into slavery by his jealous brothers and ended up a servant in the home of Potiphar, an Egyptian officer. Potiphar's wife was physically attracted to Joseph and one day the two were in the home alone. *And she caught him by his garment, saying, "Lie with me!" And he left his garment in her hand and fled, and went outside.*[1] Joseph chose to flee youthful lusts and pursue righteousness. The wife accused him of attempted rape and he was unjustly thrown in prison. Two years later, God miraculously gave Joseph favor in Pharaoh's eyes and he was placed second in command in Egypt.

Now when evening came David arose from his bed and walked around on the roof of the king's house, and from the roof he saw a woman bathing; and the woman was very beautiful in appearance. And David sent messengers and took her, and when she came to him, he lay with her.[2] David opted to pursue youthful lusts and flee from righteousness. He also chose to murder Bathsheba's husband in an attempt to hide the sin. David suffered the consequences of his lustful pursuit the rest of his life.

The Bible says that you reap what you sow. If you really believe that, flee immorality and run to righteousness! Learn from both Joseph and David.

[1]Genesis 39:12   [2]II Samuel 11:2, 4a

Then the Lord said to me, "Go again, love a woman who is loved by her husband, yet an adulteress, even as the Lord loves the sons of Israel, though they turn to other gods and love raisin cakes."

Hosea 3:1

God sometimes used events in the lives of Biblical characters to portray a spiritual message. As an example, He asked Abraham to offer his son on the altar and used that as a picture of the sacrifice God the Father would one day make using His Son Jesus. In essence, these situations are allegories.

Hosea was a prophet to the kingdom of Israel whose ministry started during the mid-eighth century B.C., and continued for over fifty years. God used Hosea's marriage to an adulteress to communicate how He felt when the nation of Israel was unfaithful to Him. The first two commandments God gave to Israel were to have no other gods before Him and to not make any idols which represented those gods. God further referred to Himself as a jealous God[1]. The demands for obedience came from His heart of love which He had for Israel. He was looking out for their welfare. Yet, they disobeyed, turned to other gods, and became unfaithful to God.

In the New Testament the love relationship that God has for mankind is seen primarily through Christ's death on the cross. Christ is referred to as the bridegroom and his followers, the church, are seen as the bride[2]. Unfortunately, the bride is still unfaithful at times to the bridegroom. James addresses our unfaithfulness head on as he declares that any who have become a friend with the world are adulteresses.[3] A god in our culture is anything that has assumed a higher priority in our lives than God. It could be a person, a job, or materialism.

Among men and women in marriage relationships, either or both could be found to be unfaithful to the other. However, in our love relationship with Jesus, it is always we who have moved away.

Jesus stands ready to forgive but we have to repent of our waywardness and renew our vows. Jesus loves us and wants us to return.

[1]Exodus 20:3-5   [2]Matthew 9:14, 15   [3]James 4:4

For the commandment is a lamp, and the teaching is light; and reproofs for discipline are the way of life, to keep you from the evil woman, from the smooth tongue of the adulteress. Do not desire her beauty in your heart, ...   *Proverb 6:23-25a*

Solomon spent most of chapters 5 through 7 in Proverbs advising his son about the danger of sexual immorality. When God created man one of His commands was to be fruitful and multiply. God enabled man to carry out that command by giving him a sex drive. However, restrictions came with this sex drive: *"For this cause a man shall leave his father and his mother, and shall cleave to his wife; and they shall become one flesh."*[1] Sex was a gift to man in the context of marriage.

The term *sex drive* is appropriate. A man is not indifferent to sexual relations; he has been created to want one. One of the greatest challenges to the Christian man is to subject this sexual drive to the will and timing of God. Solomon no doubt knew of his father's adulterous affair with his mother, Bathsheba, and the consequences David paid for that moment of weakness. Therefore, he labored long to instruct and warn his son about the pitfalls of sexual immorality.

Solomon made his son fully aware of the danger and urged him not to underestimate the threat of immorality in his life. He also encouraged his son to embrace God's commands, recognizing that they were given to show us how to live a full and abundant life, free of regrets.

Unfortunately, Solomon did not take his own advice. God had commanded Israel not to marry foreigners since these women would turn the Israelites' hearts to other gods. Solomon disobeyed that command and married many foreign women who did turn his heart away from God in his old age.[2]

God grant that our lives will be sexually pure from this point forward!

[1]Genesis 2:24   [2]I Kings 11:1-4

1. The importance of self-control in avoiding immorality cannot be overstated. But as we seek to avoid sexual sins, we must also discipline ourselves to pursue righteousness. What are you doing that will give you a godly frame of mind?

2. Solomon was faithful and wise to talk to his son about sexual temptations. Children need to hear God's design regarding sex from Christian parents and grandparents. The world will feed them destructive lies. Is it time to begin discussions?

Prayer Starter: God, I want to be at the center of your will regarding my sex life. Give me wisdom to know when to run from evil, and a heart that wants to please and obey You. In particular, help me with …

And the elders of the Jews were successful in building through the prophesying of Haggai the prophet and Zechariah the son of Iddo. And they finished building according to the command of the God of Israel and the decree of Cyrus, Darius, and Artaxerxes, King of Persia. Ezra 6:14

Whenever God initiates a project, He provides the leadership to get the job done. In 586 BC the Babylonians destroyed Jerusalem and the temple Solomon had built. Fifty years later God stirred the heart of Cyrus, king of Persia (conqueror of Babylon) to allow the Jews in captivity to return to Jerusalem to rebuild the temple.

Under the leadership of Zerubbabel and other Jewish elders the work was begun. When the work stopped because of opposition, God spoke through Haggai: *Is it time for you yourselves to dwell in your paneled houses while this house lies desolate?*[1] Temple reconstruction restarted and was finished in 516 BC.

Today, God is building another temple: His Church. He is still providing the leadership required to get the job done: *And He gave some as apostles, and some as prophets, and some as evangelists, and some as pastors and teachers, for the equipping of the saints for the work of service, to the building up of the body of Christ.*[2]

God has allowed many Christians today to live in countries where the governmental leadership is not opposing Christianity and in some places supports it. If the Church is not being built, it is either because leaders are not leading or followers are not following. God has still provided everything needed to get the job done. We just need to do the part He has called us to do.

[1]Haggai 1:4   [2]Ephesians 4:11-12

You therefore, my son, be strong in the grace that is in Christ Jesus. And the things which you have heard from me in the presence of many witnesses, these entrust to faithful men, who will be able to teach others also.

                                                    II Timothy 2:1-2

Any spiritual task we undertake has to be balanced with an awareness of the grace needed from God to accomplish anything for Him. As Paul urges Timothy to make disciples, he prefaces his charge with an admonition to be strong in the grace of Jesus. We know what it looks like to fulfill the Great Commission by making disciples. What does it look like to be strong in grace?

Paul had this to say to the Corinthian church: *But by the grace of God I am what I am, and His grace toward me did not prove vain; but I labored even more than all of them, yet not I, but the grace of God with me.*[1] Is Paul crediting his success in ministry to hard work or the grace of God? I think he saw both as equally important and inextricably linked.

A person strong in the grace of Jesus will be a person with an attitude of praying without ceasing. We cannot be strong in God's grace if we seldom think of Him or pray to Him for empowerment and direction. Strength from grace also comes from receiving nourishment from God's Word on a daily basis. We need a lifeline to the Holy Scriptures to keep our minds and thoughts in the spiritual realm. Daily intake of the Word will keep us aware of our need for His presence in our lives.

In addition to exemplifying these two disciplines, the one strong in God's grace will also be humble. Pride comes from the belief that you have accomplished something in your strength. Believers are simply vessels through whom Christ works. We rely on His grace to accomplish anything spiritually significant through our lives.

I love the expression: We need to pray as though it all depends on God and work as though it all depends on us. If we can keep hard work and grace in the proper balance we will one day hear: Well done my good and faithful servant.

[1] I Corinthians 15:10

But Jesus called them to Himself, and said, "You know that the rulers of the Gentiles lord it over them, and their great men exercise authority over them. It is not so among you, but whoever wishes to become great among you shall be your servant." Matthew 20:25-26

Christians are called by Jesus to be servant-leaders. Many studies have been done to categorize the various leadership styles. One possible grouping of leadership styles is: autocratic (retains power/decision making), democratic (participative), bureaucratic (by the book), and laissez-faire (hands off). Depending on your personality and goals, you may be able to place yourself in one of these four categories. Whatever leadership style best defines you, Jesus wants servant hood to be the primary characteristic of that style.

In which category would you place the Gentile rulers that Jesus describes above? Since they are "exercising authority" over their subordinates, it sounds like autocratic to me. If you had to place Jesus in one of the four leadership styles above, which style would it be? It seems to me that autocratic best describes Jesus since He was always directing the disciples what to do. The difference between Jesus and the Gentile rulers was not the style of leadership as much as it was the attitude of leadership. A Gentile ruler would "lord it over" his subjects, whereas Jesus served His disciples. You will not find an example of a Gentile ruler washing the feet of his subjects as Jesus did for His disciples.

Jesus expects His followers to be leaders in the home, the neighborhood, the workplace, and the marketplace. As we lead, let's ensure servanthood is the cornerstone of our leadership.

And it came about that after three days they found Him in the temple, sitting in the midst of the teachers, both listening to them, and asking them questions. And He said to them, "Why is it that you were looking for Me? Did you not know that I had to be in my Father's house?"
Luke 2:46, 49

Remember the movie Home Alone in which the parents frantically left home for vacation only to realize on the plane that their son wasn't with them. Upon returning home they discovered their son was more mature and capable than they thought; all was well. That plot mirrors well with Luke's story above.

We don't know at what age Jesus was aware that He was the Messiah, but He clearly knew at age twelve that His Father had a mission for Him. His family travelled to Jerusalem once per year for Passover and Jesus took advantage of the trip to go to the temple. There He listened to the teachers of the law and asked questions. Jesus had to be in His Father's house because He was preparing Himself for the work the Father had for His life.

Jesus had two primary missions from His Father. First, He was to shepherd His people: being an example, teaching them, and leading them. Second, He was to be the spotless lamb that would offer His life for the sins of the world. Each of these tasks required that Jesus saturate Himself with the word of God so that He was equipped to teach and was a sinless offering.

We may not know how God wants to use us, but we always need to be preparing ourselves for whatever it is. Stay in the Word. Seek training. Volunteer to serve. Accept positions of leadership. Go on mission trips. The laity is most available to be used by God during retirement. How sad it is when Christians reach retirement age, have few ministry skills, and are not prepared for all that God wants to do through them. Don't let that be said of you.

And David said to Solomon, "My son, I had intended to build a
house to the name of the Lord my God. But the word of the Lord
came to me, saying, 'You have shed much blood, and have waged
great wars; you shall not build a house to My name…'"

I Chronicles 22:7-8

      King David and Nathan the prophet both discovered that just
because a work for God may be valid and worthwhile, that doesn't
mean that God wanted David to do it. When David first suggested to
Nathan that he build a temple to replace the tent tabernacle, Nathan
said that the Lord was with him. However, that night, Nathan saw a
vision in which God told him that David's son would build the
tabernacle, not David.[1]

      When David approached Nathan with the construction idea,
that action was equivalent to praying to God and asking for
direction. In fact, David refers to Nathan's vision as "the word of
the Lord came to me". So, David is to be commended for seeking
God's will in the matter before plowing ahead with his good
intentions.

      For many followers of Christ, the tendency is to be lacking in
ministry activity. But for the 20% in the church that do 80% of the
work and for the rest, wisdom says that we should pray before
committing to a work, asking God to shut the door if He so chooses.
God may want to get the inactive involved instead of you.

      God was faithful to answer David's prayer. He will answer
ours as well, but we need to ask. *In all your ways, acknowledge*
Him, and He will make your paths straight.[2]

[1]II Samuel 7:1-17   [2]Proverbs 3:6

1. Do you see yourself spiritually as a leader or a follower? If a leader, list those who are following you below. If a follower, list those who are leading you below. If neither, then ask God where He wants you now – a leader or a follower?

2. Many Christians tend not to lead out in an area because we are not aware of the grace of God available to us through Christ. Ask God to show you an area in which He wants you to offer leadership and then step out in faith and do it.

Prayer Starter: Father in Heaven, I want to be the spiritual leader You want me to be. Prepare me for the tasks ahead. Lead me one step at a time to trust in Your grace for the strength and wisdom to lead others. Open doors if you want me to …

I have many more things to say to you, but you cannot bear them now. But when he, the Spirit of truth, comes, he will guide you into all the truth; for He will not speak on His own initiative, but whatever He hears, he will speak; and he will disclose to you what is to come.   *John 16:12-13*

What are some examples of truth that Jesus did not reveal to His disciples when He was with them on Earth? Said another way, what doctrines do we find in the New Testament that are not found in the Gospels? Jesus promised that the Holy Spirit would reveal these previously undisclosed truths to the disciples after Jesus' return to the Father.

Many of these truths dealt with the Holy Spirit Who had not yet been given. The disciples knew little about the gifts of the Spirit or the fruit of the Spirit which would accompany the Spirit's presence in their lives. They didn't understand the coming spiritual struggle between the old nature and the new nature. Jesus only refers to the church twice in the Gospels, both in Matthew, and makes no mention of church structure or that it will include Gentile believers. So, the Holy Spirit provided the inspiration needed to the authors of the New Testament letters to reveal these and other truths. The Spirit also communicated "what is to come" to John through an angel and The Revelation resulted.

Jesus also promised that the Holy Spirit would *bring to your remembrance all that I said to you.*[1] This promise allowed Matthew and John to supernaturally recall incidents, discourses and conversations regarding their time with Jesus. Mark and Luke similarly benefited by being in the company of other eye-witnesses who were Spirit-guided. Thus the four Gospels have the imprint of the Holy Spirit on each page.

The same Spirit that inspired New Testament writers is in our hearts today if we have been saved by grace through faith in the atoning work of Jesus on the cross.[2] Our responsibility is to immerse ourselves in the word of God so the work of God can be accomplished in our lives through the Spirit of Truth.

[1]John 14:26b   [2]Ephesians 2:8-9

Do not quench the Spirit.   *I Thessalonians 5:19*

The Greek word for quench used here is found two other places in the New Testament. In both places the context deals with putting out a fire. John the Baptist referred to Jesus as One that would baptize with the Holy Spirit and fire. When this promised Holy Spirit first descended on the 120 disciples at Pentecost, the physical manifestation of the Spirit was described as *tongues as of fire.*[1] Paul is telling the church at Thessalonica not to pour water on what the Holy Spirit is trying to do in them individually and corporately.

Perhaps we could think of quenching the Spirit as committing sins of omission. These sins occur when we are prompted by the Spirit to some action but don't respond. In the verses prior to this one, Paul challenges the believers to admonish and encourage each other, to rejoice always, to pray without ceasing and to be thankful in everything. The Holy Spirit within will prompt the believer to engage in these actions and attitudes. We need to respond in obedience.

Jesus' visit to His hometown in Nazareth was summarized as follows: *And He did not do many miracles there because of their unbelief.*[2] A lack of faith will quench the Spirit. When the Holy Spirit calls us to some action related to personal growth or ministry and we don't believe He can change us or use us then we quench the Spirit.

And for this reason I remind you to kindle afresh the gift of God which is in you through the laying on of my hands.[3] Fan the flame, don't douse it!

[1]Acts 2:3   [2]Matthew 13:58   [3]II Timothy 1:6

And do not grieve the Holy Spirit of God, by whom you were sealed for the day of redemption.   *Ephesians 4:30*

If we quench the Spirit by sins of omission then perhaps we grieve the Spirit by sins of commission. In the verses surrounding our text, Paul encourages the Ephesians to lay aside falsehood, anger, stealing, and unwholesome speech. When we commit these and other overt sins we grieve the Holy Spirit within.

How does a parent respond when a child willfully disobeys? Among the many emotions present in these situations is grief. The parent is saddened and hurt that the child disregarded the parent's direction and chose their own course of action. The parent realizes that the child's disobedience has the potential of causing harm to the child. Further, the child's rebellion will cause a temporary breech between the parent and the child. The child is still a member of the family, but there will be consequences and uneasiness between the parent and child until the disobedience can be confessed and forgiven.

We are children of our heavenly Father and the Holy Spirit within us is grieved when we willfully disobey the Father's commands. The same Holy Spirit has sealed us for the day of redemption so we do not fear being cast out of the family of God. However, we can expect consequences to our acts of disobedience. Our goal should be to confess the sin and ask forgiveness as soon as we recognize we have grieved the Spirit.

Paul gave this advice to the Galatians: *Walk by the Spirit, and you will not carry out the desire of the flesh.*[1] Just as the child who has a close, personal relationship with the parent is less likely to disobey, so also the child of God who walks by the Spirit.

[1]Galatians 5:16

Truly, truly, I say to you, he who believes in Me, the works that I do shall he do also; and greater works than these shall he do; because I go to the Father.

John 14:12

Maybe Jesus said "truly, truly" here because He suspected we would not take Him seriously. After all, how could disciples living after Jesus' ascension do greater works than Jesus did? The answer is tied to the phrase "because I go to the Father." When Jesus left earth, the Holy Spirit came to earth and took up residence in the followers of Jesus. Let's look at two ways these disciples did greater works than Jesus.

During Jesus' earthly ministry, Jesus and His disciples focused on *the lost sheep of the house of Israel.*[1] When the Spirit entered the disciples their mission changed to include Jews and Gentiles.[2] Thus the scope of their ministry became greater. Previously they concentrated on Israel, now the world.

Jesus' ministry was primarily sowing, not reaping. At the close of His three year ministry, there were 120 disciples in the upper room prior to Pentecost. That attendance would represent an average church size in America today. When the Holy Spirit empowered these believers at Pentecost, Peter preached and 3,000 people were baptized and added to the church. Thus in one day, Jesus' church became a mega church by today's standards. The disciple's impact was greater with the Holy Spirit's presence.

When the Holy Spirit was given to the believers, spiritual gifts and the fruit of the Spirit were part of the package deal. A supernatural empowerment now accompanied the followers of Christ. They had greater potential with the Spirit than when they were with Jesus without the Spirit. Thus they could tackle a mission that was greater in scope and find greater success numerically than when with Jesus.

Today followers of Christ have the same indwelling Spirit that existed with the first disciples. If our works are not greater than those of Christ, then the problem lies with us, not the Holy Spirit. What needs to be done today to make Jesus' statement a reality?

[1]Matthew 10:5-6   [2]Acts 1:8

For I have no one else of kindred spirit who will genuinely be concerned for you welfare. For they all seek after their own interests, not those of Christ Jesus.   *Philippians 2:20-21*

An easy way to divide items into categories is by use of "not" or "non". For example, there are two categories of people in this world: Christians and non-Christians. Further, Christians can be divided into two categories: spiritual and non-spiritual. Or Paul would say spiritual and carnal[1].

Since carnal means fleshly, as in carnivorous, I tend to think of carnal Christians as those who display various acts of the flesh. In fact, when Paul discusses carnal Christians he refers to the jealousy and strife that was among them. So, when I seem to have the flesh under control, I tend to consider myself spiritual, since if I am not fleshly then I must be spiritual.

In the above passage, Paul uses different terms to subdivide Christians. Namely, Christians are divided into those who are seeking the things of Christ, and those who are seeking their own interests and not the things of Christ. I find it harder to classify myself as spiritual using these criteria. To be spiritual, my interests and Christ's interest should be in perfect alignment?

When Paul was imprisoned in Rome he considered whom he should send to Philippi to minister to their needs. Earlier in his letter to Philippi, Paul refers to Christians in Rome who preach Christ out of love and others who preach out of self ambition.[2]   Out of all the Christians in Rome, Timothy was the only one Paul felt would genuinely care for the needs of the church in Philippi. (Perhaps Titus and other young pastors were committed elsewhere.)

Christian spirituality is not so much the absence of the flesh as it is the presence of the Spirit. If we are Spirit controlled then we will not only abstain from fleshy lusts, but we will also be led by the Spirit into unselfish acts of love and service for the Kingdom.

[1]I Corinthians 3:1-3 (NKJV)   [2]Philippians 1:15-17

1. Are you aware of any ways you have recently grieved or quenched the Spirit? If so, what are they? Do they appear to be sins of omission, commission, or both? What do you conclude from your observations?

2. Do you think it is more valid to characterize yourself as a "spiritual" Christian based on what you are doing (ministry) rather than what you are not doing (evil)? Why?

Prayer Starter: Holy Spirit, I want to be more and more sensitive to your presence in my life. Prick my heart when I grieve or quench your Spirit. Forgive me for recent situations when I …

And having summoned His twelve disciples, he gave them authority over unclean sprits, to cast them out, and to heal every kind of disease and every kind of sickness. Now the names of the twelve apostles are these ... These twelve Jesus sent out ...
                                                    Matthew 10:1-2a,5a

There came a day when the disciples were referred to as apostles. Since apostle means "one sent forth", this new designation occurred when Jesus sent them out in pairs to preach. It appears Jesus sent them on mission early in His ministry since Matthew recorded his decision to follow Jesus in the previous chapter. At this point the gospel message was still forthcoming and the Holy Spirit had not been given, so the message shared was "The kingdom of God is at hand". Jesus gave them authority to heal to validate the message they were sharing.

Matthew records the Great Commission in the last three verses of his gospel. At this point Jesus has been crucified, buried, and raised from the dead. Sin's penalty has been paid and the offer of salvation can now be made in earnest. Since Jesus has all authority in heaven and on earth, He has commissioned His followers to go and make disciples. His disciples have transformed lives and the working of the Spirit to validate the message being shared.

Many in the Church today have not made the transition from being disciples to being sent forth into the world with the gospel. If you have a testimony of how you heard and responded to the gospel, then you have all you need to share the message of salvation. Jesus trained His disciples before sending them out, and getting training is appropriate for today as well. But, in reality, no follower of Christ has a legitimate excuse for not making disciples. Do you need to take any action to become "one sent forth"?

"If the foundations are destroyed, what can the righteous do?" The Lord is in His holy temple; the Lord's throne is in heaven.

Psalm 11:3-4a

Most people would agree today that the foundations are destroyed – there is no "if". Families are disintegrating; crime is becoming more and more heinous; and the moral fabric of society is ripping apart. Hence the question: What can the righteous do?

The first step for the righteous is to repent. The foundations are destroyed because followers of Jesus, individually and collectively, have not been sharing truth and winning the lost to Christ. Satan is having a heyday throughout the world with little opposition from the army of God. Christians are enjoying fellowship with each other in the church while the rest of the world is starving spiritually.

Believers must take the Great Commission seriously if the breach in the foundation is to be repaired. Government is not going to solve our problems because our problems are spiritual. Fortunately, the Lord is on His throne and more than willing to work through us to effect revival in the land.

If My people who are called by My name humble themselves and pray, and seek My face and turn from their wicked ways, then I will hear from heaven, will forgive their sin, and will heal their land.[1] Israel was suffering because they had sinned against God. Since Jesus commanded us to be disciples and make disciples, if a believer doesn't obey, sin results. The good news is that God will forgive and heal the land if we repent and obey.

[1] II Chronicles 7:14

*In order that He might redeem those who were under the Law, that
we might receive the adoption as sons. And because you are sons,
God has sent forth the Spirit of His Son into our hearts, crying,
"Abba! Father!"*   Galatians 4:5-6

    And God said, "Let Us make man in Our image."[1] The
Trinity was acting in a parent role when they created man. Thus
Adam and Eve could be considered children and part of the family of
God. However, sin entered the human race and when Adam and Eve
brought forth after their kind, the children had a sin nature and were
no longer part of God's family. They became part of a worldly
family with Satan as their father. Adoption was now required if
humanity was ever to rejoin the family of God.
    Jesus' death on the cross opened the door of adoption into
God's family to all who believe and desire to be in that family.
However, we can refuse adoption by a heavenly Father. *But as many
as received Him, to them He gave the right to become children of
God, even to those who believe in His name.*[2]
    Consider the benefits of adoption. You receive the Holy
Spirit into your life which provides regeneration and renewal.[3] While
still on Earth you are surrounded by the friendship and
encouragement of fellow brothers and sisters in Christ. The
presence of the Spirit in your life guarantees that you will live
forever with that family and your loving heavenly Father. Finally,
because you are family, an inheritance is reserved in heaven for
you.[4]
    Let's invite someone else today to be a part of our heavenly
family.

[1]Genesis 1:26a   [2]John 1:12   [3]Titus 3:5   [4]I Peter 1:4

But if a stranger sojourns with you, and celebrates the Passover to the Lord, let all his males be circumcised, and then let him come near to celebrate it; and he shall be like a native of the land. But no uncircumcised person may eat of it.   *Exodus 12:48*

When God first called Abram He promised to make him a great nation and to bless all families of the earth through him.[1] The promise to bless all families was culminated with the life and death of Jesus Christ. However the above verse provides an Old Testament opportunity for that blessing to come on whoever chooses to follow Jehovah God.

There is a remarkable parallel between the requirements to become a follower of Jehovah in Old Testament times and the New Testament requirements. Israel celebrated Passover because that was the night the death angel judged Egypt by killing the firstborn in every household. The provision for escaping judgment was applying lamb's blood to the doorposts of the house. Those who believed in that solution applied the blood and remained in their house that night. The judgment "passed over" them. Additionally, they were released from slavery in Egypt and allowed to go free. In the New Testament, belief in Jesus' atoning death on the cross as the Lamb of God saves us from judgment and delivers us from slavery to sin.

Circumcision was also required to become a follower of the God of Israel. When God changed Abram's name to Abraham He instituted circumcision as a sign of the covenant between Him and Abraham.[2] It was an outward sign of the new person Abraham had become through faith in the promises of God. Today water baptism is the outward sign that God prescribes to symbolize the death, burial and resurrection of Jesus and the corresponding new life that we have in Christ.

From the foundation of the world God had a plan to redeem mankind from the fall. We see that plan unfold in the Old Testament and come to perfection in the New Testament. The Passover and circumcision were fulfilled in the crucifixion and baptism, respectively. Followers of Christ have been entrusted with communicating the sin solution to all mankind. Who will you tell?

[1]Genesis 12:1-3   [2]Genesis 17:11

Practicing hospitality.   Romans 12:13b

Friends of Internationals is a parachurch organization that shows hospitality to international students who come to Tampa to study at the University of South Florida or the University of Tampa. My wife and I have picked up a young man from Viet Nam at the airport; several days later I gave him a ride to get a driver's license. We have had students from China, India, London, and Egypt in our home for a Thanksgiving meal. We have spent a day with international students visiting the Edison and Ford winter estates in Fort Myers. All of these encounters were coordinated by Friends of Internationals.

The goal is simple: Connect international students with local Christians who will demonstrate the love of Christ and pray for opportunities to share the gospel. The vehicle used to achieve this goal is showing acts of kindness, including hospitality. That strategy is effective with internationals because assistance and friendships are very important to a student, alone and far from home.

Our society today is becoming more and more withdrawn. Technology plays a big part in our reclusive behavior. Growing up, I remember couples dropping by our house unannounced to visit for a while. That is unheard of today. Yet, the human soul longs for relationships, even as we substitute other venues to meet that need.

Don't give up on hospitality, even though it is practiced less and less. When was the last time you invited an unsaved friend or neighbor to your house or a local restaurant for coffee or a meal? Have you ever asked an unbeliever to accompany you on an outing? Those outside the family of God need to experience a Christian up close and personal. It is unlikely that they will initiate that interaction, so that means we must be intentional in making that connection.

1. Do you see yourself as a disciple, an apostle, or both or neither? Why? Has God placed some individual(s) on your heart so that you feel "sent forth" to them? Who?

2. On a scale of 1 to 5 (highest) how would you rate yourself on "practicing hospitality"? Within the next week, which unsaved friend or neighbor can you connect with for a cup of coffee or a meal?

Prayer Starter: Lord, I acknowledge that You have sent me into the world with the gospel. Give me your burden for people. Orchestrate events in my life this next week so I can meet with …

The twenty-four elders will fall down before Him who sits on the throne and will worship Him who lives forever and ever, and will cast their crowns before the throne, saying, "Worthy art Thou, our Lord and our God, to receive glory and honor and power; for Thou didst create all things and because of Thy will they existed, and were created."   *Revelation 4:10-11*

"Worship" comes from the Old English word "worthship" which means to recognize the worth of another and to respond accordingly. Part of the elders' worship was declaring that God was worthy to receive glory, honor, and power. They recognized His worthiness. The elders also fell down and cast their crowns before God's throne, thereby responding to His worthiness. Worship involves both recognition and response to God's worthiness.

We learn in verse 4 of this chapter that the elders were clothed in white garments and seated on thrones with golden crowns on their heads. The elders were created by God and all that they have of value was given to them by God. No wonder they viewed God as worthy and responded accordingly.

When we take time to remember that God is our Creator and the Redeemer of our souls, we likewise will deem Him worthy. That recognition should cause us to vacate the throne of our lives and fall down before His throne of grace in worship. Whatever we are and have today that we consider good and beautiful is from His hand. As our Creator and Redeemer, He is worthy of all our praise and adoration.

Then Hezekiah took the letter from the hand of the messengers and read it, and he went up to the house of the Lord and spread it out before the Lord. And Hezekiah prayed before the Lord and said, "O Lord, the God of Israel, who art enthroned above the cherubim, Thou art the God, Thou alone, of all the kingdoms of the earth. Thou hast made heaven and earth."   II Kings 19:14-15.

King Hezekiah received high marks from God as a king of Judah. Noteworthy traits were his trust in God and his obedience. Scripture records two prayers of Hezekiah that reflect his trust and dependence on God. One prayer is primarily focused on others and one is personal.

The above passage details how he has received a letter from the King of Assyria demanding surrender with eventual exile to another land. Bearing the weight of responsibility for his people, Hezekiah takes the parchment into the temple and spreads it out before the Lord. After a time of worship and adoration before God, the king asks for deliverance from his enemy and God grants his request.

Later Hezekiah becomes sick and is told by Isaiah that he will die from the sickness.[2] Hezekiah is 39 years old and is understandably distraught over the news. He prays to God, weeping, and reminding Him of his obedience throughout his kingship. God hears and grants him fifteen more years.

Today, many Christians are carrying heavy burdens, whether it is for themselves or someone else! We could learn from Hezekiah if we would take something that represents the concern and physically lay it before the Lord. Let's worship Him for who He is. Let's be transparent before Him and not hide our emotions. Let's make our request and trust that He is mighty to deliver in our particular situation in accordance with His will.

We have Jesus as our high priest: *Let us therefore draw near with confidence to the throne of grace, that we may receive mercy and may find grace to help in time of need.*[3]

[1]II Kings 18:5-6   [2]II Kings 20:1-6   [3]Hebrew 4:16

Remember Jesus Christ, risen from the dead, descendant of David,
according to my gospel.   *II Timothy 2:8*

My wife and I were driving down the main thoroughfare of Brandon, Florida and saw a pick-up truck to our right. In bold letters on the rear windshield were the words "Remember Pearl Harbor". We considered that a rare sighting. "Remember the Lusitania" is a slogan I have never seen in public. Today, they have been largely replaced by "Never Forget…9/11". These tragic events claimed the lives of 2403, 1198, and 2977 innocent souls, respectively. These slogans were both a rallying cry against the enemy and a call to remember those who were lost.

With time, remembrance slogans fade away. Over time, the enemy may become an ally. As time passes, the loved ones of those tragically lost also pass away and no one remains who personally knew the victims. In time, the slogan enters the history books and no longer tugs at anyone's heart.

"Remember Jesus Christ" is unique. It also calls to remembrance a perfectly innocent man who was tragically killed by wicked men. However, Jesus is risen from the dead and is alive today. Jesus lives inside whoever believes the gospel message, repents, and asks Him to be the Savior and Lord of his or her life.[1] As a result, the memory of Jesus never fades. He still tugs at our hearts. Even with the passage of time, the enemy is still Satan and sin.

When Paul penned these words, many lived who could visualize the man Jesus Christ. Two thousand years later, the mental image is gone, but the heart image lives. Whatever your need is today, remember Jesus Christ!

[1]Romans 10:9-13

But the Lord said to him, "Go, for he is a chosen instrument of Mine, to bear My name before the Gentiles and kings and the sons of Israel."

Acts 9:15

And all the circumcised believers who had come with Peter were amazed, because the gift of the Holy Spirit had been poured out upon the Gentiles also.

Acts 10:45

When Jesus gave the Great Commission to the disciples, they assumed it applied only to fellow Jews. They had heard Jesus say to the Syrophoenician woman: *I was sent only to the lost sheep of the house of Israel.*[1] So prior to Acts 10, the disciples and other believers had only shared the gospel with Jews. But a change was coming. In fact, Mark's account regarding this woman has Jesus alluding to the change by saying: *Let the children be satisfied first, for it is not good to take the children's bread and throw it to the dogs.*[2] Salvation was offered first to Jews, then to Gentiles.

But Jesus had not clearly communicated this change to His followers. That job was left to the Holy Spirit after Jesus' departure. And so above we have God's explanation of Paul's conversion and the events accompanying Peter's vision of the unclean animals. These two events ushered the world into the next step of its spiritual journey.

So Paul was certain he had been appointed as the apostle to the Gentiles, and Peter was certain that God no longer considered Gentiles unclean. When Peter shared his story with the apostles in Jerusalem, they glorified God that Gentiles were now included. The abundance of visions, angels, miraculous events, and acts by the Holy Spirit sealed the deal.

Since Jews make up less than one percent of the world population, there is a good chance that you are a Gentile. Rejoice, glorify and worship God with me because we have been included in God's marvelous plan of redemption!

[1]Matthew 15:24   [2]Mark 7:27

In everything give thanks; for this is God's will for you in Christ
Jesus.   *I Thessalonians 5:18*

And when He had taken a cup and given thanks, He gave it to them,
saying, "Drink from it, all of you; for this is My blood of the
covenant, which is poured out for many for forgiveness of sins."
                                    Matthew 26:27-28

   "Everything" obviously includes what we would consider
good and bad. We have no problem thanking God for the good, but
thanking Him for what we deem bad is challenging. Whenever we
encounter a hard command to obey, we can go to Jesus as our
example of how to do it.
   Jesus gave thanks for the bread and drink in recognition of
God's provision for their basic needs. However, Jesus was also
giving thanks to His Father for what the bread and drink represented:
His body and blood to be offered up within the next 24 hours for the
forgiveness of sins. A few hours later in the Garden of Gethsemane
He would pray: *My Father, if it is possible, let this cup pass from*
Me; yet not as I will, but as Thou wilt.[1]
   Jesus was thanking His Father for what He viewed as bad.
No one would consider crucifixion as a good event in their lives, and
Jesus was no different. Jesus' ability to thank God for His imminent
death came from His understanding that God's will was the best
thing for His life. When that fact grips our souls then we can thank
God in everything also.
   The Psalmist said: *My times are in Thy hand.*[2] Whatever
happens in our lives passes through the hand of God to reach us.
Since God loves His children, He intends to use all events in our
lives to grow us into the likeness of His Son Jesus. For that we can
give thanks.

[1]Matthew 26:39b   [2]Psalm 31:15a

1. *Be still and know that I am God* (Psalm 46:10). To recognize the majesty of God, solitude is often required. Set aside some time to recognize and respond to the worthiness of God.

2. Are you burdened by someone or something to day? Take something that represents your burden and surrender it before the Lord. Worship God, make your request, and leave your cares with Him.

Prayer Starter: O Lord, the God of Israel, who are enthroned above the cherubim, Thou art the God, Thou alone, of all the kingdoms of the earth. Thou hast made heaven and earth. Worthy art Thou, our Lord and our God, to receive glory and honor and power. Lord, I worship you today because You are …

*Now these things happened as examples for us, that we should not
crave evil things, as they also craved.*   *I Corinthians 10:6*

Are you a student of the mistakes of others? Do you
solemnly consider the consequences of those who have gone astray
and vow to never follow that path? Scripture encourages us to learn
from the shortcomings of others. In fact, Bible characters are
portrayed in wide-screen Technicolor showing the good, the bad,
and the ugly. *And there is no creature hidden from His sight, but all
things are open and laid bare to the eyes of Him with whom we have
to do.*[1] God places their actions on full display, and sometimes, even
their motives. We are given details about their struggles and failures
to help us be victorious in similar temptations.

It is one thing to read the command: *You shall not commit
adultery.* It is quite another to observe David's temptation on the
rooftop of his house, to watch as he snatched the lure and committed
adultery, to wince as he ordered Uriah's murder to cover his sin, to
blush as he confessed his sin when the prophet, Nathan, confronted
him, and to sorrow when the baby dies as the first of many
consequences of his sin. You want to shout: Don't do it, David. But
the event is history; written for our instruction. So we make a fresh
commitment to shun adultery at all costs.

A common expression among Christians is: There but for the
grace of God, goes I. This statement is a humble acknowledgement
that each of us is capable of any example of wrongdoing found in the
Bible. We can learn from the failure of others, but our victory rests
in a dependence on the Spirit in our lives.

[1]Hebrews 4:13

It is a trustworthy statement, deserving full acceptance, that Christ
Jesus came into the world to save sinners, among whom I am
foremost of all.   *I Timothy 1:15*

Be imitators of me, just as I also am of Christ.   *I Corinthians 11:1*

How can Paul view himself as the chief of all sinners and yet
tell the Corinthian believers to imitate him? Notice that Paul doesn't
say he **was** foremost of all sinners. That we could understand
because earlier in life he sought to imprison and kill Christians.
Rather he says, I am the foremost of sinners – present tense.

One description of Jesus is the Light of the world. Light is a
source of heat. As one gets closer to light, the individual gets
warmer as he or she absorbs heat from the light. But the light also
allows one to see oneself more clearly. The closer one gets to the
light, the better one can see the imperfections and flaws, because
light reveals. These two dynamics are at work in Paul's seemingly
incompatible statements.

Paul had been a close follower of Jesus since his conversion
on the Damascus Road. As the years passed, Paul's life became
more and more like that of His Master, through the presence of the
Holy Spirit within him. Since Paul was following Jesus, he asked
others to follow him. However, the closer Paul got to Jesus, the
more Paul realized how sinful he was. Paul wasn't comparing
himself to others. He was only comparing himself to his perfect
Lord and Savior. The more Paul understood the incomparable
holiness of Jesus, the more unworthy he became in his own sight.

If a growing sense of humility does not accompany spiritual
growth, then something is wrong. Further, if spiritual maturity does
not result in more people being influenced by your life, then
something is wrong. Growing in Christ-likeness means influence
and humility.

How blessed is the man who does not walk in the counsel of the wicked, nor stand in the path of sinners, nor sit in the seat of scoffers! But his delight is in the law of the Lord, and in His law he meditates day and night.   *Psalm 1:1-2*

The Psalmist blesses the man who is careful where he walks, stands, and sits. He instructs the reader on where not to walk, stand, or sit. The person who spends considerable time with ungodly people can easily be influenced by their philosophy and actions. Paul warned: Do not be deceived: *Bad company corrupts good morals.*[1] We want to be accepted and liked by those we are around, and that disposition leads to conformity in thought and deed.

If a man walks in the counsel of the wicked it will not be long before he is standing with them in their sin. He has moved from considering what they do and think, to participating in their evil with them. As he partakes in their sin, he becomes comfortable and finds himself sitting and scoffing at others who are living righteously. He starts the process of ungodly living by considering the ungodly man's way of life, and ends up by showing contempt for the godly man or woman.

The person who consistently meditates in the law of the Lord will not be influenced by ungodly friends and succumb to the lures of the world. Daily exposure to God's thoughts and ways will help keep him or her on a righteous path. God's word will provide the wisdom and strength needed to live for God on a moment by moment basis. If you are being negatively impacted by ungodly friends, then either disassociate with them or restrict your interactions to situations where the impact is minimal.

[1] I Corinthians 15:33

In all things show yourself to be an example of good deeds, with purity in doctrine, dignified.
                                                                                    Titus 2:7

Paul's admonition for Titus to be a good example implies that we are positively impacted by the example of others. When was the last time you noted a good example in another's life? Did that example motivate you to do likewise?

And let us consider how to stimulate one another to love and good deeds, not forsaking our own assembling together.[1] I find that being in the company of believers who are kind and thoughtful, motivates me towards acts of kindness. I learn from their example. A common expression today is that life lessons are better caught than taught. Effective preachers and teachers share illustrations to give life to their words. Godly examples are three-dimensional sermons. Their impact is more powerful than words alone.

Brethren, join in following my example, and observe those who walk according to the pattern you have in us.[2] How often are you in the company of godly believers? Is there a Paul or Titus in your church that you could spend some time with and learn from his example? As we discipline ourselves to learn from the example of godly men and women, we in turn become an example others can emulate.

[1]Hebrews 10:24-25a   [2]Philippians 3:17

*For I do not want you to be unaware, brethren, that our fathers were
all under the cloud, and all passed through the sea; ...and all drank
the same spiritual drink, for they were drinking from a spiritual rock
which followed them; and the rock was Christ. Nevertheless, with
most of them God was not well-pleased; for they were laid low in the
wilderness.*   *I Corinthians 10:1, 4-5*

Most followers of Christ spend time in the wilderness. Our
goal should be zero wilderness detours. However our flesh is weak,
our spiritual perspective dim, and our adversary formidable. So the
question for most is not if we venture into the wilderness, but how
long we stay there.

When the children of Israel left Egypt, God declared them
free. These individuals had applied the lamb's blood to their
doorposts and the death angel had passed over their homes. They
were baptized under the cloud and in the sea. Their experiences
leaving Egypt, Satan's dominion, foreshadowed the salvation offered
to future believers of Christ. Unfortunately, their disobedience and
lack of faith after leaving Egypt also reflect the state of carnal
Christians today.

Paul is encouraging us to learn from their poor example, not
to imitate them. When believers follow the course of the world
rather than Christ, God provides a wilderness experience until
repentance occurs. He chastises us today when we wander, just like
He disciplined the Israelites in the wilderness. We would expect a
loving Father to correct a wayward child, so He is faithful in that
regard. If you are far away from God and it doesn't bother you, then
maybe you are not His child after all.

Joshua and Caleb were the only two of an accountable age
from the freed slaves that made it into the Promised Land. May we
reject the example of the masses, and follow these two men's
examples of faith and obedience.

1. We need to be in the world, not of it. (John 17:15-16) We walk a fine line when we associate with the ungodly to share our faith, and yet try to remain unaffected by their unbelief and lifestyle. Do you have a healthy balance of Christian and non-Christian friends? Or, are you too isolated from the ungodly or being negatively impacted by unbelievers?

2. To whom in your family, workplace, or neighborhood can you be a positive example?

Prayer Starter: Father God, provide someone in my life as a godly example for me. Help me to also be a positive example in the life of another. I am thinking, in particular, about …

And without faith it is impossible to please Him, for he who comes to God must believe that He is, and that He is a rewarder of those who seek Him.   *Hebrews 11:6*

Faith is interwoven through the Christian life from start to finish because that pleases God. God is pleased when we see *His invisible attributes, His eternal power and divine nature*[1] through creation. *By faith we understand that the worlds were prepared by the word of God, so that what is seen was not made out of things which are visible.*[2] We have to recognize that God exists before we can believe God sent His Son to save the world.

When we pray and ask Jesus to be Lord and Savior of our lives, we act in faith. We believe the Biblical account and see it as historically and theologically true. God invites us to pray to Him for our needs and the needs of others. When we spend time praying we exercise faith, saying that God exists, and He hears and answers my prayers. God wants us to give our financial resources to support His Kingdom, promising us that we cannot out give Him. As we develop more and more faith in that promise, we look for opportunities to give sacrificially.

When Jesus left us with the Great Commission, He promised to be with us always. Witnessing is scary. Those who do it actually believe that Jesus is with them as they share their faith. They believe Jesus will providentially give them opportunities to share, and the boldness and ability to represent Him.

As you have therefore received Christ Jesus the Lord, so walk in Him.[3] Are you walking daily by faith? Are you pleasing God?

[1]Romans 1:20a   [2]Hebrews 11:3   [3]Colossians 2:6

I am my beloved's, and his desire if for me.   *Song of Solomon 7:10*

The Song of Solomon is an allegory of Christ's love for the Church, His heavenly bride. At some point in the courting relationship, the future groom will express his love for the future bride and ask if she will marry him. Jesus, the future groom, expressed His love and extended the invitation to marriage as He hung on the cross, hands outstretched. *And I, if I be lifted up from the earth, will draw all men to Myself.*[1] His desire is for all mankind to be wed to Him, to live happily ever after with Him in heaven.

However for the marriage to occur, she has to accept the wedding proposal. Knowing that he loves her and desires to marry her is not enough; she must say "I do". She must be willing to commit herself to this man for the rest of her life. She must receive his love and extend her love to him. She must say: *My beloved is mine, and I am his.*[2]

Now that they are husband and wife, her goal should be to remain faithful to him for the rest of her life. Paul said: *For I am jealous for you with a godly jealousy; for I betrothed you to one husband, that to Christ I might present you as a pure virgin.*[3] When Paul introduced the Corinthians to their future husband, Jesus, he was not content with just the marriage. Paul discipled these new believers so they would receive the full benefit of the marital relationship.

Are you married to Christ by faith? Have you continued to get to know Him after you said "I do"? Will you run to embrace Him when you see Him face to face, or will you shrink away from Him in shame?

[1]John 12:32   [2]Song of Solomon 2:16   [3]II Corinthians 11:2

*Then Mordecai told them to reply to Esther, "Do not imagine that
you in the king's palace can escape any more that all the Jews. For
if you remain silent at this time, relief and deliverance will arise for
the Jews from another place and you and your father's house will
perish. And who knows whether you have not attained royalty for
such a time as this?"*   *Esther 4:13-14*

    The Book of Esther is the last historical book and occurs
during the reign of Ahasuerus (Xerex I) when the Jews were captive
in Persia. Esther was a Jewish orphan who had been reared by her
cousin, Mordecai. The king divorced his wife and chose Esther from
among all the beautiful women in the kingdom as his new queen, not
knowing that she was a Jew. Haman, the king's right-hand man,
despised the Jews and convinced Ahasuerus to approve a law which
established a date for all Jews in the kingdom to be killed.

    Mordecai asked Esther to approach the king on behalf of the
Jews, but she was reluctant since anyone approaching the king
without being invited was subject to death. Mordecai was not
positive his suggestion was God's plan for delivering the Jews, but
he felt confident enough to suggest it to Esther.

    Esther then had to decide whether it was God's will to risk
her life by approaching the king on behalf of her people. She had
received godly counsel from Mordecai. Circumstances seemed to
support Mordecai's suggestion since she had been providentially
placed in a position to have an audience with the king. Esther just
needed a peace within herself that God would bless this plan. So she
asked all the Jews in the area to fast and pray for three days while
she did the same. When Esther made herself visible to the king, he
invited her to approach him. The Jews were spared, and Haman and
all those who wished harm to the Jews were killed.

    As we seek God's will in the various decisions we must
make, we are asked to walk by faith. As with Mordecai and Esther,
there will be an element of uncertainty when making decisions.
However, if the counsel of godly friends and Scripture align with
circumstances and an inner peace, step out in faith and act. For who
knows whether you were not placed in that circumstance for such a
time as this.

"But if You can do anything, take pity on us and help us!" And Jesus said to him, " 'If You can!' All things are possible to him who believes." Immediately the boy's father cried out and began saying, "I do believe; help my unbelief."   *Mark 9:22b-24*

A father had brought his demon-possessed son to Jesus' disciples but they were unable to cast out the demon. When Jesus arrived on the scene, the father asked Jesus for help. At this point in the story, the father had demonstrated both belief and unbelief. Belief was shown when he brought his son to Jesus in that there was some expectation that Jesus might help. However, unbelief was veiled in his statement: *If you can do anything.*

The author of Hebrews describes faith as the conviction of things not seen[1]. Since Jesus cannot be seen or touched today, faith in Him may never be at a 100% confidence level. The mature follower of Christ may have a surety close to 100%, and the individual exploring the claims of Christ may rank his belief at the other end of the scale. But both the mature follower and the seeker likely have some combination of both belief and unbelief.

When Jesus appeared in bodily form to the disciples after His resurrection, Thomas was absent. Thomas refused to believe unless he could touch Jesus' scars. Jesus later appeared to Thomas and said: *"Because you have seen Me, have you believed? Blessed are they who did not see, and yet believed"*.[2] The blessing Jesus gave falls on believers today.

When sharing our faith with an unbeliever who cannot commit, perhaps it would be better to focus on the little belief they have rather than their mountain of unbelief. Encourage them to pray (or pray for them) and admit that they want to fully believe and ask God to help their unbelief. Ask Jesus to manifest Himself to the seeker so he or she can believe. That is always a good prayer to God.

[1]Hebrews 11:1   [2]John 20:29

Though the fig tree should not blossom, and there be no fruit on the vines, though the yield of the olive should fail, and the fields produce no food, though the flock should be cut off from the fold, and there be no cattle in the stalls, yet I will exult in the Lord, I will rejoice in the God of my salvation.   *Habakkuk 3:17-18*

The Book of Habakkuk is a dialogue between the prophet Habakkuk and God. Habakkuk asks God why He is delaying judgment on Judah based on the violence and injustice in the land. God responds that Chaldean invaders will bring judgment on Judah. Habakkuk is perplexed since God is using a wicked nation to bring judgment on the less wicked Judah. The key verse of the Book is *the righteous will live by his faith*[1]. The righteous are asked to trust God even when we don't understand what He is allowing in our lives.

Trials enter our lives from two sources. Sometimes trials are the consequence of our sin. We sow the wind and reap the whirlwind.[2] We bring difficulty on ourselves by our bad choices. Other times, trials occur as part of life, through no fault of our own. If a family member errs and suffers from it, it is likely that other family members will be negatively impacted although they did nothing wrong. Unpleasant life events are considered trials and seem like random misfortunes.

In the trials of life, we Christians must remember that God has promised to never leave or forsake us.[3] If the trial is caused by our wrongdoing, God is trying to get our attention. We need to confess the sin, receive forgiveness, and move on. We may still have to live with the consequences but God will be there with us. If the trial is just part of life, we need to trust that God will use it to make us more like His Son. Once again, God promises to be with us through the trial.

Habakkuk could be viewed as the family member who did no wrong but is about to suffer for the sins of others in the family. God is about to bring judgment on Judah and Habakkuk finds himself as part of the family. In the face of bad times ahead, Habakkuk determines to trust and rejoice in the God of his salvation. He made a decision to trust because that is what the righteous do.

[1]Habakkuk 2:4b   [2]Hosea 8:7a   [3]Hebrews 13:5b

1. Hebrews 11:6 can be stated this way: If you please God, then you have faith. Why do you think God requires faith as criteria for pleasing Him?

2. If you sense God is leading you to initiate some action for the kingdom, how do you determine when you have enough faith to start? How do your criteria align with those used by Mordecai and Esther?

Prayer Starter: Lord Jesus, I believe, help my unbelief. Strengthen my faith to accomplish what you want me to do for the Kingdom this week. Open and shut doors as I seek your will regarding …

*If anyone comes to you and does not bring this teaching, do not
receive him into your house, and do not give him a greeting; for the
one who gives him a greeting participates in his evil deeds.*

II John 10-11

Many have experienced a visit from well-meaning
proselytizers who represent sects that are not considered part of
mainline Christianity. The passage above is not discussing that
situation. To apply these verses properly, we must understand the
customs of Biblical times.

When Jesus sent His disciples out in pairs to preach and heal,
He instructed them: *And in whatever city or village you enter,
inquire who is worthy in it; and abide there until you go away.*[1] It
was customary for travelers to be welcomed into homes. So John is
warning his readers not to invite false teachers into their home for
the night since they would be supporting the deceptive teachings of
these individuals.

In our present day situation, only the mature Christian should
invite proselytizers into their home for a religious discussion. Paul
describes immature Christians as *carried about by every wind of
doctrine, by the trickery of men, by craftiness in deceitful scheming.*[2]
The new or immature believer does not have the Biblical knowledge
and experience to refute these well-trained ambassadors of false
doctrine. However, the believer with years of studying the
Scriptures and the doctrines of the Christian faith, with God's grace,
may be able to reveal truth to those who have been deceived.

[1]Matthew 10:11   [2]Ephesians 4:14

"Is it a time to receive money and to receive clothes and olive groves and vineyards and sheep and oxen and male and female servants? Therefore, the leprosy of Naaman shall cleave to you and to your descendants forever." So he went out from his presence a leper as white as snow.   II Kings 5:26b-27

Elisha, the prophet of God who succeeded Elijah, had refused any payment for cleansing Naaman of his leprosy. When Gehazi, Elisha's servant, observed this refusal, he secretly followed Naaman and concocted a story to get part of the booty for himself. Gehazi hid the silver and clothing, stood before Elisha and heard the above words from Elisha. Gehazi's life was forever changed for the worse because of his love of materialism.

Christians are susceptible to the lure of materialism. Gehazi had witnessed God's power as Elisha raised a man from the dead, and later cured Naaman's leprosy. Yet in a moment of weakness he succumbed to the idea of getting silver and clothing through a simple act of deceit. His spiritual world view was overcome by a materialistic world view. The next and last time we read of Gehazi, he is relating to the king all the great things that Elisha had done.[1] Imagine the regret as Gehazi relived the past while beholding his leprosy, a stark reminder of his materialistic weakness.

As Christians, we would do well to remember Elisha's question to Gehazi. God is working through many Christian organizations and churches which are underfunded. Is it a time for materialism? Over one billion people are undernourished. Is it a time for materialism? People are dying and going to hell. Is it a time for materialism? Jesus may soon return. Is it a time for materialism? We will one day stand before God and give account of what we have done with the resources entrusted to us. Is it a time for materialism? Is it?

[1] II Kings 8:4

But certain ones of the sect of the Pharisees who had believed, stood up, saying, "It is necessary to circumcise them, and to direct them to observe the Law of Moses."   Acts 15:5

Does it bother you that there are 41,000 denominations worldwide that ascribe to the Christian faith? If it does, you should recognize that our inability to agree on doctrinal issues goes all the way back to the early church. The Apostolic Council of Jerusalem convened around A.D. 49 to address a doctrinal issue raised by the Judaizers, an extrabiblical term for those requiring circumcision for Gentile believers. After testimony from Peter, Paul and Barnabas, the Council agreed not to require Gentiles to be circumcised.

In a perfect world the Judaizers would say: Since this Council with its recognized authority has decided that we have erred doctrinally, we will abandon our views and convictions and agree with your ruling. Do you think that is what happened? Apparently not, because Paul's letter to the churches of Galatia references the decision of the Jerusalem Council[1] and he states: *I am amazed that you are so quickly deserting Him who called you by the grace of Christ, for a different gospel.*[2] The Judaizers were obviously at work in Galatia spreading their doctrinal views of salvation based on faith in Christ plus works. If they had renounced these views there would be no need for Paul to address the issue in his letter.

What is your Biblical understanding of church order, being filled with the Spirit, baptism, end time events, corporate worship, the Lord's Supper, and the free will of man? Whatever your views are, there is probably a denomination that will endorse your beliefs. Christian denominations will disagree on a variety of doctrinal issues but they should all agree that *there is one God, and one mediator also between God and men, the man Christ Jesus.*[3]

Jesus' prayer to His Father for future believers shortly before His crucifixion was: *that they may all be one ... that the world may believe that Thou didst send Me.*[4] The focus of Jesus' prayer was that followers of Christ today would be sharing Him with the world. Regardless of our individual denominations, we can all be united in our mission to share Christ with the world.

[1]Galatians 2:1-10   [2]Galatians 1:6   [3]I Timothy 2:5   [4]John 17:21

Peter said to Him, "Never shall You wash my feet!" Jesus answered him, "If I do not wash you, you have no part with Me." Simon Peter said to Him, "Lord, not my feet only, but also my hands and my head." Jesus said to him, "He who has bathed needs only to wash his feet, but is completely clean; and you are clean, but not all of you."

John 13:8-10

During supper the night before His crucifixion, Jesus rose and washed each of the disciple's feet. Jesus was giving them an example of servanthood, but was also teaching them about the various facets of being cleansed from sin.

When a person receives Jesus into his or her life as Savior and Lord, that person is washed, sanctified, and justified.[1] The blood of Jesus has satisfied a Holy God so that the sin debt has been paid. He or she is adopted into the family of God and is now heaven-bound. At that instant the Holy Spirit of God takes up residence in that life.

However, the old sinful nature is still present and the believer chooses on a moment by moment basis whether to follow the leading of the old nature or the Spirit. Feet represent our contact with the world. When the old nature is in charge, the feet run to sin. Sin breaks our fellowship with God. Fellowship is restored when sin is confessed.[2]

Jesus washed all the disciple's feet, but not all were clean. Judas had been in the ministry and company of Jesus for the past three years but was not a true follower of Jesus. Judas had his own agenda and accompanied Jesus to benefit that agenda. The penalty for his sin had not been washed away so he was not clean. Washing his feet was irrelevant and inconsequential.

The Judas persona sits in many churches today. An excellent way to identify and help this individual is to ask him or her to share their personal testimony of how they became a follower of Jesus. If the answer is vague and general, then present the gospel because this individual probably needs to be washed, not have the feet cleansed.

[1] I Corinthians 6:11   [2] I John 1:7-9

The thief comes only to steal, and kill, and destroy.   *John 10:10a*

The thief here represents the religious rulers, of whom Jesus said "*You are of your father, the devil.*"[1] So these terms are apt descriptions of Satan as well. Satan's purpose is to steal, kill, and destroy but his method is lying – he is *the father of lies.*[1]

The first recorded incident of Satan interacting with mankind was when the serpent talked with Eve in the Garden of Eden. He first questioned what God said: *Indeed, has God said, 'You shall not eat from any tree of the garden'?*[2] Next came the lie: *You shall not surely die!*[3] Every word attributed to Satan was intended to deceive Eve.

What was the result of Satan's deception? He was able to steal the innocence of Adam and Eve and their intimate relationship with God. They had now experienced evil which was previously unknown to them. Satan destroyed their quality of life. They were expelled from the garden where all their needs had been readily met. Now they have to toil for food by the sweat of their face in a cursed ground. Finally, Adam and Eve died just as God had said. They died twice. First, their spirit died when sin entered their heart. Secondly, their body died when the curse of sin ran its course.

Do you believe any of Satan's lies? Is he causing you to question what God has said? Satan can tempt using an attractive package with a beautiful bow, but once opened you experience a taste of Hell on earth. In the last half of the above verse Jesus says: *I came that they might have life, and might have it abundantly.* Jesus has the best offer. Take it!

[1]John 8:44   [2]Genesis 3:1   [3]Genesis 3:4

1. *The god of this world has blinded the minds of the unbelieving* (II Corinthians 4:4). The unsaved world is deceived by Satan. Our mission is to engage the unbeliever and confront him or her with truth. Read II Timothy 2:23-26 and list below the various traits we should display during these conversations.

2. *For he who lacks these qualities is blind or short-sighted* (II Peter 1:9). Satan wants to deceive believers also. He finds fertile ground for deception in the hearts of believers who are not abiding in Christ and not growing in their faith. Read II Peter 1:5-8 and list below the qualities in which you should be growing.

Prayer Starter: Father, I pray today for believers and unbelievers I know who are deceived by Satan. Specifically, I pray for ...

Son of man, behold, I am about to take from you the desire of your eyes with a blow; but you shall not mourn, and you shall not weep, and your tears shall not come. ... So I spoke to the people in the morning, and in the evening my wife died. And in the morning I did as I was commanded.   *Ezekiel 24:16, 18*

Ezekiel's wife died so God could communicate a message to Israel through his stoical response to her death. Previously God had required Ezekiel to lay 390 days on his left side and then 40 days on his right side to portray the upcoming siege of Jerusalem.[1] If Ezekiel had not viewed himself as an instrument in the hands of God, he would never have been able to thrive under the emotional stress and physical discomfort God placed on him.

Christians can be broadly placed into one of two categories. Some see God solely as the One who meets their needs and gives them joy and peace in the midst of trials. This view of God primarily has an inward focus on self. Others acknowledge God's blessings in their lives, but also see themselves in God's army in the battle for the souls of men and women. This view of God has an outward focus on others. The difference in the two categories boils down to spiritual maturity.

Let's say you were to represent your spiritual life by a ship on the sea with God as your Captain. Do you see yourself on a cruise ship or a battleship? The captain on the cruise ship is concerned with the safety of the ship and the comfort of his passengers. The battleship captain wants a disciplined crew who are willing to lay down their lives to defeat the enemy.

Lord Jesus, help us to join Ezekiel on the battleship!

[1]Ezekiel 4:1-8

Be strong and courageous, for you shall give this people possession of the land which I swore to their fathers to give them. Only be strong and very courageous; be careful to do according to all the law which Moses My servant commanded you.   Joshua 1:6-7a

Courage is defined as the attitude of facing anything recognized as dangerous, difficult, or painful, instead of withdrawing from it. Three times in this chapter the Lord commands Joshua to be courageous. God has given Joshua his marching orders. Joshua must lead Israel across the Jordan River and possess the land which is occupied by enemy nations. Courage will be needed. As believers, we have been commissioned to assault Satan's territory and set captives free by the power of the gospel of Jesus Christ. Such action will require courage.

Joshua was also commanded to be courageous as he and his people sought to be obedient to the Law of Moses. Israel's track record regarding obedience was poor so Joshua would need courage to confront disobedience and to maintain an obedient heart in his own life. Today, the allure of conformity to the world has never been stronger. Every believer needs courage to say no to temptation and yes to any action the Spirit leads us to do.

So, how can we find courage to accomplish these tasks? The answer is found in the Lord's third command to be courageous: *Be strong and courageous! Do not tremble or be dismayed, for the Lord your God is with you wherever you go.*[1] The Spirit of God within the believer provides the courage needed to face any task that God has placed before us. The Lord God was with Joshua and the same Lord promises to be with us. The Apostle Paul reminds us: *For God has not given us a spirit of timidity, but of power and love and discipline.*[2] As we walk with Jesus and rely on the Holy Spirit we will find the courage needed for every situation. Be encouraged!

[1]Joshua 1:9   [2]II Timothy 1:7

As for the builders, each wore his sword girded at his side as he built, while the trumpeter stood near me. "At whatever place you hear the sound of the trumpet, rally to us there. Our God will fight for us."   Nehemiah 4:18, 20

These verses remind us of the necessity to balance our labor for the Lord with attentiveness to our personal walk in our battle with Satan. It is about 446 B.C., and Nehemiah has returned to Jerusalem to plan and execute the rebuilding of its wall. Nehemiah knows that he has been commissioned and empowered by God to accomplish this mission. The enemies of the Jews in the surrounding area oppose the rebuilding effort since it would provide more security for the Jewish population. These opponents threaten to attack if the construction proceeds.

In verse 17, the builders are described with *one hand doing the work and the other holding a weapon.* When Nehemiah planned the work, he ensured that the workers were prepared to fight at a moment's notice if the enemy attacked. As believers are involved in God-ordained projects, it is possible that the work becomes so paramount that we neglect our personal walk with God. If so we are unprepared for an assault from our enemy. If Satan is successful in attacking our personal life, our involvement in God's work may cease.

Samson accomplished God's will on many occasions by performing acts that required his supernatural physical strength. However, he was lax and undisciplined in his personal life with sexual temptations. This personal weakness led to his enemies getting the upper hand. His work for God stopped and he toiled the rest of his life, blinded, and acting as a beast of burden. Through God's grace he was given strength to avenge his enemies but much of his life had been wasted due to inattention to his personal walk with God.

As we are involved in building Christ's Church, let's not neglect our personal time with God. Satan wants to halt the construction effort and will attack the workers to accomplish his goal. We are not engaging in skirmishes with Satan in our own strength but are relying on the Holy Spirit to battle for us.

I do not ask Thee to take them out of the world, but to keep them from the evil one. They are not of the world, even as I am not of the world. Sanctify them in the truth; Thy word is truth. John 17:15-17

It is commonly said that the follower of Christ has three adversaries: the flesh, the world, and Satan.[1] The flesh refers to the carnal nature or old man in every believer. The world represents the fallen world system composed of lust, pride, and selfish ambition. Satan, or the evil one, wanted to sift Peter like wheat, and was later described by Peter as an adversary and a roaring lion seeking someone to devour.[2] All three are separate entities but they interact in an effort to dethrone Christ in the believer's life.

The world and Satan are external forces pursuing our harm. The flesh is an internal adversary desiring mastery by rendering the indwelling Holy Spirit inconsequential. In His high priestly prayer to the Father, Jesus asks that His disciples be protected from the evil one and the world.[3]

We protect ourselves from the flesh by walking in the Spirit. When Jesus asks the Father to sanctify us in the truth, He wants us to be set apart for His use through immersion in the word of God. The Psalmist said: *How can a young man keep his way pure? By keeping it according to Thy word.*[4] It is impossible to be victorious over the flesh without a regular, meaningful intake of God's word, the Bible. When you have His thoughts in your mind, it enables you to walk in His Spirit.

The author of Hebrews says that Jesus, our High Priest, *always lives to make intercession for them.*[5] As we battle our spiritual adversaries on Earth, we can be encouraged to know that Jesus is praying for us to be victorious. Let's do our part also.

[1]Ephesians 2:2-3   [2]I Peter 5:8   [3]John 17:11   [4]Psalm 119:9
[5]Hebrews 7:25b

And the Lord was with Joseph...   *Genesis 39:2a*

Joseph was able to make the correct decisions during his trial in Egypt because the Lord was with him. Most of us would be so fixated on the unjustness of being sold into slavery by the brothers that our decision-making process would be negatively impacted. But the Lord was with Joseph and that ensured sound thinking.

When tempted by Potiphar's wife, Joseph was able to see the situation from God's perspective and respond in a godly fashion. The ungodly man longs to be placed in the situation in which Joseph found himself. But Joseph responded to the temptation: *How then could I do this great evil, and sin against God?*[1] The abiding presence of God in his life was very real and the thought of sinning against God was abhorrent.

After Jacob died, Joseph's brothers concocted a story saying that their father requested that Joseph forgive the brothers before he died. The brothers knew that if they had been wronged the way Joseph had, they would be seeking revenge. But, the Lord was with Joseph, so he reacted differently: *Do not be afraid, for am I in God's place?*[2] Even though Joseph had the power and opportunity to get revenge, he realized that vengeance was God's responsibility, not his. Further, he knew now that God used their evil intent for good. The Lord who was with him was sovereign.

But we have the mind of Christ.[3] Today, we have the same advantage that Joseph had in that the Lord is with us. The Holy Spirit's presence in our lives allows us to have the mind of Christ. We can resist temptations and be victorious in trials because we can view them from God's perspective. Take time to connect with Jesus each day to remind yourself that the Lord is with you.

[1]Genesis 39:9b   [2]Genesis 50:19   [3]I Corinthians 2:16b

1. Spiritual warfare can refer to a battle with Satan in your personal life (defensive) or battling Satan through kingdom ministry and evangelism (offensive). Which do you identify with most? Why?

2. How many of these five devotionals on warfare emphasize the importance of your personal walk with God? What is the significance of your answer?

Prayer Starter: Holy Spirit of God, empower me with courage and wisdom to engage the enemy for the kingdom of God. Help me to guard my personal life, walking closely with Jesus, as I seek to do Your will. Open my eyes to see opportunities to interact spiritually with people, especially in …

And let us consider how to stimulate one another to love and good deeds, not forsaking our own assembling together, as is the habit of some, but encouraging one another, and all the more, as you see the day drawing near.   Hebrews 10:24-25

Fellowship means companionship with others based on something held in common. The apostle John said: *what we have seen and heard we proclaim to you also, that you also may have fellowship with us; and indeed our fellowship is with the Father, and with His Son Jesus Christ.*[1] Fellowship among Christians is an extension of what we have in common: fellowship with God through Jesus.

In the Christian community today fellowship is synonymous with getting together, usually over a meal. Experiencing a feeling of community during a meal is an encouragement in itself, but the above verses seek more than mere companionship. We are asked to consider how we can stimulate each other to love and good works. "Pass the potato salad" is stimulating, but we are asked to do better than that.

Our primary point of concurrency is Jesus, not food. Food is a social lubricant. As the opportunity presents itself, let's be open to sharing with others what we have learned recently from our time in the Bible. Let's be honest and talk about a struggle in our lives and ask for prayer to overcome it. Let's take time to humbly share an opportunity God gave us to help someone in need. Let's tell about a witnessing opportunity we either took advantage of or let slip away. Let's talk about spiritual matters so that after the meal is finished, our soul has been nourished as well as our body.

[1] I John 1:3

Can two walk together, except they be agreed?   *Hosea 3:3 (KJV)*

Although Hosea is referring to Israel's fellowship with God, I want to apply this truth to the marriage relationship. The most important area of agreement in a Christian marriage is that each spouse is committed to growing as a believer in Christ. If Christian maturity is the goal of each spouse then all other disagreements will be resolved as they look to Jesus for the answers. Let's learn from the lives of two Christian couples that are mentioned in Acts.

Aquila and Priscilla[1] allowed the apostle Paul to stay in their home while he ministered in Corinth. When Paul left for Ephesus he took the couple with him since they had become part of his ministry team. While in Ephesus this couple encountered Apollos, an eloquent teacher of the things of the Lord, and instructed him in some doctrinal issues. They remained in Ephesus to minister when Paul left for Jerusalem. God used this married couple mightily because they both desired to grow as Christians and be used in building His kingdom.

Ananias and Sapphira[2] sold a possession and presented a portion of the income to the apostles to aid the poor. Unfortunately, the couple had conspired to lie, and claimed that the amount given was the selling price. Both were struck dead by God. This couple was in agreement, but their desire was to look like a godly couple rather than to be a godly couple.

These two couples' lives are two points on the continuum between the two endpoints represented by lives lived totally for self and lives lived totally for God. Which endpoint are you walking toward today with your spouse?

[1]Acts 18   [2]Acts 5:1-11

But if you show partiality, you are committing sin and are convicted by the law as transgressors.   *James 2:9*

James used the example of how the poor were treated compared to how the rich were treated to illustrate the presence of partiality in his day. Nothing has changed. Most people today are still enamored with the rich over the poor, and thus the rich receive preferential treatment. At the heart of preferential treatment is "How can this relationship benefit me?" The focus on self rather than others makes partiality a sin. The "law" James cites is: *You shall love your neighbor as yourself.*[1] Would you want to be snubbed because you lacked wealth, prestige, or good looks?

Jesus once gave some advice at a dinner He attended. *When you give a luncheon or a dinner, do not invite your friends or your brothers or your relatives or rich neighbors, lest they also invite you in return, and repayment come to you.*[2] Rather, invite those who don't have the means to repay you, and you will be repaid by God. Whenever we act out of a selfish motive, we have our payment.

Our challenge is to view people as God views them – precious creations with eternal souls. By dying on the cross for all mankind, Jesus assigned equal value to each soul. As we look to God for our reward and our fulfillment, and not people, we will be better able to view people impartially.

So speak and so act, as those who are to be judged by the law of liberty.[3] Speak and act with mercy; affirm and accept all.

[1]James 2:8b   [2]Luke 14:12   [3]James 2:12

Do not judge lest you be judged. ... You hypocrite, first take the log out of your own eye, and then you will see clearly to take the speck out of your brother's eye.   Matthew 7:1, 5

Consider two professions: a judge and a marriage counselor. A judge is charged with ensuring that the accused receives a fair trial and, if guilty, receives a just sentence. A marriage counselor must evaluate the source of the problem in the marriage and offer solutions. There is a sense in which the counselor is judging the married couple, but the purpose is reconciliation, not condemnation.

Followers of Jesus are called to be counselors, not judges. As such, we must be able to recognize weaknesses or sin in another's life before we can help. To do so, we have to be walking in the Spirit and of sufficient spiritual maturity to be able to offer solutions to the hurting believer. We must have a log-free eye before we can hope to help with the speck in a brother's eye.

As it turns out, we are fairly adept at recognizing weaknesses, or perceived weaknesses, in another person's life. The human reaction to this awareness is to condemn or ostracize, whereas the Biblical reaction is to pray for the person and seek opportunity to help.

The verses above are not promoting tolerance of sin. Rather, they are encouraging us to call sin, sin; but not let that evaluation lead to condemnation of the sinner. *For God did not send the Son into the world to judge the world, but that the world should be saved through Him.* [1] May we also have God's heart toward others, both believers and non-believers.

[1] John 3:17

There should be no division in the body, but the members should have the same care for one another. And if one member suffers, all the members suffer with it; if one member is honored, all the members rejoice with it.   *I Corinthians 12:25-26*

Imagine what heaven will be like for a moment with regard to personal relationships. You will carry no grudges against anyone. You will never say anything that offends others or hear anything that offends you. You will not be turned off by someone's personality. You will not like one person more than another person. In short, you will treat everyone, all the time, in a Christ-like manner. It will be heaven!

Now back to earth. Not that way here. But as believers in Jesus, our goal should be to exhibit the same care for one another in the Body of Christ. We should be impartial in our relationship with other Christians. What does that look like?

Paul says it looks like the parts of the human body. When I stub my big toe, my nerves alert me, my eye inspects the damage, my hands massage the toe, my leg favors the toe, and my mind considers how best to heal the toe. When my toe suffers, the members of the body unite to bring comfort and healing to the toe. No body part snubs the toe. The same should be true in the Body of Christ.

Paul was more direct with the Church at Rome: *Rejoice with those who rejoice, and weep with those who weep. Be of the same mind toward one another.*[1] When at odds with a fellow believer, we may find ourselves rejoicing when he or she weeps and vice versa. If that is ever your reaction, confess it as sin, and seek to do something caring for the person.

[1]Romans 12:15-16a

1. Which do you struggle with the most: partiality, judging others, or being uncaring? Select a verse from the pertinent devotional and memorize it to get God's thought in your mind and heart.

2. When was the last time you broached a spiritual topic at the dinner table? If you don't do that regularly, then initiate that conversation this week.

Prayer Starter: Lord Jesus, thank You for your body, the church. May I be edified by my association with fellow believers and may I be an encouragement to them also. Help me as I deal with …

For you have not received a spirit of slavery leading to fear again,
but you have received a spirit of adoption as sons by which we cry
out, "Abba! Father!"   Romans 8:15

      Who or what do you fear? The unbeliever will fear death and
the disastrous uncertainties of life. The mature follower of Christ
will fear only God. For the unbeliever, fear is a dread. For the
believer fear is a reverential awe of God, leading to peace and
security.
      Picture the servant of a wicked master and also the son of a
loving father. Both the servant and the son have fear in their lives.
The servant fears because he never knows when his master will harm
him. Harm may come when the servant errs or it could arrive
because his master is having a bad day and vents on the servant. The
son respects his father greatly. The son fears disappointing his dad
and knows that consequences await any disobedience.
      The Bible portrays mankind as slaves to sin before coming to
Christ. Sin and Satan are evil masters that seek to destroy – a
legitimate reason for fear. When we receive forgiveness of sin
through trust in Jesus Christ we are adopted into a family with a
loving Father. Our heavenly Father is so powerful, majestic and
holy when compared to us, that we must respond with a awe-
inspiring fear of God. But our fear is directed toward a loving Father
who is committed to our best interest. Discipline and seemingly
unfavorable circumstances may cross our paths but we trust our
Father to work all things together for our good.
      One of Isaiah's Messianic prophesies states: *And He will*
delight in the fear of the Lord.[1] Jesus is our example in all things
pertaining to this life on Earth. If Jesus delighted in the fear of God,
then we should also. We should not just have the fear of God, but it
should be a joy to us because of the loving protection it affords.
Choose to fear God and you automatically choose not to fear the
world.

[1]Isaiah 11:3a

When I am afraid, I will put my trust in Thee. In God, whose word I praise, In God I have put my trust; I shall not be afraid. What can mere man do to me?   *Psalm 56:3-4*

Fear is a feeling of uneasiness or apprehension. Fear does not have to be summoned by us; rather it arrives automatically, whether we want it or not. When danger is present, fear is beneficial and should be heeded. However, we should allow a healthy fear and trust in God to override the human emotion of fear whenever God so directs.

When David wrote Psalm 56, he was running for his life from King Saul. God had already told Saul that the kingdom would be taken from him and given to another. Saul knew that David was that man and thus was determined to kill him. David was alone and fled to Gath, a Philistine city, hoping that being in another country would provide protection from Saul. However, he was recognized in Gath as a great Israelite warrior and a legitimate fear gripped him. He disguised himself as a madman and was able to escape unharmed.[1]

David was afraid for his life in Gath so he made a conscious choice ("I shall not be afraid") to put his trust in God. David had been anointed by the prophet Samuel and had received the Spirit of the Lord at that time.[2] David knew that God had a future plan for him that didn't include dying in Gath at the hands of the Philistines. He chose to trust God for his deliverance and God provided the way of escape. David recognized that if God had a plan for his life, no man would be able to thwart that plan.

Christians who walk with God in the center of His will need not fear, for our lives on this earth are in God's hands until He calls us home. As believers we must fear and trust God, not man.

[1] I Samuel 21:10-15   [2] I Samuel 16:1-13

They feared the Lord and served their own gods according to the custom of the nations from among whom they had been carried away into exile. To this day they do according to the earlier customs: they do not fear the Lord...   II Kings 17:33-34a

These two verses contradict each other because they are stated from two different perspectives. Israel, the ten northern tribes, has been exiled by Assyria and the cities of Samaria where they lived have been repopulated by foreigners. To appease the "god of the land," an Israelite priest was sent to the foreigners to teach them the customs of Jehovah. The new inhabitants believed that by adding the customs of Jehovah to the order of worship for the gods from their former homeland, they would placate Jehovah. Thus verse 33 says "they feared the Lord" because from their perspective they were serving the Lord. However verse 34 gives God's perspective and it declares "they do not fear the Lord". Jehovah God demands that there be no other gods before Him and the new inhabitants either didn't understand that or refused to obey it.

Fast forward 700 years and Jesus encounters a woman at a well in Samaria. He tells her: *You worship that which you do not know.*[1] Not much changed in 700 years.

Christianity involves a changed mind and heart. We cannot just add some new Christian activities into our old lifestyle and expect to please God. The lifestyle has to be revamped so that it conforms to the image of Christ, not the world. The gods from our pre-Christ life are often hard to dethrone but as God brings them to our attention we must seek His help to remove them from our lives. Only then will we truly fear the Lord.

[1]John 4:22

And not only this, but we also exult in our tribulations, knowing that tribulation brings about perseverance; and perseverance, proven character; and proven character, hope.   *Romans 5:3-4*

Mankind in general prefers life that is calm, not hectic; easy, not difficult; and pleasant, not painful. Most of us would sign up in a heartbeat for a life in the Garden of Eden before the Fall. Food, water and shelter were readily available at no cost. The entire animal kingdom was subservient to you. Your spouse was perfect in your eyes and there was no one else with whom to compare him or her. There were no thorns or thistles – imagine a weed-free landscape. There were no hurricanes or tornadoes to disrupt, damage or destroy. It was heaven on Earth.

But mankind did sin; the Fall did occur; and tribulation has reigned ever since. The good news is that God uses tribulation in our lives to grow us into Christ-likeness. Tribulation encourages us to be dependent on God and look to Him for answers. God builds patience and endurance in our lives as we trust Him to show up. We become more caring and empathetic with others who are going through deep waters. In short, we learn to live like Christ lived in the midst of His pain and suffering.

If a golf ball were manufactured with a smooth exterior, it would travel less distance than a golf ball with the standard dimples on it. The dimples on a golf ball create air disturbance near the ball's surface which produces a smaller air wake that creates less air drag and the ball goes farther. God uses the pockmarks of our lives created by tribulation to get us farther down the road to Christ-likeness. Let's courageously embrace distress, rather than fear it.

In the world you have tribulation, but take courage; I have overcome the world.[1]

[1]John 16:33b

Now David became aware that Saul had come out to seek his life while David was in the wilderness of Ziph at Horesh. And Jonathan, Saul's son, arose and went to David at Horesh, and encouraged him in God.   *I Samuel 23: 15-16*

God often uses people to help us deal with our fears. In the midst of fear it is easy to lose perspective and become discouraged. Jonathan knew that his friend David was stressed out and fearful since his father King Saul sought David's life. Jonathan made a special trip to come and visit David with words of encouragement. He affirmed that his father would never be able to kill David and shared how he believed David would one day be king. Jonathan helped turn David's eyes to God and see God as his deliverer.

Paul played a similar role in Timothy's life but as a mentor more so than as a friend. Paul sent word ahead of Timothy's arrival in Corinth to ensure that Timothy was not despised and thus made fearful.[1] Paul was attempting to minimize the effects of fear in Timothy's life and ministry by removing the source of the fear.

Paul would later write to Timothy: *For God has not given us a spirit of fear, but of power, and of love, and a sound mind*[1]. Paul reminds Timothy that if he is experiencing fear, it is not from God. Paul encouraged Timothy to be bold as he proclaimed the gospel, not shirking back in an attitude of fear.

There will be times in life when we face fearful situations. We need to be honest about our fears to our spouse or close friends. They can help us trust God. There will also be times where we can act as a friend or mentor to help turn someone's focus to God rather than on the destructive fear they face. "Fear not" occurs over thirty times in the Bible. Let's heed God's command and face fear whether it is found in our life or the life of a friend or spouse.

[1] I Corinthians 16:10-11   [2] II Timothy 1:7 (KJV)

1. Jesus sent His disciples out, but first He told them: *And do not fear those who kill the body, but are unable to kill the soul; but rather fear Him who is able to destroy both soul and body in hell.* (Matthew 10:28) What must you believe before you are successful in not fearing man?

2. Do you have a spouse or close friend with whom you have shared fears? Has anyone ever confided with you about a fear they had? What was the result of either or both interactions?

Prayer Starter: Lord God, I don't want to live in fear of evil circumstances or people. I want to trust You as my sovereign, loving Father. Please remove the fears I have regarding ...

You are the light of the world.   *Matthew 5:14a*

   As Christians we should be both a lighthouse and a searchlight. Both emit light and both result in lives being saved but one is passive and the other is active.

   The lighthouse consistently sends light over the waters to safely guide seafarers home or warn of approaching land. It is not targeting any particular ship or person. It is simply providing light to anyone who may be in need of that light.

   Paul challenged the Philippians to be *"blameless and innocent, children of God above reproach in the midst of a crooked and perverse generation, among who you appear as lights in the world."*[1] As we live in this dark world, the light of Christ in our lives should be evident to all who know us. We don't know who among us is searching for light; it is just our duty to shine. Each Christian is praying that those in his/her sphere of influence will be attracted to the light and *ask you to give an account for the hope that is in you.*[2]

   However, being a consistent Christian witness through the life we lead is not enough. We must also be a searchlight, specifically targeting those whom Christ has laid on our hearts. The Great Commission says *Go into all the world and preach the gospel to all creation.*[3] We have been commanded to actively share the Good News. What do you need to do to be able to clearly share the gospel message when the Holy Spirit presents the opportunity?

[1]Philippians 3:15   [2]I Peter 3:15b   [3]Mark 16:15

And even if our gospel is veiled, it is veiled to those who are
perishing, in whose case the god of this world has blinded the minds
of the unbelieving, that they might not see the light of the gospel of
the glory of Christ, who is the image of God.   II Corinthians 4:3-4

     God's instructions to Moses for building the tabernacle
included a veil which separated the holy place from the holy of
holies.[1] The holy place was accessed and maintained by the priests
on a regular basis. The holy of holies, containing the Ark of the
Covenant and the mercy seat, was entered only once a year by the
high priest who sprinkled blood on the mercy seat to obtain
forgiveness for the sins of the people. The veil served as a protective
barrier between a holy God and unholy man.
     When Moses came down from Mount Sinai with the second set
of tablets, he was unaware that the skin of his face shown because he
had been speaking with God.[2] When Aaron and the other Israelites
saw his face shining they were afraid. So Moses placed a veil over
his face whenever he needed to talk to the people. Once again a veil
shielded mankind from the radiance of God's glory.
     When Christ died on the cross, the veil of the temple in
Jerusalem, which had long since replaced the tabernacle tent, was
torn in two from top to bottom.[3] It was as though God reached
down from heaven and ripped the veil, demonstrating that the
sacrificial, atoning work of His Son's blood had removed the wall of
sin's separation between God and man forever.
     God has removed that veil, however a veil from Satan has
blinded the minds of the unbelieving. Paul describes Christians as
follows: *But we all, with unveiled face beholding as in a mirror the*
glory of the Lord, are being transformed into the same image from
glory to glory, just as from the Lord, the Spirit.[4] As Christians spend
time with Jesus in the Word and prayer, we are gradually changed
into Christ's image. Lord, may the lost around us be compelled to
see Christ in us as we share Your Good News with them.

[1]Exodus 26:31-33   [2]Exodus 34:29   [3]Matthew 27:51
[4]II Corinthians 3:18

And they said to me, "The remnant there in the province who
survived the captivity are in great distress and reproach, and the
wall of Jerusalem is broken down and its gates are burned with fire.
Now it came about when I heard these words, I sat down and wept
and mourned for days; and I was fasting and praying before the God
of heaven.   *Nehemiah 1:3-4*

Nehemiah was deeply burdened by the defenseless nature of
Jerusalem and the distress of the Jewish remnant that lived in the
region. The temple in Jerusalem had been rebuilt as discussed in the
Book of Ezra, but the disrepair of the city walls and gates had never
been addressed. As cupbearer to the Persian king, Nehemiah knew
he was in a position to possibly solve the problem so he prayed to
that end. God provided an opportunity to share his burden with the
king who authorized him to return to Jerusalem with the resources
needed to do the job.

The New Testament church is portrayed more as an offensive
force rather than a defensive one. Jesus told Peter that He would
build His church and the gates of hell would not prevail against it.[1]
That description pictures the church attacking hell. Jesus declared
early in His ministry that He had come to preach the gospel to the
poor, proclaim release to the captives, give sight to the blind, and set
free the downtrodden.[2] He commissioned His followers to finish
the task He started.

How often do we weep over people or situations, thereby
reflecting God's heart for the matter? How often do we fast and
pray, asking God to use us to be part of the solution? If we are
walking closely with God, shouldn't we have His heart for the
people and situations that surround us?

From a spiritual perspective we are surrounded daily by the
poor, the captives, the blind and the downtrodden. Lord, help us to
see these people as You see them and have Your heart toward them.
Then give us the strength and wisdom to attack Satan's strongholds
with the gospel message.

[1]Matthew 16:18   [2]Luke 4:18

Save others, snatching them out of the fire…   *Jude 23a*

A middle-aged man once asked me if I ever wanted to be an action hero. I thought he was kidding so I said, no, too much responsibility. Turns out, he was serious. He shared how he thought it would be cool to have powers like Superman or Spiderman and to be able to help people in danger. I thought later that it seems God has instilled in mankind a need for adventure and to feel that you are making a difference.

I predict that one of my greatest disappointments when I reach heaven is that I didn't share my faith more while on planet Earth. For the follower of Christ, that is where the action lies. God has enlisted all believers in a cosmic battle with Satan and his evil forces over the souls of mankind. Unfortunately, too many of us never put on the armor of God and join in the battle. We seldom pray for the supernatural power and wisdom of the Holy Spirit while looking for opportunities to share the gospel.

People without Christ are headed for the fire of Hell and need someone to share with them the gospel of salvation. Jesus did all the heavy lifting required on the cross. Our job is simply to share what He has already done. Only then, do we truly experience the abundant life that Jesus promised. What greater adventure in life can one have than to co-labor with the God of the universe for the souls of mankind?

Paul said at the end of his life: *I have fought the good fight, I have finished the course, I have kept the faith.*[1] May we say the same!

[1]II Timothy 4:7

But I say unto you, that unless your righteousness surpasses that of the scribes and Pharisees, you shall not enter the kingdom of heaven.
                                                    Matthew 5:20

Jesus made this statement early on in His Sermon on the Mount. This declaration must have been quite a shock to the audience. After all, the scribes were the teachers of the law and the Pharisees were their religious rulers who came from the ranks of the scribes. Both groups knew the Law thoroughly and were very careful to keep every aspect of the Law to the best of their ability. What chance did a commoner have of entering heaven if they had to keep the law better than their super-religious leaders?

Christianity is the only religion in which getting to heaven is not based on doing good works. As an example, the Koran says: "Then those whose balance of good deeds is heavy, they will be successful. But those whose balance is light, will be those who have lost their souls; in Hell will they abide."[1] To mankind, it is logical to assume that a holy god would require that they do good to get to heaven. Although the statement holds some truth, it is also true that the standard God requires to enter heaven is perfection. *Since all have sinned and fallen short of the glory of God*[2] no one can reach heaven on their own merit.

The second diagnostic question in Evangelism Explosion is "If you were to stand before God and He asked you 'Why should I let you into My heaven?' what would you say?" The purpose of this question is to determine the individual's reason for why he or she will go to heaven. As we talk to people about spiritual matters, it is important to remember that many will have a works-based mentality when it comes to going to heaven. The truth of the Gospel is that Jesus provides the righteousness we need to enter heaven and that righteousness is available through faith in the redemptive work of Christ on the cross. Jesus didn't hesitate to shock his listeners with the truth; neither should we.

[1]Surat 23 (Al-Muminun): 102-103   [2]Romans 3:23

1. Would you describe yourself as both a lighthouse and a searchlight? If not, what do you need to do to be a more effective light to a lost world?

2. Who are some people in your sphere of influence that have a works-based mentality regarding going to heaven? Salvation based on faith in Christ alone is not politically correct, but it is true. Ask God for a burden to see them saved.

Prayer Starter: Father, use Your light from my life and the gospel to remove the veil of unbelief from my unsaved friends and family. Give me a burden for the souls of the following people: ...

Then Caleb quieted the people before Moses, and said, "We should by all means go up and take possession of it, for we shall surely overcome it." But the men who had gone up with him said, "We are not able to go up against the people, for they are too strong for us."
Numbers 13:30-31

When God commanded Abram to leave his country and his family, He promised to make him a great nation in a new land.[1] After 400 years in Egypt, Abraham's descendents left Egypt as a nation. Israel was now numerous enough to conquer and occupy the land that God had initially shown to Abram. At God's direction, Moses sent twelve men, one from each tribe, into Canaan to spy out the land and its people.

The spies agreed that the land was good, the people were strong, and the cities were fortified. Caleb and Joshua were ready to obey God and claim the Promised Land. The other ten wanted to disobey God and return to Egypt since the inhabitants were stronger than they were. The people sided with the ten and their fate was sealed: forty years of wandering in the wilderness.

Consider what Israel had witnessed in the recent past. They saw God break Pharaoh's hold on them with ten miraculous plagues. They witnessed the Red Sea part, their march across its dry riverbed, and the destruction of Pharaoh's army. They enjoyed God's provision of daily manna and water provided from a rock. Yet, only a few chose obedience and believed that God was able to accomplish what He had promised to them.[2] Why?

Perhaps the majority never had a personal relationship with God and thus never involved Him in every aspect of their daily lives. Maybe they saw God's miracles of the past from a national perspective, not a personal one. Now each man may be asked to take sword and shield and attack a stronger enemy. Will God be with me in hand-to-hand combat?

Obedience is easier if it is based on relationship rather than requirement. We need to ask ourselves why we are obedient or disobedient. The answer may lead back to how personal our relationship is with God.

[1]Genesis 12:1-3   [2]Exodus 3:16-17

And Amaziah said to the man of God, "But what shall we do for the hundred talents which I have given to the troops of Israel?" And the man of God answered, "The Lord has much more to give you than this."
                                                    II Chronicles 25:9

Amaziah was a king of Judah with a warlike temperament. He paid over 6,000 pounds of silver to hire 100,000 soldiers out of Israel to fight with him against the Edomites. A man of God came to Amaziah and told him that God was not with Israel and he should send the mercenaries home. The king obeyed, but only after considering the financial investment he had already made to the campaign.

Amaziah erred when he neglected to ask God whether it would be wise to hire the mercenaries. God was faithful and gracious to send someone to him to warn him of his mistake. Once he understood his error, he had to decide whether he was going to cut his losses and face the Edomites with only God's help.

The king considered his sizable investment in his previous plan and perhaps wondered if it would be wise to walk away from that investment. The man of God essentially told Amaziah that finances should not factor in the equation when deciding whether or not to obey God. Obey God and leave the finances to the One who owns creation.

When God reveals sin to us, it is human nature to do a cost-benefit analysis on whether and/or when we will obey. Biblically speaking, the cost of disobedience will always be more than you want to pay and the benefit will be less than you imagined. We need to ask the Spirit of God to train us to skip the rationalization phase and go directly to obedience.

Now the word of the Lord came to Jonah the second time, saying,
"Arise, go to Nineveh the great city and proclaim to it the
proclamation which I am going to tell you."   Jonah 3:1-2

God issues six direct commands in the book of Jonah. The first command is in chapter one and is identical to the one above. Jonah chose to disobey the first time. God then commanded a storm to threaten the ship Jonah was on and a fish to swallow Jonah. These commands were needed to convince Jonah that he should obey and preach to Nineveh. After the city repented, God commanded a plant to shade Jonah, a worm to kill the plant, and a hot wind to make Jonah uncomfortable. These commands were needed to show Jonah that even in obedience his heart was evil.

God's commands given to nature and the plant/animal kingdom were readily obeyed and were directed at Jonah who represented the only part of God's creation with free will. As Jonah exercised his free will and fled, God pursued him. An excerpt from Francis Thompson's 'The Hound of Heaven' reads: "All which I took from thee I did but take, not for thy harms, but just that thou might'st seek it in My arms." God took Jonah's life and returned it to him to show that real life is found in obedience to God. God removed comfort from Jonah's life to remind him that God is compassionate toward all and desires that all men be saved.

If Jonah had obeyed the Lord the first time with a good heart, the verses above, minus "the second time", would be the lead-in to the only chapter in the book. How often do we add extra, unpleasant chapters to the book of our lives because we refuse to obey God the first time?

He has told you, O man, what is good; and what does the Lord require of you but to do justice, to love kindness, and to walk humbly with your God?
                                                                                    Micah 6:8

Jesus summarized God's commands with love God and love people.[1] Here Micah summarized God's requirements by showing what loving people and loving God look like. We love people when we treat them impartially with kindness. We love God as we walk with Him in humility and obedience.

Loving God and loving people are inextricably linked. Jesus said: *if you love Me, you will keep My commandments.*[2] He also said: *a new commandment I give you, that you love one another.*[3] So, if we love Jesus, we will love one another.

Jesus illustrated this connection when He told the story of the person who brought a gift to the altar and there remembered that someone was at odds with him or her. Jesus commanded that person to leave the gift at the altar, go and be reconciled to the brother, then return to the altar.[4] Our relationships with other believers impact our relationship with God, either positively or negatively.

Saul of Tarsus did not have a walk with God, nor was he just and kind toward Christians. After his conversion, Paul the Apostle said: *I also do my best to maintain always a blameless conscience both before God and before men.*[5]

As we truly seek to walk with God, He will give us His heart for people and will use us to advance His kingdom.

[1]Mark 12:30-31   [2]John 14:15   [3]John 13:34   [4]Matthew 5:23-24
[5]Act 24:16

"If it be so, our God whom we serve is able to deliver us from the furnace of blazing fire; and He will deliver us out of your hand, O king. But even if He does not, let it be known to you, O king, that we are not going to serve your gods or worship the golden image that you have set up."   *Daniel 3:17-18*
But Peter and John answered and said to them, "Whether it is right in the sight of God to give heed to you rather than to God, you be the judge;..."   *Acts 4:19*

At times the laws of government or religious institutions may contradict the laws of God. In those situations we are bound by God's laws as believers.

Around 600 B.C., many Jewish youths were deported to Babylon as potential servants of the king. Among these were three young men who refused to obey the law of the land and bow down to King Nebuchadnezzar's golden image.[1] They knew the penalty was to be thrown into a fiery furnace.

They could have rationalized: "We are no good to God dead, so we might as well bow down even though in our hearts we will be standing up." But they didn't. They actually believed that God could deliver them if He chose to and if He didn't, well, that was also OK. God did choose to save them and as a result the king made a decree that anyone disrespectful to their God would lose their life. That result would never have occurred if they had just blended into the scenery through compromise.

Fast forward six centuries when Peter and John found themselves in a similar situation, dealing with religious authorities rather than civil. The high priest in Jerusalem had just ordered them not to speak or teach in the name of Jesus. When Jesus left the disciples He commanded them to preach the gospel, so Jesus' command trumped that of the high priest. They continued to teach about Jesus and were later flogged for their disobedience[2].

As our world continues its march toward one government and one religion, there will be more and more pressure to conform to man-made laws which contradict God-given laws. Let's stand our ground and watch God work!

[1]Exodus 20:3   [2]Acts 5:40

1. Have you ever disobeyed God because your cost-benefit analysis of the situation convinced you? What is the problem with relying on your wisdom regarding obeying God?

2. Are you dealing now with any man-made laws or traditions that contradict God's laws? Name one and write below how you can honor God in this situation.

Prayer Starter: Lord Jesus, I know You said: *If you love me, you will keep my commandments.* (John 14:15) Help me to express my love for You as I obey you in …

And Pilate answered them, saying, "Do you want me to release for you the King of the Jews?" for he was aware that the chief priests had delivered Him up because of envy.   Mark 15:9-10

       Envy is a feeling of discontent and ill will toward another who has something that you desire. The first sin was due in part to envy. One reason Eve ate the fruit was because Satan told her it would make her like God, knowing good and evil. The first murder resulted when Cain reacted in envy and anger because his offering to God was not accepted but Abel's was. Even the perfect Lamb of God was crucified as a result of the religious leaders' envious reaction to Jesus' teachings, miracles, and popularity among the people.

       Envy looks up with desire to those viewed as superior; pride looks down with disdain from those who consider themselves superior. Since the envious place importance on what they are striving to attain; once attained, pride can result. The remedy for envy is being content and thankful for what you have.

       The author of Hebrews advises: be *content with what you have; for He Himself has said, "I will never desert you, nor will I ever forsake you."*[1] The presence of envy in our lives simply means that we have taken our eyes off God as the provider of our needs. The carnal man is in charge, not the spiritual man. Repent, refocus on Christ, and rejoice in what God has blessed you with already. Envy may appear to be leading you to a pleasant place, but at the end of that road lies disaster.

[1]Hebrews 13:5b

Therefore consider the members of your earthly body as dead to immorality, impurity, passion, evil desire, and greed, which amounts to idolatry.
                                                                    Colossians 3:5

Why does Paul equate greed to idolatry? An idolater is anyone who substitutes an object, an idea, or a person for the one true God. Since a greedy or covetous person is treating an object as more important than God, he or she is an idolater. Jesus warned: *Beware, and be on your guard against every form of greed; for not even when one has an abundance does his life consist of his possessions.*[1] The person who believes that materialism will provide happiness and meaning in life is serving Satan, and that is idolatry.

The Ten Commandments start with *have no other gods before Me* and end with *you shall not covet.* God's primary concern is that He is first in our lives, above all else. Jesus said: *But seek first His kingdom and His righteousness; and all these things shall be added to you.*[2] Here Jesus presents a cure for idolatry by presenting a positive command to obey. If we always seek God's kingdom first, then by definition, we cannot fall into idolatry and we conquer greed.

Everyone needs "things". Jesus promises to provide the basic needs of life, and blesses with much more, if we put Him first. Satan tries to convince us that our priority in life should be to seek an abundance of things. *No one can serve two masters; for either he will hate the one and love the other, or he will hold to one and despise the other. You cannot serve God and mammon* (riches).[3] Who is your master?

[1]Luke 12:15   [2]Matthew 6:33   [3]Matthew 6:24

God gave them over to a depraved mind ... full of envy, murder,
strife, deceit, malice; they are gossips, slanderers, haters of God,
insolent, arrogant, boastful, inventors of evil, disobedient to parents.
                                              Romans 1:28b-30

     Paul lists characteristics of the ungodly. Many of these traits
could be indirectly linked to speech but four of them deal directly
with the tongue: deceit, gossip, slander, and boasting. James is
addressing followers of Christ when he states that no one can tame
the tongue[1]. We are constantly in a battle with the old man over
control of our speech. Let's address these four evils in an effort to
reduce their impact and frequency in our lives.
     Deceit and boastfulness focus on self. We typically lie when
we try to hide our wrongdoings or indiscretions. Boasting is an
attempt to magnify self in the eyes of another. The goal of deception
and boasting is either to protect our reputation by covering that
which would detract, or to advance our standing by bragging on our
achievements. A spirit of humility would help us admit
shortcomings and refrain from self-aggrandizement.
     Gossip and slander spray their venom on others. Gossip
usually attempts to portray another in a negative way. Slander's aim
is to harm another's reputation with false or damaging words. Many
times, the objective of gossip or slander is to make oneself look
better by making others look worse. A spirit of love would starve
these two evils as the purpose for words would shift to constructive
rather than destructive talk.
     Jesus reminded us that *the mouth speaks out of that which*
fills the heart.[2] If our hearts and minds are led by the Spirit of God,
then our words will encourage and edify. *But I say, walk by the*
Spirit, and you will not carry out the desire of the flesh.[3]

[1]James 3:8   [2]Matthew 12:34b   [3]Galatians 5:16

Now accept the one who is weak in faith, but not for the purpose of passing judgment on his opinions. Let not him who eats regard with contempt him who does not eat, and let not him who does not eat judge him who eats, for God has accepted him.   Romans 14:1, 3

Food was a subject of much discussion and controversy in the life of the early church. Some Jewish believers had a difficult time grasping their new liberty in Christ and the concept that all foods were now clean[1]. Some Gentile believers' conscience bothered them when they were offered food that had been placed before pagan idols they once worshipped[2]. Many believers gave no thought to what they ate and received all food with thanksgiving. Paul challenged these various groups to bear with each other, recognizing that each group is acting in good conscience toward God and that we will all one day give account to God, not to each other.

In our culture today food fights have been replaced by other contentious issues. Conflicts arise when believers develop different convictions or opinions about topics that are not directly addressed in Scripture as being immoral. Denominations are formed over doctrinal differences but most also have their lists of acceptable and unacceptable practices based on the collective conscience.

Today opinions vary over using praise songs for worship, attending movies, reading Harry Potter books, and participating in Halloween activities, to name a few. Those who feel at liberty to participate in these activities should not look down on their brothers and sisters in the faith who have a conviction from the Lord to abstain. Similarly, those abstaining should not judge and condemn those who sense liberty from the Spirit to participate.

Can you think of any areas in life about which you have convictions that are not specifically addressed in Scripture? Do you have a tendency to look down on or judge another believer who doesn't share your conviction? God has called us to unity as believers. Let's focus on what unites us as followers of Christ rather than on what makes us different. One day, God will judge the intent and motive of each servant's heart.

[1]Mark 7:18-20   [2]I Corinthians 8

If we live by the Spirit, let us also walk by the Spirit. Let us not become boastful, challenging one another, envying one another.
                                        Galatians 5:25-26

          The Spirit is in all believers but doesn't control all believers. When Paul discussed the concept of a carnal Christian, the context was the occurrence of boasting and envy in the Corinthian church: *For since there is jealousy and strife among you, are you not fleshly* (carnal)*, and are you not walking like mere men.*[1] The one who is boastful or envious is not acknowledging the Spirit's work in believers' lives and is thus not walking in the Spirit.
          The boaster is filled with pride. Pride, like sin, has "I" as its center. The leader of a men's Bible study I attend, often asks if anyone present would like to brag on God. Men may share how God is working in or through them but the focus is on what God is doing, not what they have done. It is impossible to give God too much credit for anything positive you have experienced because *it is God who is at work in you, both to will and to work for His good pleasure.*[2] When sharing, seek to glorify God and not self.
          When Paul wrote to the church at Philippi, he mentioned that some in Rome were preaching Christ from envy and strife. Perhaps they were envious of his reputation or his success in leading people to Christ and were trying to outdo him. Clearly they were focused on self and not God.
          Whenever envy and boasting are present, strife is not far behind. Believers challenge one another as they seek to elevate self. Church unity is disrupted and the cause of Christ is hindered. As we seek to walk in the Spirit and glorify God in our thoughts and actions, the Kingdom of God will be advanced. Problem solved!

[1] I Corinthians 3:3   [2] Philippians 2:13

1. Which of these do you have the most problem controlling: envy, boasting, greed, evil speech, or judging? What can you do this week to surrender this area to the Spirit's control?

2. Are you aware of any convictions you have or don't have that put you at odds with another Christian? If the conviction at issue is not addressed in Scripture, find a way to live in harmony with your brother or sister.

Prayer Starter: Father God, I want to die to the flesh and walk in the Spirit. By the power of the Holy Spirit help me to control …

*Who once were disobedient, when the patience of God kept waiting
in the days of Noah, during the construction of the ark, in which a
few, that is, eight persons, were brought safely through the water.*
                                                        I Peter 3:20

Noah came from a godly, distinguished heritage. His great
grandfather was Enoch who walked with God and was taken directly
to heaven by God. His grandfather was Methuselah whose lifespan
of 969 years made him the oldest recorded person in the Bible. His
father was Lamech.

When God instructed Noah to build the ark He also promised
Noah that his wife, his three sons and their wives would be delivered
from death by the ark. Since the construction of the ark was a multi-
year project, it is certain that both his father and grandfather were
alive when God made His covenant with Noah. The implication is
that Noah's father and grandfather would be dead when the flood
came since otherwise they would have been included as part of the
family in the ark.

Perhaps Methuselah's advanced age was a picture of the
patience of God toward those who were awaiting God's judgment.
Genesis 5 provides this information: Methuselah fathered Lamech at
age 187; Lamech fathered Noah at age 182; and the flood came
when Noah was 600 years old. The sum of these three numbers
gives the time from Methuselah's birth to the beginning of the flood:
969 years. So Methuselah died in the year of the flood (Lamech died
five years earlier). If Methuselah's death and the completion of the
ark were the trip wires for the flood, then God provided ample time
for sinners to repent.

Peter refers to Noah as a preacher of righteousness.[1] Noah's
preaching and the construction of the ark were powerful testimonies
of God's impending judgment. Peter also looks ahead to God's next
worldwide judgment when he says: *The Lord is not slow about His
promise, as some count slowness, but is patient toward you, not
wishing for any to perish but for all to come to repentance.*[2] As
Christians we must hold in tension the anticipation of "Come, Lord
Jesus"[3] with the urgency of "now is the day of salvation."[4]

[1]II Peter 2:5   [2]II Peter 3:9   [3]Revelation 22:20   [4]II Corinthians 6:2

For God is not unjust so as to forget your work and the love which you have shown toward His name, in having ministered and in still ministering to the saints. Hebrews 6:10

When we think of our God being just, it is typically in the context of judging sin. Another aspect of God's justice, mentioned above, is remembering and rewarding the Christian's good works. Justice is both punishing wrong and rewarding right.

God often required memorials in the Old Testament to help the Israelites remember God's mighty deeds on their behalf. There are two incidents in the New Testament where God memorializes godly actions of individuals. In other words, He makes a point of remembering our good deeds done for His sake.

In one incident Mary of Bethany anoints Jesus' head with costly perfume shortly before His crucifixion. The disciples were indignant at the apparent waste of money which could have been given to the poor. Jesus commended her actions and said her good work would always be remembered.[1]

The second situation involved a Roman centurion. An angel declared to Cornelius that his prayers and monetary gifts to the Jewish people had "ascended as a memorial before God".[2] God responded by sending Peter to Cornelius with the gospel message which he and his family gladly received.

Since Jesus is no longer physically among us we cannot minister to Jesus as Mary did. However, we can all follow Cornelius' example and pray and give to the needs of others. When we do these acts in Jesus' name, God promises to remember them.

Jesus told his disciples that whoever gave a cup of water for them to drink would not lose his or her reward.[3] As Christians, we can be thankful that the penalty for all our unrighteousness has been paid for by Jesus. When we humbly live out that thankfulness through righteous acts of charity to advance the Kingdom of God, we can be sure that God will remember those deeds and reward us accordingly.

[1]Mark 14:1-9   [2]Acts 10:4   [3]Mark 9:41

And in the generations gone by He permitted all the nations to go their own ways; and yet He did not leave Himself without witness, in that He did good and gave you rains from heaven and fruitful seasons, satisfying your hearts with food and gladness.

Acts14:16-17

Why do good things happen to bad people? The moment we commit our first sin we deserve death and eternal separation from God. In fact, when Satan and his cohort sinned, God *cast them into hell and committed them to pits of darkness.*[1] Theologians refer to God's blessings to mankind who deserve death as common grace. This grace differs from saving grace which allows people to have salvation.

When God gave mankind a conscience to know right from wrong, He demonstrated common grace. Without our conscience the sinful nature would be unrestrained and the world would be flooded with evil. God's gift of government and social laws further restrict evil and encourage good.

Since the wages of sin is death, we all live our lives using time loaned to us from the common grace account. God doesn't want anyone to perish and has granted time so that each of us has the opportunity to recognize His common grace and His saving grace. God's goodness provides rain, crops and abundant food to sustain us and demonstrates His love for undeserving people.

If you have trusted Jesus, you are doubly blessed. While living in a world of common grace, you have also experienced saving grace. Thank God right now for that blessing! If you have only been enjoying God's common grace, please repent of your sins and ask Jesus to be your Lord and Savior! Saving grace is available.

[1] II Peter 2:4b

The secret things belong to the Lord our God, but the things revealed belong to us and to our sons forever, that we may observe all the words of this law.   Deuteronomy 29:29

      I use this verse whenever asked a question about God for which I have no answer. You have probably also heard these type questions many times. "How can God exist as three separate entities: Father, Son and Holy Spirit?" "Why did my loved one die prematurely?" "How can God's foreknowledge and man's free will coexist?" "When will the rapture of believers and Second Coming of Jesus Christ occur?"

      The fact is that God has chosen not to reveal everything about Himself and how He works to His creation. If that bothers us, then we need to get over it. Does it even make sense that a created being would know as much as the Creator? The good news is that believers will have eternity to have the entire glory and secrets of God revealed to us. The apostle Paul said: *Now I know in part, but then I shall know fully just as I also have been fully known.*[1]

      Notice the second part of the Deuteronomy verse. God has chosen to reveal much to His created beings and we will be held accountable for what has been revealed. We should focus on obeying what He has revealed and not concern ourselves with what He hasn't revealed. In the end, we will be judged by our Creator based on what we were able to know, not on what we had no way of knowing.

[1] I Corinthians 13:12b

*The Lord's lovingkindnesses indeed never cease, for His
compassions never fail. They are new every morning; great is Thy
faithfulness.*   *Lamentations 3:22-23*

Jeremiah begins his lamentation with: *How lonely sits the
city that was full of people!*[1] He is broken hearted that Jerusalem lies
desolate after the overthrow of the city in 586 B.C. by King
Nebuchadnezzar. Many of its citizens have been deported to
Babylon. Jeremiah recognizes that it was the sin of the people that
brought God's judgment upon them, and that makes him even more
sorrowful. This catastrophe could have been averted had the people
repented, but they didn't.

Six centuries later, Jesus begins his lamentation with: *O
Jerusalem, Jerusalem, who kills the prophets and stones those who
are sent to her! How often I wanted to gather your children
together, the way a hen gathers her chicks under her wings, and you
were unwilling.*[2] We feel Jesus' longing for His people to return to
the God of Israel. Instead, they chose to crucify the Son of God.

Half-way through his five-chapter lamentation, Jeremiah
pauses to recall the character of God. He knows the end goal of
God's judgment on Jerusalem was correction and restoration.
Indeed, seventy years later, repentant exiles would return to
Jerusalem to begin reconstruction. Jeremiah rejoices that God is
faithful to be the same every day. God had been heavy handed with
Israel, but that did not affect His ever-present loving and
compassionate nature.

Twenty centuries latter, Jesus desires to gather everyone
under His wing. Every morning that you awaken, Jesus wants you to
experience His love and compassion toward you. Will you nestle
close to Him? If your tendency is to run the other way, know that
He will not change, but you need to change. The choice is yours.

[1]Lamentations 1:1a   [2]Matthew 23:37

1. We would do well to be more mindful and thankful for God's grace in our lives. Take a moment now and thank God for specific examples of His grace to you.

2. When you think of God being just, do you normally think in terms of God punishing wrong or rewarding right? Which aspect of God's justice is a greater motivator in your life? Why?

Prayer Starter: Father God, I am amazed in your presence as I think of who You are, compared to me. I praise and thank You for your grace and patience that are daily extended to me. Specifically, I praise You for …

*But if you have bitter jealousy and selfish ambition in your heart, do
not be arrogant and so lie against the truth. This wisdom is not that
which comes down from above, but is earthly, natural, demonic.*
James 3:14-15

    Person A invests 10% of income and gives 0% to God;
Person B gives 10% of income to God and invests 0%. Who is
wiser? The answer to that question depends on your world view. If
you have an earthly world view, Person A is wiser. If you have a
heavenly world view, person B is wiser. Both realms recognize
wisdom which is defined as "the power of judging rightly and
following the soundest course of action based on knowledge,
experience, understanding, etc".

    Heavenly wisdom operates with eternity in mind. Earthly
wisdom focuses only on the finite and temporal. The problem with
earthy wisdom is that a focus on the finite can easily lead to a focus
on self. When self is centermost, jealousy and selfish ambition are
not far behind.

    Since the Christian lives in the world, he or she is bombarded
daily with worldly wisdom. The challenge is to be in the world but
not influenced by the world. Do we want revenge when we are
wronged or do we commit the outcome to God? Do we worry when
the concerns of life weigh us down, or do we cast all of our care
upon Him? Do we invest our time and resources in eternity, or are
our spending habits more focused on self?

    James describes heavenly wisdom as pure, peaceable, gentle,
reasonable, full of mercy and good fruits, unwavering, and without
hypocrisy. If our lives are characterized by these traits then there is
a good chance that we are operating primarily using the wisdom
from above. If not, then more time in the Word and prayer would be
in order. The best way to counter the effects of the world is to offset
them with heavenly thoughts by immersing ourselves in the word of
God and prayer.

So give Thy servant an understanding heart to judge Thy people to discern between good and evil. For who is able to judge this great people of Thine?   *I Kings 3:9*

But solid food is for the mature, who because of practice have their senses trained to discern good and evil.   *Hebrews 5:14*

Discern means to see and identify by noting differences. A Christ follower needs to see the difference between good and evil, between truth and falsehood, so that he or she can choose good and truth. Discernment is available to us from God through prayer and is a byproduct of Christian maturity.

Above we see King Solomon's answer when God asked him what he would like to receive from God. Solomon recognized his inadequacy to rightly judge the people and humbly asked God for wisdom and discernment as king. His request focused on his desire to serve those of his kingdom to the best of his ability. God granted him discernment beyond his natural ability. Do you need discernment as you face the challenges of the day? James tells us that godly wisdom is available from asking in faith.[1]

The writer of Hebrews contrasts our mastery of God's Word and Biblical principles by using a mature believer who eats solid food and a babe in Christ who is fed milk. God's will is that all Christians progress toward the ability to feed themselves from God's Word and to be able to teach others. As this growth occurs, we better grasp God's view of right and wrong, of truth and error. We take on the mind of Christ and as we walk in the Spirit we learn through experience and observation what is good and what is true. We filter every decision and circumstance through the word of God.

God is our source of discernment. Whether through a prayer like Solomon or the provision of wisdom through maturity, we are totally dependent on God for discerning good from evil, truth from falsehood.

[1]James 1:5-6

The men of David said to him, "Behold, this is the day of which the Lord said to you, 'Behold, I am about to give your enemy into your hand, and you shall do to him as it seems good to you.'" Then David arose, and cut off the edge of Saul's robe secretly.
I Samuel 24:4

As we seek God's will in our lives, we must be careful not to give too much weight to the circumstances of life. While it is true that God does open and shut doors to direct us, it is also true that godly wisdom must be applied to correctly discern God's intent.

As King Saul was pursuing David with the intent to kill him, nature called and the king had to find a private place. He happened to choose the same cave in which David and his men were hiding. David's men interpreted this favorable circumstance as David's God-given opportunity to kill Saul. They even referenced a promise that God had given David as justification for the action.

After secretly cutting off a portion of King Saul's robe, David's conscience convicted him and he concluded that it was not right to kill the Lord's anointed. David instructed his men that they were not to harm King Saul.

David viewed Saul's choice of his cave as God's providential work, but his interpretation of the circumstance was different from that of his men. David allowed the principle of respecting God's anointed to trump the circumstantial opportunity to kill his avowed enemy. David's conscience and respect for God's ways overrode the circumstances and the counsel of his men.

David used the circumstance to show that he valued Saul's life and was not his enemy. The temptation to use this situation to end his time on the lam had to be great. He and his men could have returned to a normal life and could even have claimed that it was God's will as evidenced by the circumstances. However, David followed his Spirit-led conscience and did the right thing, even though it cost him more time on the run.

Charm is deceitful and beauty is vain, but a woman who fears the Lord, she shall be praised.

Proverbs 31:30

God created beauty. He created physical beauty. He created spiritual beauty. Physical beauty is determined largely by the arrangement of the chromosomes God selects from His gene pool at conception. Spiritual beauty is from His Spirit working in cooperation with an obedient follower of Jesus Christ. In the end, physical beauty is vain and spiritual beauty is eternal.

Unfortunately, mankind tends to place more importance on physical beauty than spiritual. We acknowledge the shallowness of physical beauty when we say beauty is only skin deep. If you have ever been to a Bodies Exhibit, you have seen the body without the skin and there is nothing very attractive about it. God reminded Samuel of man's obsession with beauty when He said *God sees not as man sees, for man looks at the outward appearance, but the Lord looks at the heart.*[1]

When a man or woman is seeking God's mate for his or her life, wisdom would say to pay more attention to the inner person than the outer person. Once married, as the outer appearance begins to slowly deteriorate, wisdom would say the same thing again. If being beautiful or handsome were the most important ingredient in a good marriage then Hollywood celebrities should have the lowest divorce rate, and we know that isn't true.

As you interact with the children and youth of today, make more observations about and give more importance to inner beauty than outer beauty. Remember, God is the creator of both and He gives more value to the heart than the heart-throb.

[1] I Samuel 16:7b

So teach us to number our days, that we may present to Thee a heart
of wisdom.   *Psalm 90:12*

When I was a high school math teacher, a common practice among teachers and students was to count down the days to the end of school. Perhaps you have counted down the days to a long-awaited vacation, or maybe retirement. In Psalm 90, Moses asks God to teach us to number or count down our days. We need to make each day count for the Kingdom of God because we are accountable to God for each day and how we live it.

Let's say that tomorrow you are told that you have an incurable disease and only have one month to live. Jack Nicholson found himself in a similar situation in the movie "Bucket List". He records the things he wants to do before he "kicks the bucket". What would be on your list? Would they be material or spiritual or a combination of both? Fortunately or unfortunately, most of us will not have a countdown to our death. We must live each day with the awareness that it could be our last. As much as possible, we should live each day with no regrets.

Solomon offers a practical way to help us number our days: *It is better to go to a house of mourning than to go to a house of feasting, because that is the end of every man, and the living takes it to heart.*[1] Whenever we attend funerals or read the daily obituaries we are reminded of our own mortality and of our limited time to contribute to eternal matters.

The idea of numbering our days is not intended to make us morbid. *This is the day the Lord has made; let us rejoice and be glad in it.*[2] Lord, give us a daily, joyful focus on investing our time in Kingdom work.

[1]Ecclesiastes 7:2   [2]Psalm118:24

1. What method do you use to make decisions? Do you employ earthly or heavenly wisdom? Is your first step to pray for wisdom or to rationally weigh the pros and cons? Why?

2. How much weight do you typically give to circumstances in making a decision? Do you also consider inner peace, God's Word, and godly counsel?

Prayer Starter: Father, help me to instinctively seek your will first in my decision-making process. Give me heavenly wisdom now as I need to decide about …

*By this is My Father glorified, that you bear much fruit, and so
prove to be My disciples.*   *John 15:8*

A follower of Christ who bears fruit glorifies God and
authenticates his or her discipleship. A fruit-bearing tree or plant is
a common analogy in Scripture for a productive spiritual life. Let's
investigate the New Testament use of "fruit" to further explore this
verse.

Paul mentions both the fruit of the Spirit and the fruit of
righteousness in his letters. The nine fruit of the Spirit[1] listed by
Paul are internal qualities like love, joy and peace. Although they
describe an inner godly character they nevertheless are manifested,
for example, by acts of love and a joyful, peaceful countenance.
Paul challenged the Colossians to *bear fruit in every good work*[2].
Perhaps this is what Paul has in mind with fruit of righteousness[3] –
the external good works. The internal character and the external
actions reflect the life of Christ and glorify God.

After Jesus told his disciples that the fields (of souls) were
white for harvest, He said: *Already he who reaps is receiving wages,
and is gathering fruit for life eternal.*[4] Here Jesus is reminding us
that we are charged with sowing the gospel and that seed will
sometime land on good soil and produce fruit. The amount of fruit
in terms of souls saved is largely dependent on the amount of seed
sown. God is always glorified and we are affirmed as disciples of
Christ when we faithfully sow the seed and see the fruit that results.

Finally, let's consider the *fruit of lips that give thanks to His
name.*[5] The natural reaction to our internal and external
transformation over time to the likeness of Jesus should be one of
praise and thanks to God. After all, we just submit to the Spirit's
control in our lives and He does the rest. How fruitful is your life?

[1]Galatians 5:22-23   [2]Colossians 1:10   [3]Philippians 1:11
[4]John 4:36a   [5]Hebrews 13:15b

Nevertheless do not rejoice in this, that the spirits are subject to you, but rejoice that your names are recorded in heaven.   *Luke 10:20*

In this verse, Jesus is ranking two sources of joy. The seventy had just returned from a short term mission trip in which they had experienced power over demons. They were understandably joyful because they had seen God use them to set demon-possessed people free. Surely Jesus rejoiced with them but He also reminded them that their greatest source of joy should be that they were heaven-bound. Because Jesus was Lord of their lives, they would spend eternity fellowshipping and enjoying the family of God in the presence of a loving, holy God. It doesn't get any better than that. Jesus would soon die to ensure that future joy was a reality. He wanted them to appreciate and rejoice in His upcoming sacrifice for them.

The apostle John said this: *I have no greater joy than this, to hear of my children walking in the truth.*[1] John was focused on the present by declaring that his greatest joy was to know that those he invested in spiritually were walking with Jesus. Paul expressed a similar sentiment when he told the Thessalonians: *you are our glory and joy*[2]. Both of these men derived much joy from knowing they made a spiritual difference in others' lives.

The well-known acrostic for joy (Jesus, Others, You) prioritizes our focus and is consistent with Scripture. As we deny self and walk with Jesus while serving others, we maximize our joy.

[1]III John 4   [2]I Thessalonians 2:20

Now when the people saw that Moses delayed to come down from the mountain, the people assembled about Aaron, and said to him, "Come, make us a god who will go before us; as for this Moses, the man who brought us up from the land of Egypt, we do not know what has become of him."   *Exodus 32:1*

Have you noticed that God is not in a hurry? Why should He be? He has an infinite amount of time available to Him. Mankind, on the other hand, is very much constrained by time. Our sensitivity to that fact makes us uneasy when it comes to waiting and being patient.

The children of Israel arrived at the base of Mount Sinai two months after they left Egypt.[1] God descended on Mount Sinai, spoke the Ten Commandments, and later instructed Moses to come up the mountain to receive the law written on stone tablets. Moses, in turn, instructed the seventy elders to wait for him and Joshua to return and placed Aaron in charge.

Moses was on the mountain forty days and forty nights.[2] That is a long time! Before the availability of cell phones, do you remember waiting for someone to arrive at a predetermined place and time? If they didn't show up, how long would you wait? At what point would you take action and leave or go looking for them? The children of Israel were apparently willing to wait forty days and then took action. Moses had been their tangible representative from God and now he was gone, possibly dead. So, a vocal subgroup reverted to what they had seen in Egypt and what God had forbidden: a golden idol fashioned as a calf.

Whenever we choose not to wait on the Lord, whatever action we take will be wrong. Patience is a fruit of the Spirit and God will grant us that fruit if we ask. Don't rush and settle for an imitation. Wait on God and receive His best.

[1]Exodus 19:1   [2]Exodus 24:18

You younger men, likewise, be subject to your elders; and all of you clothe yourselves with humility toward one another, for God is opposed to the proud, but gives grace to the humble. Humble yourselves, therefore, under the mighty hand of God, that He may exalt you at the proper time.　　　　　*I Peter 5:5-6*

Humble is used above as a noun and a verb. Humility is a mental attitude of lowliness in which we don't think of ourselves more highly than we should. We recognize that all we are and have is given to us by an act of God's grace. However, if our humility is genuine then it will be demonstrated by acts of humility. Both the attitude and actions are needed for Biblical humility.

If you struggle with maintaining an attitude of humility, try Peter's suggestion and humble yourself. Submitting to another person is one way to humble oneself. Other Biblical examples are choosing a seat of lesser honor and considering others as better than you.

Jesus said: *For who is greater, the one who reclines at the table, or the one who serves? Is it not the one who reclines at the table? But I am among you as the one who serves.*[1] By serving, Jesus demonstrated humility. Serving others is an excellent way to humble oneself.

Pride is the opposite of humility. The proud person is arrogant and often seeks to be exalted. Notice that God, in His timing, exalts the humble. To be honored by God is far greater than the praise of man or any self-aggrandizement. If we live with the awareness that we are under God's mighty hand, how can we not be humble?

[1]Luke 22:27

Now it came about when they had crossed over, that Elijah said to Elisha, "Ask what I shall do for you before I am taken from you." And Elisha said, "Please, let a double portion of your spirit be upon me." And he said, "You have asked a hard thing. Nevertheless, if you see me when I am taken from you, it shall be so for you; but if not, it shall not be so."   *II Kings 2:9-10*

God had already directed Elijah to anoint Elisha as the prophet to replace him.[1] The two men had just crossed the Jordan River when this conversation took place. I interpret Elisha's request as wanting to be Spirit filled to the extent that he would be even more useful to God that Elijah was. If so, why was seeing Elijah taken to heaven the condition under which the request would be granted?

How would it affect your faith and walk with God if you were to witness your mentor being transported to heaven in a fiery chariot drawn by fiery horses? Would it deepen your commitment to God's purpose for your life on earth? To what extent did the Damascus Road experience shape the Apostle Paul's resolve to give his life unreservedly to preaching the gospel message?

Chances are that you and I will never see a fiery chariot or a blinding light from heaven. Instead, our faith grows when we obediently follow God into situations that we deem uncomfortable or beyond our ability. God asks us to place ourselves in positions where if the Spirit doesn't show up, we fail. But the Spirit will be present and our faith will grow because of the experience of seeing God come through on our behalf. We don't need a double portion of the Spirit, we just need to obey when the Spirit beckons.

[1] I Kings 19:16

1. Which category of fruitfulness do you sense needs more growth: internal qualities, good works, souls saved, or thankfulness? What can you do to improve in this area?

2. When was the last time the Holy Spirit prompted you to step out in faith and do something that was not necessarily in your comfort zone? How did it work out?

Prayer Starter: Spirit of God, I want to experience more fully the fruit and the works of the Spirit in my life. Deepen my thankfulness for the Spirit residing in me. As I seek to grow in this area, help me to …

Faithful are the wounds of a friend, but deceitful are the kisses of an enemy.
                                                              Proverbs 27:6

God is often pictured as a Father disciplining the son or daughter whom He loves. All children at times need correction and it is best done at the loving hands of a parent. As Christians we are no different. We still sin and sometimes the sin is not immediately recognized and confessed. When that occurs, correction is needed to get us back on the right path.

God uses a variety of methods to get our attention when we have strayed off course. One of those ways is confrontation from other people. We may be confronted with our sin from a preacher in church or a sermon on the radio or television. It might also be from someone you know, perhaps a friend. Friends know our routine and our disposition, and can sense when something is wrong. We trust our friends, so when they share we believe that they have our best interest at heart, and that makes the correction easier to take.

Some of us naturally have a critical spirit; it's a gift from below. If so, we need to be especially careful that our words of correction are from the Spirit of God and not our spirit. Humans have an uncanny ability to detect when someone is sincerely interested in their welfare versus simply satisfying an urge to find fault. When correction comes from the heart of a compassionate, loving friend, the wound will heal quickly.

If we find ourselves on the receiving end of correction from someone, we need to be thankful that the person cared enough to risk alienation and share. As mentioned earlier, God has many resources to get our attention. If we don't respond to someone he sends to us, the other options may not be as pleasant. God our Father will continue to pursue us until we respond to His correction.

All discipline for the moment seems not to be joyful, but sorrowful; yet to those who have been trained by it, afterwards it yields the peaceful fruit of righteousness.[1] Remember, His goal is the peaceful fruit of righteousness, which should be our goal as well.

[1]Hebrews 12:11

So Achan answered Joshua and said, "Truly, I have sinned against the Lord..." And all Israel stoned them with stones.
                                            Joshua 7:20a; 25b

And as he heard these words, Ananias fell down and breathed his last; and great fear come upon all who heard of it.   *Acts 5:5*

Two prominent works of God recorded in the Bible are Israel's entrance into the Promised Land and the origin of the New Testament church. Both were new beginnings, born of God, and integral to His overall redemptive plan. It is interesting to note that at the beginning of each of these two critical historical events, the Holy Spirit records God's severe judgment against an individual's sin.

The expression "sin in the camp" is not found in the Bible. Rather it was apparently coined to refer to Achan's sin of taking some plunder during the battle of Jericho which caused the defeat at Ai and the death of 36 Israelites. The expression would also be appropriate to reference the sin of Ananias who lied to the apostles when he said he was donating the full selling price of some property. Both sins dealt with materialism and today would probably not register very high on our sin-ometer. However, God viewed these sins very seriously and took decisive action against them.

New beginnings are often fragile, susceptible to numerous opposing forces that seek to derail and stop the momentum. For godly institutions the greatest threat is sin in the camp. Satan attacks the Church from without and within but the more effective strategy is from within. The sins of Achan and Ananias were the first recorded sins in Israel or the Church in each of these new beginnings. God sent a message at the onset of each sin: I will not allow sin to impede the work I am doing in your midst. The public judgment of God against the sin resulted in a healthy respect to the dangers of sin for both the Israelites and the Church.

Today, God is still fulfilling His redemptive plan. Sin in the Church impedes that effort. May each of us take seriously our role in maintaining personal purity and responding appropriately to known sin in the Church.

But take care lest this liberty of yours somehow become a stumbling block to the weak. Therefore, if food causes my brother to stumble, I will never eat meat again, that I might not cause my brother to stumble.   *I Corinthians 8:9, 13*

The church at Corinth had written Paul seeking his guidance on several spiritual issues they had encountered. One of these issues dealt with Gentiles who formerly worshipped pagan gods but were now believers in Christ and part of the Corinthian church. Part of the Gentile worship was to offer food to their idols. Some of this food was later sold on the open market and the Jewish Christians would buy it. When Gentile Christians, who were trying to separate themselves from their ungodly past practices, saw Jewish Christians eating this food that was once offered to idols, it troubled them.

Paul and the Jewish Christians recognized that the pagan idols were just wood and stone so eating food that had been offered to these inanimate objects was of no consequence to them. Their knowledge of this fact gave them liberty to buy and eat this food with no guilty conscience. However, the religious background of the Gentile Christian presented a conflict when they observed fellow Christians eating this food.

Paul counseled the church not to eat food offered to idols if it offended their Gentile brothers and sisters in Christ. Our Christian liberty should be made subservient to the needs of others. If our actions, considered lawful in Christ, cause a fellow believer to stumble, then we set our rights aside and do what is best for the fellow believer.

This principle is really a practical outworking of what Jesus termed the second greatest commandment: *You shall love your neighbor as yourself;*[1] and what we have coined the Golden Rule: *And just as you want people to treat you, treat them in the same way.*[2] Lord, help us to see and correct any way that we may be a stumbling block to others.

[1]Mark 12:31   [2]Luke 6:31

For even when we were with you, we used to give you this order: if anyone will not work, neither let him eat. For we hear that some among you are leading an undisciplined life, doing no work at all, but acting like busybodies.   *II Thessalonians 3:10-11*

A spirit of discernment is required to determine whether to help someone in need. Not every need in the Body of Christ should be readily met. Paul ordered the church in Thessalonica not to feed the brother who was not willing to work.

Enabling a brother or sister in Christ to continue in a destructive lifestyle is not compassion. Instead, "helpful" actions may remove the opportunity for God's discipline to be at work in their lives. Appropriate consequences may never be realized because of intervention by some well-meaning individual. Harsh consequences push us to the end of our rope so that we reach out to God to help us. In the long run, the needy individual may be truly helped when we decide not to help in a material way.

Paul describes those that are not willing to work as undisciplined and notes that they spend their time as busybodies. When a brother is enabled to continue a harmful habit it becomes a poor witness to the unbelieving world. In the section immediately prior to the verses above, Paul reminds the readers of his example to them in this area. He worked tirelessly while among them and paid for all his food so he would not be a burden to them. Being a Christian model of what to do, is more beneficial than subsidizing an improper model.

When confronted with questionable needs in the body of Christ, ask God for discernment. The proper action may be to bend our knees in prayer for the situation, rather than bend our elbow to grab the wallet.

When it is My desire, I will chastise them; and the peoples will be gathered against them when they are bound for their double guilt. You have plowed wickedness, you have reaped injustice, you have eaten the fruit of lies, because you have trusted in your way, in your numerous warriors.   *Hosea 10:10, 13*

Hosea was a prophet to Israel, the Northern Kingdom, from 750-725 BC. He warned Israel of God's discipline which was forthcoming if they didn't repent. The Assyrians gathered against them and bound them in 722 BC. Hosea also reminded Israel that they had already reaped what they had sown. God's discipline was a future event, but sin's consequences were an event of the past. Perhaps if the consequences of sin don't change our heart, God intervenes with His own discipline in an effort to turn believers' hearts back to Him.

It seems that when God created the physical laws that rule the universe, He also implemented spiritual laws that govern mankind's morality. *Do not be deceived, God is not mocked; for whatever a man sows, this he will also reap.*[1] This spiritual law is universally accepted as true. When did you last hear: "What goes around, comes around."? Even the oriental notion of Karma deals with cause and effect in our lives. God's discipline appears to be separate and distinct from simply reaping what you sow.

Discipline is used to correct or restore, not to punish. Let's say a student is caught cheating at school on a test. The teacher gives the student a zero on the test which dramatically lowers the student's grade in the class. The student reaped the consequences for his or her actions. When the student arrives home, the parents have a decision to make about discipline. If the student is obviously remorseful and repentant, the parents may decide further action is not required. If however, there is little evidence of repentance, discipline is required.

Furthermore, we had earthly fathers to discipline us, and we respected them; shall we not much rather be subject to the Father of spirits, and live?[2]

[1]Galatians 6:7   [2]Hebrews 12:9

1. When was the last time you either received spiritual correction or corrected someone else? How was the correction received, either by you or the other person? What value came from the confrontation?

2. How would you distinguish between reaping what you sow and spiritual discipline from your heavenly Father, or do you view them as the same?

Prayer Starter: Father God, I want to be quick to respond to your correction in my life when I stray. Give me a soft heart of wisdom to know when I am being corrected or when You want me to correct others.

*And He was transfigured before them; and His face shone like the
sun, and His garments became as white as light.   Matthew 17:2
And do not be conformed to this world but be transformed by the
renewing of your mind.   Romans 12:2a*

The words transfigured and transformed in these verses are
both translated from the Greek word METAMOPϕOψ, shown in
upper case letters. You probably recognize our English word
metamorphosis which is used to describe the transformation from a
tadpole to a frog or from a caterpillar to a butterfly. Both of these
physical transformations are quite remarkable, as are the changes
described in the verses above.

I appreciate the translators of our Bible using different words
to convey a metamorphosis because the transfiguration and the
transformation discussed are dramatically different. Jesus was
transfigured into what He already was, whereas we are transformed
into what we never have been. Paul describes Jesus as one who
*emptied Himself, taking the form of a servant, and being made in the
likeness of men.*[1] On the mountain, those present saw the refilling of
the glory and majesty of the Son of God.

If Jesus had not set aside His visible glory, He would not
have been able to walk shoulder to shoulder with mankind on earth.
Instead, we would have recoiled in fear as the Israelites did when
Moses face shone after being in God's presence on Mount Sinai.[2]
Thankfully, Jesus did humble Himself so He could walk where we
walk and we could learn how to walk by following His steps.

One day we will see the transfigured Christ face to face. Our
goal in the here and now should be to allow His Spirit to transform
us. We need to become what we have never been: transformed into
the image of Christ.

[1]Philippians 2:7   [2]Exodus 34:30

But we all, with unveiled face beholding as in a mirror the glory of the Lord, are being transformed into the same image from glory to glory, just as from the Lord, the Spirit.   *II Corinthians 3:18*

So how does the Spirit transform us into the image of Christ? One way is through our obedient exposure to the word of God. Remember the veil that covered Moses' face so the people wouldn't fear the manifestation of God's glory? For the believer that veil has been removed and we can look intently at God's glory without fear. God's glory has been revealed to us in the Bible, God's mirror. The Spirit of God works in and through the w ord of God to change us into the image of the Son of God. It is a long, gradual process taking us from one degree of glory to another.

James also uses the mirror analogy: *But one who looks intently at the perfect law, the law of liberty, and abides by it, not having become a forgetful hearer bur an effectual doer, this man shall be blessed in what he does.*[1] James emphasizes the importance of obedience to what we read. Is there a sin to confess, a promise to claim, an example to follow, a command to obey? In short, is there some application to my life that the Spirit is trying to convey to me?

The metamorphosis of a tadpole to a frog is stunning. After six weeks or so, tiny legs start to sprout. The head becomes more distinct and the body elongates. The limbs begin to bulge where they will eventually pop out. By 12 weeks, the tadpole has only a small tail stub and looks like a miniature version of the adult frog. This transformation is accomplished by adding food and water to God's design.

In the same way the babe in Christ undergoes metamorphosis to a mature believer by the design of God. However, if sustenance from God's word is withheld, maturity will not occur and the babe remains a babe. It is always tragic when God's design is thwarted by a lack of action on our part. Let's devote ourselves to an obedient, intentional intake of the Bible. Let's morph into Christ-likeness!

[1]James 1:23-25

Therefore be careful how you walk, not as unwise men, but as wise, making the most of your time, because the days are evil.
                                                    Ephesians 5:15-16

The Apostle Paul used the analogy of walking, standing, and sitting in his letter to the Ephesians. He urged the Ephesians to walk or live in a careful way which implies they should be thoughtful about how they spend their time. Are they investing their lives in matters that will have eternal significance and impart righteousness in an evil world?

He also encouraged them to put on the full armor of God and *stand firm against the schemes of the devil.*[1] Here, standing portrays the idea of being prepared to fight, always alert and on guard against the enemy's attack. As we walk and advance God's kingdom, times will come when we have to stand and do battle with Satan.

Finally, Paul reminded them that they have been saved by Christ and are *seated with Him in the heavenly places*[2]. The Christian's sin debt has been paid by Christ and we are resting or seated with Him. Physically we are on earth, but spiritually we are with Christ. We are secure.

Since we are seated with Christ, we have the ability to walk wisely and to stand firmly. Never forget that it is our seated position that allows spiritual maturity and productivity. *I, therefore, the prisoner of the Lord, entreat you to walk in a manner worthy of the calling with which you have been called.* [3]

[1]Ephesians 6:11b   [2]Ephesians 2:6   [3]Ephesians 4:1

But like the Holy One who called you, be holy yourselves also in all your behavior; because it is written, "You shall be holy, for I am holy."   *I Peter 1:15-16*

"Holy" means to be separate from all that is sinful. Holiness is an overarching attribute of God. Glimpses of worship of God in heaven are often accompanied by a chorus of "holy, holy, holy". The Bible uses "holy" to describe God, certain things, and certain people. Each Person of the Trinity is holy. In the Old Testament, God declared the Sabbath, the tithe, the temple, the sacrifices, and other objects as holy because they had been set apart for a holy purpose. The priests and the Nazarites were also referred to as holy because they also were set apart for a holy work.

In the New Testament there are fewer references to holy objects, and references to holy people are not restricted to a vocation or a vow. The reason for this change is that the holy objects in the Old Testament were pointing to the sacrifice of Christ which enabled believers to become holy. Once Jesus paid the penalty for our sins, the holy objects were no longer needed. Whereas God previously declared certain objects to be holy, He now declares those who trust in His Son's sacrificial death to be holy.

He made Him who knew no sin to be sin on our behalf, that we might become the righteousness of God in Him.[1] This verse speaks of a positional righteousness that believers have before God as a result of Christ's substitutionary death. Christians also have positional holiness because we have been set apart in Christ.

We now must become who we are. Hence, we have Peter's admonition to be holy in all your behavior. We are given a lifetime and the Holy Spirit's presence to make God's declaration of our imputed holiness as close to a visible reality as possible. The goal: Christ-likeness. Time is short. Let's press toward the goal!

[1] II Corinthians 5:21

For the eyes of the Lord move to and fro throughout the earth that
He may strongly support those whose heart is completely His. You
have acted foolishly in this. Indeed, from now on you will surely
have wars.   *II Chronicles 16:9*

     Asa, king of Judah, was described as one who *did good and*
right in the sight of the Lord his God.[1] During the eleventh year of
his reign, Ethiopia came against him with an army twice as big as
his. Asa called on God for help and Judah routed the Ethiopians.
Then Asa led his nation to enter into a covenant to seek the Lord
God with all their heart.[2] For the next twenty years or so the nation
enjoyed peace and prosperity.
     Have you noticed that during times of plenty in which there
is little or no conflict, we can drift away from the Lord. When we
don't sense a need for His help in our lives, our relationship with
Him can take a back-burner as we live the good life. Perhaps that is
what happened to King Asa. The next time we hear of him, he is in
the thirty-sixth year of his reign and he seems like a totally different
person.
     In that year, the king of Israel came to war against the king of
Judah. Asa's response was to take gold and silver from the house of
the Lord and send it to the king of Aram in Damascus with a plea for
help. Asa devised his own plan and it worked. However he should
have sought the Lord in this situation as he did with the Ethiopians.
Perhaps during the twenty years of peace and prosperity he had lost
his devotion to the Lord and thus reacted in the flesh.
     After this incident the prophet Hanani confronted Asa with
the words above. The foolish act mentioned was seeking the help of
Aram and not God. Asa's response was to throw Hanani in prison.
Asa died a few years later with a disease with which he sought help
from physicians, not the Lord.
     A strong start does not ensure a strong finish. As we keep
our hearts focused on the Lord, He promises His strong support.
With His support we can finish well.

[1]II Chronicles 14:2   [2]II Chronicles 15:12

1. An obedient, consistent intake of God's word is one key way to mature spiritually. List several other disciplines below that lead to maturity. How many of them are active in your life?

2. If you have an average life span, are you in the first third, middle third or last third of your life? Regardless of where you are, commit to God that you will run your race to full maturity in Christ till your last breath.

Prayer Starter: Lord, Paul said prior to his death: *I have fought the fight, I have finished my course, I have kept the faith.* May I say the same to You as I prepare to exit this world.

A new commandment I give to you, that you love one another, even as I have loved you, that you also love one another. By this all men will know that you are My disciples, if you have love for one another.   John 13:34-35

When Jesus was asked what the greatest commandment was, He said: love God. He then offered that the second greatest was: love others.[1] In essence He summarized the Ten Commandments in two verses. Now on the night before His crucifixion He gives the disciples a new command: love one another. It was new, in part, because Jesus offered His life as the standard for loving one another.

The Biblical view of love is not an easy term to define. A dictionary would express love as a feeling or affection but God portrays it as an action. Most of the commands in the Decalogue are negative so it is easy to know when we have kept them. Honor your father and mother is a positive command and we are less certain where we stand. Love one another is another positive command and thus difficult to wrap your arms around. So, when Jesus gave them the command, He told them to love each other as He had loved them. For the past three years the disciples observed Jesus' acts of love toward them and others. Love had been personified and they had seen love in action.

Dr. Don McMinn has written a workbook focusing on the above verses and entitled The 11th Commandment. He observes that there are 35 distinct "one another" verses in the New Testament of which "love one another" is the overarching verse. The other 34 "one another" verses flesh out what love one another looks like. Some of the verbs used with one another to show the action involved in love are: encourage, comfort, pray for, forgive, admonish and serve.

Jesus noted that as we act in love toward one another, those around us will know that we belong to Jesus. Since love is an action, we must be intentional in loving one another. Be on the lookout for the presence of the "one anothers" in Scripture and for opportunities to employ the "one anothers" in the lives of others.

[1]Mark 12:28-31

I urge Euodia and I urge Syntyche to live in harmony in the Lord.
                                                        Philippians 4:2

How would you like your failure to resolve disagreements in the church highlighted in print two thousand years later? The two women Paul mentioned either had a conflict between themselves or with the church. The situation had exacerbated to the point that Paul was informed and felt the need to address the problem.

Earlier in the letter Paul requested that he might hear *that you are standing firm in one spirit, with one mind striving together for the faith of the gospel.*[1] Paul wanted the church's spirit and mind focused on advancing the gospel message. A gospel focus was hard to achieve with distractions in the church caused by these two ladies. Resolution was needed for the sake of God's Kingdom.

I have come to appreciate the simple statement: Let's agree to disagree. When Paul and Barnabas disagreed over whether to take Mark on their second missionary journey, they decided to form two teams; Barnabas with Mark, Paul with Silas. They couldn't agree, but they found a solution to advance the gospel in spite of their disagreement. The tragedy in many churches is that their reputation in the community is tarnished over internal arguments and the Kingdom of God is negatively impacted.

We do well to remember that a permanent record of our disagreements is kept in heaven so *that each one may be recompensed for his deeds in the body, according to what he has done, whether good or bad.*[2]

[1]Philippians 1:27b   [2]II Corinthians 5:10b

"For John the Baptist has come eating no bread and drinking no wine; and you say, 'he has a demon!' The Son of Man has come eating and drinking; and you say, 'Behold, a gluttonous man, and a drunkard, a friend of tax-gatherers and sinners!'" Luke 7:33-34

Every person is unique. When God saves an individual that individual remains unique. God uses our uniqueness to reach others with the gospel. John the Baptist and Jesus were very different, and yet each had an effective ministry in reaching people for the Kingdom. John was a solitary man who had taken the vow of a Nazarite which means he drank no wine and didn't cut his hair. Jesus however was very social and had taken no such vow.

In a 24-hour period, I encountered a Christian man with a ponytail, a Christian woman with a prominent tattoo, and a group of Christians out for a ride on their motorcycles. How do you react when you meet someone who is very different from you? Would you have been more attracted to the lifestyle of Jesus or John the Baptist?

We need to recognize that diversity among Christians is a good thing and should be embraced rather than shunned. God works through that diversity to build bridges of relationships with people who have a variety of interests and walks of life.

Paul said *"I have become all things to all men, that I may by all means save some."*[1] He built relationships with as many people as possible by living outside the boundaries with which he was normally comfortable. He diversified himself trusting that would result in a better return on his investment in the lives of others.

When we in love reach out to unbelievers in our circle of influence and beyond, we attempt to advance the Kingdom of God. When we encourage and love those fellow Christians who would not normally be in our circle of friendships, we attempt to advance the Kingdom of God. As in the passage above, people do not always respond positively to the gospel message regardless of who they hear it from. However, we are not responsible for how people respond to the gospel. We are responsible for doing whatever we can to get the gospel to the unsaved.

[1] I Corinthians 9:22b

And I pray that the fellowship of your faith may become effective
through the knowledge of every good thing which is in you for
Christ's sake. For I have come to have much joy and comfort in
your love, because the hearts of the saints have been refreshed
through you, brother.   *Philemon 6-7*

     The Greek word *koinonia* is translated "fellowship" here and means partnership or participation. Some churches jokingly refer to fellowship as "bellyship" since it is often thought of in the context of sharing a meal together. True Christian fellowship always has our faith in Jesus as the central focus of our time together.

     The church in Colossae met in Philemon's home[1] and Paul knew him personally. Notice that Paul prayed that the fellowship of Philemon's faith would be effective. Many Christians just view fellowship as a social time and are not concerned with the effectiveness of the time spent together. The source of the effectiveness was to be the knowledge of every good thing which was in Philemon for Christ's sake. Philemon was exhibiting the love of Christ and employing the gifts and fruit of the Spirit as he fellowshipped with others.

     Therefore, the result of the fellowship time was that the hearts of the saints had been refreshed by Philemon's presence. Conversation didn't just focus on the weather and arena ball. People present for fellowship shared their spiritual struggles and victories. *And if one member suffers, all the members suffer with it; if one member is honored, all the members rejoice with it.*[2]

     At your next gathering with believers, share something spiritually significant going on in your life and see how God might use that to encourage you or to strengthen others.

[1]Philemon 2   [2]I Corinthians 12:26

And concerning you, my brethren, I myself also am convinced that
you yourselves are full of goodness, filled with all knowledge, and
able also to admonish one another.   Romans 15:14

"Admonish" is used scripturally in two different contexts.
One situation deals with instructing others with Scriptural truths as
when Paul encourages the Corinthians to learn from the mistakes of
the Israelites and avoid immorality.[1] The other relates to warning
others who are in sin or heading toward sin as when Paul advised
Titus to reject a factious man after a first and second warning.[2] The
prerequisites of goodness and knowledge are especially helpful when
admonishing in the context dealing with sin.

A spirit of goodness communicates a loving attitude toward
the one being admonished. If the one on the path toward sin or in sin
senses a lack of genuine concern, the admonition will be less
effective. A judgmental or condemning spirit is likely to harden the
recipient to what is being shared.

The one involved in admonishing another must know when
and how to admonish. The admonisher must be able to distinguish a
sin or steps in sin's direction from his or her own personal opinions
and convictions. He or she must know both the spirit and the letter
of God's commands, and be able to recognize what disobedience
looks like.

When was the last time you were admonished or you
admonished someone about a sin issue? If we are to mature as
believers, we must actively depend on the Spirit to fill us with
goodness and knowledge. Let's ask that same Spirit to give us eyes
to see those who need admonishment and the grace to receive
admonishment when it is shared with us.

[1] I Corinthians 10:11   [2] Titus 3:10

1. The "one anothers" that are mentioned in this week's devotionals are: love, encourage, comfort, pray for, forgive, admonish, serve, accept, live in harmony with, fellowship with one another. Select one that you would like to focus on this week. Why did you choose the one you did?

2. Are you currently in a disagreement with a fellow brother or sister in Christ? What can you do to resolve it?

Prayer Starter: Lord Jesus, thank you for the Body of Christ and how You have made us interdependent on each other. Help me to fulfill my function in the local church by …

Go therefore and make disciples of all the nations, baptizing them in the name of the Father and the Son and the Holy Spirit, teaching them to observe all that I commanded you; and lo I am with you always, even to the end of the age.   Matthew 28:19-20

   If you are a Trekkie, you will remember the Prime Directive from Star Trek. It dictates that there can be no interference with the internal development of alien civilizations, lest this exposure alter the natural development of the civilization. Sometimes it seems that we followers of Christ (citizens of heaven) are operating by the Prime Directive rather than the Great Commission. We avoid any meaningful contact with the natural[1] man or woman on planet Earth as if we didn't want to influence them to live in our spiritual realm.
   Jesus instituted the Great Commission specifically because there was an urgent need to alter the natural development of Earth's citizenry. Our internal development has been flawed by sin and we are headed for destruction without a course correction. The imperative Jesus gives us to make disciples, baptize them, and teach them requires us to intentionally interact with those around us. We have been sent on a mission to save the world, not explore it.
   The Prime Directive is fiction; the Great Commission is fact. Let's ask God to help us live today in the reality of His presence as we seek to influence our world for Christ. Let's pray for the souls of those we know, share the gospel as the opportunity arises, and give financially so that those beyond our reach may hear.

[1] I Corinthians 2:14

And He said to them, "Follow Me, and I will make you fishers of men."

Matthew 4:19

Jesus' statement transforms easily to a conditional statement: If you follow Me, then I will make you fishers of men. In logic, the contrapositive of a conditional statement is formed by switching and negating the two parts of the sentence. If the original statement is true, then logic demands that the contrapositive is also true. The contrapositive of Jesus' statement is: If I have not made you fishers of men, then you have not followed Me. A true disciple of Christ will be actively seeking to connect people with God.

Consider the example Jesus lived before His followers. He welcomed Nicodemus and the rich young ruler and engaged them in a spiritual discussion. He intentionally sought out the woman at the well and Zaccheus; then led each one to repentance and salvation. During His agony on the cross, Jesus conversed with a dying thief and assured him that he would soon be in paradise.

As He demonstrated a compassion for people, He also sent out the twelve disciples two-by-two to preach the need for repentance. Later, He sent out seventy disciples two-by-two to preach the kingdom of God. Finally, His last words to His disciples before returning to the Father were to go and make disciples. Jesus demonstrated how to interact spiritually with people and then sent the disciples out to do it.

If you are a Christian, do you have the heart and actions of a fisher for souls? If not, then ask Jesus to show you how to get there, because that is where He wants you to be.

For since in the wisdom of God the world through its wisdom did not come to know God, God was well-pleased through the foolishness of the message preached to save those who believe. I Corinthians 1:21

Perhaps you have heard stories of a man and a woman marrying each other without ever meeting face-to-face. In decades past, they may have communicated through letters. But, the fact is, there are people who agree to the marriage covenant prior to ever holding the hand of their betrothed. God has arranged salvation in much the same way. We come to God, and the church is married to His Son, by faith, not by sight.

We read God's love letter, the Bible, and we learn what He is like. We come to understand what causes Him joy and what makes Him angry. We perceive His sacrificial love for us and His desire to draw us to Himself. When we study the animate and inanimate things of His creation, we see His matchless wisdom and creativity. As we explore our conscience, we recognize His view of right and wrong is implanted in us. We see evidence of God all around us and can even discern His invisible attributes.[1] We sense God wooing us to Himself even though we cannot see or touch Him.

Since God initiates the love relationship, He chooses how He does it. Paul tells us that it pleased God to stipulate the relationship based on our faith response to the gospel message. The author of Hebrews reinforces this idea: *And without faith it is impossible to please Him, for he who comes to God must believe that He is, and that He is a rewarder of those who seek Him.*[2]

Once we enter into the marriage relationship with Christ, we are commissioned to encourage others to enter also. Not everyone will respond positively but we align ourselves with God's wisdom when we seek their welfare by unashamedly sharing the gospel with them.

[1]Romans 1:20   [2]Hebrews 11:6

And may these words of mine, with which I have made supplication before the Lord, be near to the Lord our God day and night, that He may maintain the cause of His servant and the cause of His people Israel, as each day requires, so that all the peoples of the earth may know that the Lord is God; there is no one else.   *I Kings 8:59-60*

We are very familiar with Jesus' Great Commission: make disciples of all nations. The Old Testament counterpart could easily be called the Great Cause: *that all the peoples of the earth may know that the Lord is God.* When God called Abraham, the father of the Jews, He promised that *in you all families of the earth shall be blessed.*[1] This promise was fulfilled by the birth of Jesus of the tribe of Judah. However, Solomon refers to an additional blessing that God intended all people to have.

God wanted to showcase to the world how blessed a nation could be whose god was the Lord. Through Israel's obedience to God, all their needs would be abundantly supplied. All nations would recognize that the God of Israel was the one true God. Solomon prays that he, as king, and all of Israel, would focus daily on the cause of manifesting the glory of God so all nations could know Him.

Unfortunately, throughout Israel's history, their disobedience led to times of cursing rather than blessing. Instead of nations being drawn to Israel's godly example, God incited those nations to war against Israel as punishment. When David committed his great sin with Bathsheba, Nathan told David: *because by this deed you have given occasion to the enemies of the Lord to blaspheme, the child born to you shall surely die.*[2] Israel continually misrepresented God to the surrounding nations and thus negatively impacted the Great Cause.

Is your life promoting or hindering the Great Commission?

[1]Genesis 12:3b   [2]II Samuel 12:14

So they answered Joshua and said, "Because it was certainly told your servants that the Lord your God had commanded His servant Moses to give you all the land, and to destroy all the inhabitants of the land before you; therefore we feared greatly for our lives because of you, and have done this thing."   Joshua 9:24

The Hivites lived in Gibeon and other nearby cities in the land of Canaan. As such, God had judged them for their sin and had commanded Moses to destroy them with all the other inhabitants of Canaan. They had heard the same information about Israel as all the other nations in Canaan, but they reacted differently. The other nations joined forces to fight Israel; the Hivites devised a plan of deception to make peace with Israel. Their plan worked and they were the only group of cities not destroyed by Israel.[1]

Gibeon was known throughout Canaan as a great city with mighty warriors.[2] Yet, because they recognized the God of Israel as the God of all, they abandoned fighting as an option. Instead they sought peace with Israel and with Israel's God. They responded to the Great Cause even though no other nation did. They received mercy instead of justice. Joshua made them *hewers of wood and drawers of water for the house of my God.*[3] They became slaves/servants in the house of God, just as we view ourselves today.

We also see limited success of the Great Cause with non-Israelite individuals. Rahab and her family were spared in Jericho because of her reaction to the God of Israel. Ruth, the Moabite, claimed the God of her mother-in-law Naomi. Naaman, the Aramean captain, believed the witness of an Israelite slave girl and was healed of his leprosy by Elisha.

We experience limited success in sharing the gospel today also. But if our lives don't reflect God's goodness and our words don't speak God's gospel, our success is probably limited to zero.

[1]Joshua 11:19   [2]Joshua 10:2   [3]Joshua 9:23b

1. If a person says they are following Jesus and yet never becomes a fisher of men, something is wrong. What could have happened along the way to prevent an individual from acquiring a heart for souls?

2. Is the purpose of your life better represented by the Prime Directive from Star Trek or the Great Cause from Solomon? Why?

Prayer Starter: Lord Jesus, thank you for your sacrifice on the cross for me. Give me your love for mankind so I will be compelled to share the gospel where you have placed me. I pray for opportunities and boldness to witness to …

For there must also be factions among you, in order that those who
are approved may have become evident among you. Therefore when
you meet together, it is not to eat the Lord's Supper, for in your
eating each one takes his own supper first; and one is hungry and
another is drunk.   *I Corinthians 11:19-21*

It was customary in Corinth for believers to gather together
to share a meal, after which the Lord's Supper was observed. This
activity promoted fellowship, but also served the poor by providing a
good meal. Unfortunately cliques developed causing separation, not
unity. Also, those who brought much food and drink refused to
share with those in need. Paul rebuked them because they had lost
their proper focus on fellowship and worship.

How easy it is, even today, to attend church with a consumer
mentality – what is in this for me? We see attendance as an
opportunity to catch up with friends or meet new social contacts.
We enjoy hearing the music and critiquing what the preacher has to
say. We view it as an activity that God wants us to do so we can
check off that box.

In truth, all believers are consumers – we have needs that
only God can fill. New believers especially need the church to grow
in their faith and knowledge of the Lord Jesus Christ. So, we all
should come to church with the expectation that God will speak to us
and grow us into the likeness of His Son. But, if singing songs of
praise and hearing sermons year after year never leads to service,
then something is wrong. At some point we have stopped focusing
on spiritual needs and we are meeting non-spiritual needs. Growing
in Christ-likeness equates to growing in stewardship.

For this is not for the ease of others and for your affliction, but by way of equality – at this present time your abundance being a supply for their want, that their abundance also may become a supply for your want, that there may be equality. II Corinthians 8:13-14

In socialism, society owns and operates the means of production and distribution with all members of society sharing in the work and the products. Paul's emphasis on equality above differs from socialism since the individual Christian is being asked to voluntarily give his/her resources to others in need. With socialism, the leadership requires that everyone participate since human nature is more selfish than altruistic.

Paul addresses the Corinthians' previous commitment to send financial aid to the poor in Jerusalem. He offers God's provision of manna in the wilderness in verse 15 above as a Biblical illustration of this giving principle: *As it is written, He that had gathered much had nothing over; and he that had gathered little had no lack.* When the Israelites went out in the morning to gather manna, some gathered more than the required amount and others gathered less.[1] The gathered manna was then apportioned so that each person received one omer of manna, about two dry quarts. Notice that God was the source of all the manna and He determined it should be allocated equally.

Today God is still the source of all that we have, whether we recognize it or not. God is also involved in the distribution of His resources to the needy but He does it principally through the leading of His Spirit in the lives of His people. Unfortunately, His people are not always sensitive to His Spirit as John observes: *But whoever has the world's goods, and beholds his brother in need and closes his heart against him, how does the love of God abide in him?*[2] The challenge for Christians who have been blessed financially is to be sensitive and obedient to the Spirit's leading in their lives. As we do, needs are met and God is glorified.

[1]Exodus 16:18   [2]I John 3:17

Thus says the Lord of hosts, 'This people says, "The time has not come, even the time for the house of the Lord to be rebuilt."'... "You look for much, but behold, it comes to little; when you bring it home, I blow it away. Why?" declares the Lord of Hosts, "Because of My house which lies desolate, while each of you runs to his own house."

Haggai 1:2, 9

God moved in the heart of Cyrus king of Persia to allow Jewish volunteers to return to Jerusalem to rebuild the temple in 538 B.C. Under the leadership of Zerubbabel, workers journeyed to Jerusalem, materials were gathered and reconstruction began. However when opposition arose from nearby Samaritans the work stopped for ten years. The Jews became preoccupied with their own homes and abandoned rebuilding the temple by saying the timing wasn't right.

Leadership was needed to get the project on track again so God sent the prophets Haggai and Zachariah to confront and challenge the Jews. God had already been at work to get the people's attention by sending drought and oppressing them economically. The people responded to the prophets' message and finally completed the temple in 516 B.C.[1]

As we walk daily with the Lord and are on mission for Him, we will encounter opposition. Satan and his forces are arrayed against us. Their goal is to sidetrack us and to get our focus on something other than God's will for our lives. Busyness, materialism, and minimizing our personal time with the Lord are common ploys. When we get off course, God may try to get our attention through unfavorable circumstances. He may also provide fresh leadership in our lives to help get us back on track.

Paul reminds us that we are the temple of God and as Christians we are each involved in a building project.[2] Paul encourages us to use materials that will last. We do this when we invest our time, talents, and treasure in Kingdom work.

[1]Ezra 6:14-15   [2]I Corinthians 3:9-16

Remember also your Creator in the days of your youth, before the evil days come and the years draw near when you will say, "I have no delight in them"; then the dust will return to the earth as it was, and the spirit will return to God who gave it.   Ecclesiastes 12:1, 7

God created man from the dust of the earth and breathed into him the breath of life and man became a living being. Mankind started as dust and upon death reverts once again to dust. Mankind started with a God-breathed spirit and upon death the spirit returns to God. Given the certainty of an eventual departure from earth with the subsequent accounting to God, are we focusing more on the body or on the spirit?

Nutritionists advise three healthy meals daily so that the body will be well nourished. Jesus reminded us that *man does not live on bread alone but on every word that proceeds from the mouth of God.*[1] Are we nourishing our spirit daily thorough the word of God?

Doctors prescribe regular exercise to keep the body fit and healthy. Paul encourages us to *discipline yourself for the purpose of godliness; for bodily discipline is only of little profit.*[2] Are we disciplined in the use of our time so that we pursue activities that train us to be effective in God's kingdom work?

Financial advisors suggest investing money regularly for retirement so the body can be properly cared for in old age. Jesus commanded *do not lay up for yourselves treasures upon earth, where moth and rust destroy, and where thieves break in and steal. But lay up for yourselves treasures in heaven.*[3] Are we investing significant financial resources in matters that are on God's heart?

Obviously nothing is wrong with following the counsel of experts regarding the body. The question is: Are we giving disciplined heed to the counsel and commands of our Creator to Whom we will one day give an accounting?

[1]Matthew 4:4   [2]I Timothy 4:7b, 8a   [3]Matthew 6:19-20a

" You are cursed with a curse, for you are robbing Me, the whole nation of you! Bring the whole tithe into the storehouse, so that there may be food in My house, and test Me now in this", says the Lord of hosts, "if I will not open for you the windows of heaven, and pour out for you a blessing until it overflows."   Malachi 3:9-10

The Book of Malachi addresses several moral and religious offenses, one of which was Israel's neglect of the tithe. A tithe is ten percent. God declared a tithe of the fruit of the land and of the livestock to be His, and thus holy to the Lord[1]. However, the custom of tithing was common among Semitic people before the Mosaic Law and was practiced by both Abraham[2] and his grandson, Jacob[3]. Since tithing was a command, there was a curse when tithing was disobeyed and a blessing when it was obeyed.

In the New Testament giving is viewed as a "gracious work."[4] The giver is reminded that the one who sows sparingly will reap sparingly and the one who sows bountifully will reap bountifully. We also must determine the amount to give, but it must be given cheerfully, not grudgingly[5]. Many Christians have determined to use the tithe as the amount they will give. That is great, but don't limit God's blessing in your life by stopping there.

In both Testaments, giving to God shares some common themes. Giving is an act that recognizes that God is the owner of all that we have, and we are simply returning a portion of that to Him. The Mosaic law of tithing provided food for the Levites and priests to eat, hence the storehouse reference above. Similarly, in the modern church age, Jesus ordained that those in full-time ministry should be paid by gifts given to Him[6]. Finally, giving to those in need is encouraged under the law and under grace.

It is more blessed to give than to receive. Do our lives demonstrate this fact?

[1]Leviticus 27:30-32   [2]Genesis 14:20   [3]Genesis 28:22
[4]II Corinthians 8:6-8   [5]II Corinthians 9:6-7   [6]I Corinthians 9:13-14

1. Every child of God is a steward of the talents and resources entrusted to him or her. *It is required of stewards that one be found trustworthy.* (I Corinthians 4:2) What emotions are evoked when you consider that God requires you to be worthy of the trust given to you?

2. How long have you been attending a local church? Look at your church involvement objectively and assess your contribution in terms of service rendered and resources given. Is the Spirit leading you to make any changes?

Prayer Starter: Father God, You have created me and purchased my salvation with the blood of Christ Jesus. I acknowledge that I am accountable to You for how I invest my time and resources. Help me to …

And by this we know that we have come to know Him, if we keep His commandments.   *I John 2:3*
Therefore, brethren, be all the more diligent to make certain about His calling and choosing you; for as long as you practice these things, you will never stumble.   *II Peter 1:10*

John and Peter wanted their readers to know for certain that they were heaven-bound. Both disciples offered our attitude toward God's commandments as proof of a legitimate conversion.

Prior to receiving Christ, many think God's commands restrict them from living the good life. After conversion we recognize His commands free us to live the abundant life. John says that *His commandments are not burdensome.*[1] We recognize the love Jesus displayed for us on the cross and we want to please Him through obedience. We have a healthy fear of God in our lives and understand that we benefit by obeying God.

As we obey Christ, our lives change is substantial ways. We begin to manifest the fruits and gifts of the Spirit. The entrapments of the world begin to lose their appeal. Peter argues that as we diligently seek God, our lives become useful and fruitful.[2] The changes in our lives are supernatural and provide evidence to us that the Spirit of God is at work in our lives.

Do you delight in obeying God? Are you confident you have eternal life? If the answer is no, you either have never been a follower of Christ or have turned away from following Christ. For the former, accept Jesus' offer to be the Savior and Lord of your life. For the later, repent and rededicate your life to God.

[1] I John 5:3b   [2] II Peter 1:8

And the commander answered, "I acquired this citizenship with a large sum of money." And Paul said, "But I was actually born a citizen."   *Acts 22:28*

Many people view acquiring citizenship in heaven the same way citizenship on earth is received: by birth or with payment. Our daughter married a Scotsman who is a citizen of the United Kingdom by birth. However, Lindsay would have to pay a large fee to become a citizen of the United Kingdom. Two thousand years ago, the same situation existed to become a Roman citizen as shown by the dialog between the Roman commander and Paul.

Those who focus only on the love of God can easily believe that everyone born into the human race will automatically go to heaven since a loving God would not condemn someone to hell. Those who see God as a just judge recognize there must be some payment for sin since we have all violated God's laws at some time. A popular approach to paying this sin debt is to assume that if our good deeds in life outweigh our bad deeds, the net effect is a positive balance sheet which earns entrance into heaven.

The Biblical truth is that God is both a loving and just God. Further, citizenship in heaven requires both birth and a payment for sin. Our loving God provided payment for our sin's penalty with the death of His Son to satisfy the just aspect of His nature.

We are born into God's family when we acknowledge Christ's death on the cross as payment for our sins, and submit our lives to Christ's lordship.[1] If you have done that, you are a citizen of heaven[2] and have reason to rejoice today! If you haven't, please accept God's gift of heavenly citizenship through Jesus and tell a fellow citizen what you have done.

[1]John 1:12   [2] Ephesians 2:19

*Test yourselves to see if you are in the faith; examine yourselves! Or
do you not recognize this about yourselves, that Jesus Christ is in
you – unless indeed you fail the test?*   *II Corinthians 13:5*

What are the tests to determine if Jesus Christ is in you?
John concludes his first epistle by saying: *These things I have
written to you who believe in the name of the Son of God, in order
that you may know that you have eternal life.*[1] Let's look at some
tests John gave in his letter which allow us to know that we have
eternal life.

*If you know that He is righteous, you know that everyone also
who practices righteousness is born of Him.*[2] When the Holy Spirit
enters our lives after we trust in Christ, He brings a new nature
which is made in the likeness of Jesus. We still sin, but we should
be quick to confess the sin and return to a walk of obedience. If we
are characterized by an overall righteous life, then we can be assured
that Christ is within us.

*We know that we have passed out of death into life, because
we love the brethren.*[3] Jesus Himself said that all men would
recognize that we are followers of Jesus by our love for one
another.[4] So our love for one another tells the world we are
Christians, and confirms in our hearts that we know God.

And it is the Spirit who bears witness.[5] Paul said the same
thing: *The Spirit Himself bears witness with our spirit that we are
children of God.*[6] The Spirit of God living within you will give you
peace, joy, and direction in life that assures your heart that you are in
the family of God.

Did you pass the test?

[1] I John 5:13   [2] I John 2:29   [3] I John 3:14a   [4] John 13:35
[5] I John 5:7a   [6] Romans 8:16

For he who lacks these qualities is blind or short-sighted, having forgotten his purification from his former sins.   *II Peter 1:9*

Does the immature believer or carnal Christian who has disconnected from Christian fellowship and been lured back into the world's system of living have assurance of salvation? I think that depends on the person and how long he or she has been immature or in a carnal state. When I went to college, I stopped going to church and was soon led down the wrong path. Fortunately, two young men came by my dorm room sharing the gospel. I knew I was saved but I was convicted of my sin and rededicated my life to the Lord. But I have known many believers that were unsure of their salvation because of their spiritual immaturity or carnality.

As Peter begins his letter, he exhorts believers to be diligent to build godly character into their lives, i.e., to grow spiritually. He notes that those who don't grow spiritually are unable to see things properly and even forget that Christ has delivered them from the power and penalty of sin. We live in a world that naturally flows toward ungodliness. Christians must be intentional in their pursuit of spiritual growth, just like a canoeist paddling upstream to reach the destination. If the believer is spiritually inactive, the world's current will draw him or her backward.

We know we are saved if we practice righteousness and love fellow believers. However the immature or carnal Christian is not experiencing spiritual victory. The only witness left of salvation is that of the Spirit in his or her life. But it is likely that the Spirit has been grieved or quenched by this believer, so that the witness has been muted.

The remedy for the professed believer who has no assurance of salvation is growing spiritually as a disciple of Christ!

In Him, you also, after listening to the message of truth, the gospel of your salvation – having also believed, you were sealed in Him with the Holy Spirit of promise.   *Ephesians 2:13*

Both the Old and New Testaments refer to using an engraved device pressed in clay or wax to form a seal. The seal signified a finished transaction and ownership. *You were bought with a price.*[1] The price paid was the precious blood of Jesus Christ and the one who trusts Jesus to pay his or her sin debt receives the indwelling Holy Spirit. In the next verse, Paul tells the Ephesian believers that the Spirit was given as a pledge, or down payment, of their inheritance.

Each member of the Trinity is actively involved in securing our eternal salvation. God, the Father, seals believers in Christ, the Son, with the Holy Spirit. The seal is permanent and unmovable. *And I give eternal life to them, and they shall never perish; and no one shall snatch them out of My hand.*[2]

The Spirit also acts as our moral compass, but we have to follow His direction. *And do not grieve the Holy Spirit of God, by who you were sealed for the day of redemption.*[3] Our disobedience will grieve the Spirit within, but He will never leave us because the Father has sealed us.

After Jesus was crucified and buried in the tomb, the religious leaders asked Pilate to secure the grave. They remembered that Jesus said He would rise from the dead after three days. *And they went and made the grave secure, and along with the guard they set a seal on the stone.*[4] The Roman government sealed the stone, asserting a finished transaction. But an angel rolled away the stone.

God can break any seal made by man. Man can break no seal made by God. Followers of Christ can be assured that the Spirit's seal is Rock-solid.

[1] I Corinthians 7:23   [2] John 10:28   [3] Ephesians 4:30   [4] Matthew 27:66

1. One of the surest signs that you are a believer bound for heaven is that you have a desire to obey God in your life. How would you rate your obedience to Christ?

2. If you vacillate about whether you are a true follower of Christ, then you probably need to focus on growing to spiritual maturity. What can you do this week to encourage spiritual growth?

Prayer Starter: Lord Jesus, I thank You for paying the penalty for my sins on the cross of Calvary. I rejoice that I have received the gift of eternal life by receiving you into my life. I want to walk in obedience each day. I ask for your help in these areas: ...

Beloved, do not be surprised at the fiery ordeal among you, which comes upon you for your testing, as though some strange thing were happening to you; but to the degree that you share the sufferings of Christ, keep on rejoicing; so that at the revelation of His glory, you may rejoice with exultation.   *I Peter 4:12-13*

Perhaps we derive the greatest benefit from joy during times of hardship. Joy is a delight of the mind arising from the consideration of a present good, or the assured possession of a future good.[1] When circumstances are favorable and we are experiencing a present good, we normally have joy and are thankful to God for His current blessings in our lives. During times of disappointment, hardship, or persecution, joy may seem elusive and yet that is when we need it most.

God has orchestrated into the symphony of our lives various times of discord. During these troubling times, our music seems off key and off beat. Joy is the ability to hear the music from a heavenly perspective and not an earthly one. We understand that God is working through the present difficulty to mature us in Christ and to advance His kingdom on earth. This joy gives us the strength to endure. We experience this joy as we seek Jesus through His Word and prayer.

Notice that Peter refers to both a joy on earth and a joy in heaven. As we suffer for Christ on earth we are to rejoice. When we get to heaven, we experience exultation – that is joy on steroids. The author of Hebrews says of Jesus: *who for the joy set before Him endured the cross….*[2] As Christians we are never asked to do anything that Jesus has not already done. He is our example and the source of our strength. *Rejoice in the Lord always; again I will say, rejoice!*[3]

[1]Unger's Bible Dictionary   [2]Hebrews 12:2   [3]Philippians 4:4

*For by grace you have been saved through faith; and that not of
yourselves, it is the gift of God; not as a result of works, that no one
should boast.*

Ephesians 2:8-9

*Let your light shine before men in such a way that they may see your
good works, and glorify your Father who is in heaven.*

Matthew 5:16

Notice that the works Paul disparages result in self-
glorification, but the works Jesus encourages result in God being
glorified. What is it about these works that makes them so different?
The key is to understand on which side of the cross they occur.

The writer of Hebrews reminds us that the blood of Christ
will *cleanse your conscience from dead works to serve the living
God.*[1] No so-called work of righteousness we do prior to trusting
Christ has any positive impact on our standing with God. God views
those works as dead on arrival. Although we and those around us
might be impressed with our works, God is not. Paul declares that
we were dead in our sins[2] prior to Christ and dead people produce
dead works. God's standard is perfection, and anything short of that
fails; it's dead.

Jesus said: *I am the light of the world; he who follows Me
shall not walk in the darkness, but shall have the light of life.*[3] The
follower of Jesus has the light of the Holy Spirit in his or her life. A
new Christian is a new creation. *The one who does good is of God.*[4]
Since the source of a believer's good works is God, it is God who is
glorified by the works.

Paul shows this contrast of dead works versus good works by
balancing the above verses with: *For we are His workmanship,
created in Christ Jesus for good works.*[5] The works mentioned in
verse 9 are nondescript; the works in verse 10 are good. If we want
our works to be viewed by God as good, we must allow the light of
Christ to shine forth in our lives.

[1]Hebrews 9:14   [2]Ephesians 2:1   [3]John 8:12   [4]III John 11b
[5]Ephesians 2:10a

*Not that I speak from want; for I have learned to be content in
whatever circumstances I am.*   *Philippians 4:11*

Biblical contentment is being totally satisfied in God.
Contentment is that disposition of mind, through grace, in which one
is independent of outward circumstances. The opposite of
contentment as applied to material goods is covetousness. The
Tenth Commandment tells us not to covet anything belonging to our
neighbor, implying that we are to be content with what God has
blessed us.

Complacency is self-satisfaction. Although the complacent
person is also unmoved by outward circumstances, there is a vast
difference between the complacent and the contented person. The
complacent individual is satisfied with where he or she is materially,
spiritually, intellectually, and socially. Smugness can often
accompany such a person.

The Christian is challenged: *Whatever you do, do your work
heartily, as for the Lord rather than for men.*[1] We should be
characterized in our workplace as go-getters and hard-chargers.
Christians should be motivated to improve in all areas of life since
our goal is to be conformed to the image of Christ. Although we
strive for improvement, we are still wholly dependent on God to
bring improvement in our lives based on His will and timetable.

Like Paul, we have to learn contentment. The only way to
learn is to be placed in uncomfortable situations where we have to
rely on God to satisfy our needs to the degree He chooses. The
complacent person reacts adversely to uncomfortable situations.
The Christian should embrace these times of trial recognizing that
God will use it to teach contentment as we rely on Him.

*Let your character be free from the love of money, being
content with what you have; for He Himself has said, "I will never
desert you, nor will I ever forsake you."*[2] The more we abide in the
awareness of Christ's presence in our lives, the easier it is to be
content with our current circumstance. Fight complacency. Strive
for contentment. Abide in Christ.

[1]Colossians 3:2   [2]Hebrews 13:5

For perhaps he was for this reason parted from you for a while, that you should have him back forever, no longer as a slave, but more than a slave, a beloved brother…   *Philemon 15-16a*

When was the last time you tried to verbalize a spiritual explanation for why something bad happened to you or someone else? That is what Paul is doing here. Philemon's slave Onesimus had run away and ended up in Rome. While in Rome, he met Paul, became a Christian, and then returned to Philemon in Colossae. For some period of time, Philemon had suffered the loss of this slave, and Onesimus had possibly stolen something of value from him.[1] From Philemon's standpoint, a bad thing had happened to him and Paul is helping him see why God might have allowed it all to happen.

We derive some consolation from knowing that God will use some bad experience in a positive way to further His kingdom. Paul himself declared: *And we know that God causes all things to work together for good to those who love God, to those who are called according to His purpose.*[2] We are called upon as Christians to believe Paul's declaration by faith, even if we cannot formulate exactly how it is working together for good. Paul's use of "perhaps" reminds us that we are speculating when we try to articulate God's purpose.

Have you ever heard someone try to console a parent who has lost a child by saying: "God must have needed another angel in heaven."? Although they mean well, that statement will probably not provide any comfort. At times, the best consolation is simply your physical presence with no attempt at explaining why some tragedy occurred. The truth is that we have no explanation, and any speculation may amplify the existing pain. Once again, we are called to walk by faith, not by sight.

[1]Philemon 18-19   [2]Romans 8:28

But not even Titus who was with me, though he was a Greek, was compelled to be circumcised.   *Galatians 2:3*

Paul wanted this man (Timothy) *to go with him; and he took him and circumcised him because of the Jews who were in those parts, for they all knew that his father was a Greek.*   *Acts 16:3*

Paul was fighting mad when some men came to Antioch from Judea and preached that circumcision must accompany belief in Christ for salvation. In response, he, Barnabas, and Titus travelled to Jerusalem to discuss the matter with the church leaders. The Jerusalem Council concluded that circumcision was not required. Thus, Titus was not required to be circumcised.

Some time later, Paul sets out on his second missionary journey and meets a young believer named Timothy, who like Titus, was also uncircumcised. However, Paul decides to circumcise Timothy so the gospel would not be hindered as they journeyed among the Jews in that region. Timothy's mother was Jewish so with circumcision he would potentially have more influence among the Jews.

For the sake of the gospel Paul took actions that caused conflict or may have appeared contradictory. Paul was committed to the integrity of the gospel message and was therefore ready to do battle when circumcision threatened to subvert a message of faith. Later he would ask a believer to be circumcised since that action would advance the gospel message.

Timothy also displayed great commitment. He was willing to undergo physical discomfort for the gospel. Timothy understood that his circumcision had nothing to do with his salvation and everything to do with being *all things to all men that he might by all means reach some.*[1] How committed are you to the integrity and advancement of the Gospel?

[1] I Corinthians 9:22

1. Recall this past week. List below some "good works" that Jesus has produced through your life. What good work is God leading you to be involved in this coming week?

2. Review the topics for this week's devotionals. In which of these areas do you sense the greatest need? What can you do to address this need?

Prayer Starter: Father God, I recognize that I am not Christ-like in certain areas of my life. Thank You for your Holy Spirit's presence with me as I seek to follow You. Help me and guide me as I seek to become more like Christ in …

"Yet even now," declares the Lord, "Return to Me with all your heart, and with fasting, weeping, and mourning; and rend your heart and not your garments." ...   *Joel 2:12-13*

For the sorrow that is according to the will of God produces a repentance without regret, leading to salvation; but the sorrow of the world produces death.   *II Corinthians 7:10*

Joel was a prophet to the Southern Kingdom of Judah. God used him to warn Judah of God's forthcoming judgment and urge them to repent of their sin. However, God was looking for more than external actions associated with repentance and wanted repentance from the heart.

The Jews of Biblical times had several ways to outwardly demonstrate repentance or grief. Sometimes the penitent or sorrowing would wear sackcloth and put ashes or earth on themselves. Other times they would tear their garments as Joel refers to in his declaration to Judah. However, these actions may or may not have been a reflection of true repentance in the heart; only God knew for certain whether the actions were sincere.

Paul makes a distinction between godly sorrow and worldly sorrow. Any sorrow for sin that leads you to sincerely come to God for forgiveness is godly sorrow. When you sin and deal with your sorrow by simply mourning, making amends or rationalizing what you did, that is a worldly sorrow. One leads to salvation; the other to death.

The English poet Alexander Pope said "To err is human, to forgive divine." His observation focuses primarily on the reaction of the person offended. If we focus on the sinner, we would say: To err is human, to repent divine. Unfortunately, sin is part of life on this earth for each of us. We must learn to deal with sin immediately and sincerely by confessing it to our Lord, and expressing our sorrow for disappointing Him once more.

For it came about when Solomon was old, his wives turned his heart away after other gods; and his heart was not wholly devoted to the Lord his God, as the heart of David his father had been.

I Kings 11:4

When Scripture says that Solomon's heart was not wholly devoted to the Lord, it implies that he was still devoted in some areas. Solomon had somehow rationalized that for him it would be okay to marry many foreign women even though God had strictly forbidden these "inter-faith" marriages. Compromise is defined as a settlement in which each side makes some concessions. For the Christian, the two sides vying for kingship are the old man and the new man. Therefore, compromising God's commands always results in sin.

If we had been privy to Solomon's thought process, it might have sounded something like this. "I am the wisest man on earth and can surely withstand the spiritual influence of these foreign wives. I am the king of a prosperous nation and can afford to have as many wives as I choose, and no one will dare say anything. Even if it does violate one of God's many laws, in degree it is not even close to the sins of adultery and murder committed by my father David. I think God will overlook this one sin."

"So the Lord said to Solomon, 'Because you have not kept My covenant and My statutes, which I have commanded you, I will surely tear the kingdom from you, and will give it to your servant.'"[1] God did not overlook the sin, just as He had not disregarded David's sin. The difference in the two sins is that David confessed and repented of his sins, whereas there is no record that Solomon ever repented.

We are all tempted to compromise in our walk with God, and we all sin. The standard God used to judge Solomon's heart was the heart of David. David's heart was exemplary, not from an absence of sin, but from a readiness to confess sin and maintain a close walk with his God. Which king's example will you choose to follow?

[1] I Kings 11:11

The backslider in heart will have his fill of his own ways.
                                                    Proverbs 14:14a

*How boastful you are about the valleys! Your valley is flowing
away, O backsliding daughter who trusts in her treasures, saying,
"Who will come against me?"*   *Jeremiah 49:4*

Backslider is a term found only in a few Old Testament
books. The New Testament equivalent is carnal or apostate. The
backslider has turned away from God and is doing his or her own
thing. This person was once moving forward, growing in a
relationship with God, but is now in full retreat. In most cases, the
slide to the rear began slowly, almost imperceptibly. But with time,
sin's slippery slope accelerated the departure from the righteous path
until there was little discernible difference between the lifestyle of
the carnal believer and the unbeliever.

The passages above indicate that the shift from forward to
backward came when life's focus shifted from God to self. At some
point, the backslider got his or her eyes off God and onto self. This
transition can be very subtle, but if not recognized and repented of,
its consequences can be disastrous.

Proverbs identifies the backslider's problem as a heart issue.
The heart's devotion to God was derailed, and devotion to self
became paramount. Time once spent seeking God is now spent
serving self. Talent and treasure once invested in God's Kingdom
now buys pleasure and recreation.

Jeremiah's audience must have lived in a valley surrounded
by mountains that provided protection against enemy forces. The
valley dwellers must also have been prosperous. They boasted of
their security and prosperity. They no longer had to rely on God;
they felt self-sufficient. They were concerned with self and meeting
their own perceived needs, apart from God.

Has there been a time when you were closer to Jesus than
you are now? If so, it is possible that you have backslidden. Please
repent and return to a life that is focused on Jesus and others.

Return, O Israel, to the Lord your God, for you have stumbled because of your iniquity. Take words with you and return to the Lord. Say to Him, "Take away all iniquity, and receive us graciously ... Nor will we say again, 'Our god,' to the work of our hands."

Hosea 14:1-3

An appropriate job description for a prophet is: *Cry loudly, do not hold back; raise your voice like a trumpet, and declare to My people their transgression.*[1] Hosea was one of God's prophets to the Northern Kingdom of Israel. The purpose of highlighting sin was to evoke repentance from Israel. Hosea addresses two elements of genuine repentance.

The first element is confession – using words to name the sin and agree with God that it is sin. Israel's sin was idolatry. They had created silver images and worshipped them as their god. Biblical confession always implies the presence of genuine sorrow for the sin. If words from the mind and mouth don't combine with sorrow from the heart, the confession is meaningless.

The second element is a desire and willingness to turn from the sin and follow God. In the military, it is called an about-face in which the unit or individual makes a 180-degree turn. The sample prayer offered by Hosea had Israel proclaim that they would not say again "Our god" to the works of their hands. If there is a heart intention to return to the sin after the confession, then repentance has not occurred. Because of our sin nature, there will be times when we may return to the sin. However, at the time of confession that thought is abhorrent to us.

The repentance process for a believer in Jesus who has sinned also applies to the unbeliever seeking salvation and eternal life. The non-Christian must confess his or her sinful life to God with genuine sorrow. Then he or she must be willing to give control of that life to Jesus as the new boss, understanding that an about-face is coming through the power of the Holy Spirit coming into the person's life. Do you need to repent?

[1]Isaiah 58:1a

If anyone sees his brother committing a sin not leading to death, he shall ask and God will for him give life to those who commit sin not leading to death. There is a sin leading to death; I do not say that he should make request for this.   *I John 5:16*

Let's say that you were present when Ananias lied to the Holy Spirit in front of Peter about the selling price of the land.[1] You immediately think of Sapphira, his wife, and pray that if she were involved in this deception, her life would be spared. Your prayer would not be answered positively because both of them had a committed a sin unto death.

We don't have in Scripture a specific list of sins that leads to the physical death of the believer. Rather there seems to be a trip wire that only God knows when it is crossed. The world in Noah's day crossed a line morally that required the population's death. God declared that *the iniquity of the Amorite is not yet complete,*[2] implying that there was a future time when judgment would fall. What applied to the world and a nation apparently also can apply to individuals.

Paul rebuked the Corinthian believers for being carnal and not spiritual. We know that the Lord disciplines those He loves. What happens when wayward believers don't respond to discipline over time? At what point will God the Father call His sheep home because of harm being done to the Kingdom?[3]

Are you walking with Jesus today or have you slipped into a carnal state? If walking with Jesus, pray now for anyone you know in that carnal state. If you are walking in the flesh, repent now so you don't approach a sin unto death.

[1]Acts 5:1-10   [2]Genesis 15:16b   [3]Ezekiel 20:9

1. Do you have a friend or family member that you would consider a backslider? If so, pray that God's discipline would soften the heart to return to God. Also, be available if God chooses to use you in the reconciliation process.

2. Is there a sin you need to confess today? Do you have a godly sorrow for your disobedience to God? Are you willing to do an about-face and wholeheartedly follow Christ? If yes, please confess your sin to God.

Prayer Starter: Father, I need to confess my sins to You and also want to pray for some who I know are backslidden. Please forgive me for …

For since the creation of the world His invisible attributes, His eternal power and divine nature, have been clearly seen, being understood through what has been made, so that they are without excuse.   Romans 1:20
In that they show the work of the Law written in their hearts, their conscience bearing witness, and their thoughts alternately accusing or else defending them.   Romans 2:15

God has revealed Himself to mankind through His creation and mankind's conscience. God's eternal power is manifested in the majesty and enormity of creation. Planet Earth is too complex and interdependent to have occurred without a Creator. Mankind instinctively recognizes God's power in creation. The invisible is clearly seen. But if we choose not to honor or give thanks to God for creation, we speculate with other theories and our heart is darkened.

God's divine nature is revealed through our conscience. We have an innate knowledge of right from wrong because we were created in God's image from a moral standpoint. God has further given us a sense of guilt when we do wrong to show us that something is not right between us and God. We can however suppress the conscience. We have the capability of rationalizing any action, regardless of how evil it might seem to the majority.

Nietzsche's declaration that God is dead in 1882 was not the first time someone had said or thought those words. Time's cover story article "Is God Dead?" in 1966 didn't resolve the question. There have always been those who have rejected God's revelation and developed their own philosophy of life. However that doesn't change the fact that *God is still not willing that any should perish.*[1] He will continue to pursue mankind externally through the marvels of His creation and internally through man's God-given conscience.

How does the believer partner with God in the area of revelation? Mankind can be viewed as God's greatest creation. In Christ we are referred to as *a new creation where the old has passes away and the new has come.*[2] As believers grow in Christ-likeness, our lives will be a compelling witness to a lost world searching for answers.

[1]II Peter 3:9   [2]II Corinthians 5:17

I will give thanks to Thee, for I am fearfully and wonderfully made; wonderful are Thy works, and my soul knows it very well.

Psalm 139:14

David had very limited knowledge of the body compared to what we know today. But he concluded in his soul that he was fearfully and wonderfully made by God. If you chose not to acknowledge God as Creator, you need another explanation. Satan has provided evolution as that explanation.

Evolutionist work very hard to convince everyone that evolution is not a theory but a fact. Discussing the evolution of the eye, Richard Dawkins, an evolutionary biologist, said "Darwin said that it was impossible to imagine that it could evolve by gradual degree, but reason tells me that if there were a series of gradual improvements then it would be easy for it to have evolved by natural selection and you find all over the animal kingdom eyes in various stages of what look like stages of evolution."[1] Translation: If you want to believe in something badly enough, you can find a way to do it.

Evolution defies common sense. I think that is what Darwin was saying. Take a few minutes and think about time, randomness, and natural selection producing a cornea, a sclera, a pupil, a lens, an iris, conjunctiva glands, lachrymal glands, a retina, a ciliary body, a choroid, vitreous humor, and aqueous humor that make up a functioning eye. Now somehow introduce the development of the optic nerve and somehow connect it to the brain at just the right place. That process is for one eye, we have two that are identical.

If anyone wants to find a reason for disbelieving in God, Satan will provide one. Reason tells me that evolution is fantasy. My heart tells me that I was created by God. If you believe in a Creator, then thankfulness is the proper response. If not, then thankfulness is not expected.

[1]"The Evolution of the Eye", uploaded on YouTube Oct 1, 2010 by dawkinschannel.

For even though they knew God, they did not honor God, or give Him thanks; but they became futile in their speculations, and their foolish heart was darkened. Professing to be wise, they became fools, and exchanged the glory of the incorruptible God for an image in the form of corruptible man and of birds and four-footed animals and crawling creatures.   Romans 1:21-23

Sin entered the angelic host when Lucifer asserted *"I will ascend above the heights of the clouds; I will make myself like the Most High."*[1] Eve was tempted to eat the forbidden fruit when Lucifer through the snake said *"You will be like God, knowing good and evil."*[2] Today we also want to be like God. Not in a moral sense but in a sovereign sense. We want to be in charge of our lives, subservient to no one.

However, there is a problem. Creation and our conscience tell us God exists and is sovereign. In Old Testament times, most civilizations chose to represent their god with an idol created by their hands. They fashioned their god into one that would best meet their perceived needs. Thus they acknowledged God but still exercised some control over their god. Paul spoke to a crowd in Athens about their idols: *"Being then the offspring of God, we ought not to think that the Divine Nature is like gold or silver or stone, an image formed by the art and thought of man. Therefore having overlooked the times of ignorance, God is now declaring to men that all everywhere should repent."*[3]

These ancient times of ignorance regarding idols have largely disappeared. Today, Satan has modernized his deception techniques and invented evolution. The beauty of evolution is that we can eliminate God altogether – He doesn't even exist. We and all that surround us are here through chance. We now have no one that we are accountable to other than the government which we have created. The more things change, the more they stay the same: Professing to be wise, they became fools.

[1]Isaiah 14:14   [2]Genesis 3:5   [3]Acts 17:29-30

And I saw a new heaven and a new earth; for the first heaven and the first earth passed away, and there is no longer any sea.

Revelation 21:1

When Adam and Eve sinned in the Garden, the consequences were far reaching. Their spiritual connection to God was immediately severed and their bodies began a gradual deterioration ending in death. God also cursed the ground. After God destroyed the world by flood in response to mankind's sin, God instilled in the animal kingdom a fear of man, and animals were given to man for food.[1] Prior to the Fall, hurricanes, tornados, earthquakes and floods didn't exist. Paul notes *that the whole creation groans and suffers the pains of childbirth together until now.*[2] Mankind, the animal kingdom, and the material creation were all negatively impacted by sin.

Because of Jesus Christ, the consequences of sin for mankind have been partially alleviated. Followers of Christ are new creatures with the Holy Spirit dwelling in their lives. However, sin is still present and death is still a future event. Nothing has been done yet to deal with creation's dilemma, but that day is coming!

The destruction of land-based life by the flood could be viewed as a second chance. But an angel revealed to John that a do-over is in the offing. God will one day destroy this corrupted earth and heaven and create a new one. Those who have gratefully accepted the Lamb's sacrifice on the cross will be inhabitants of this new earth with a glorified body that is free from sin. In the new earth, there will be no sea, no night, no sun, no death, no sorrow, and no pain. *The wolf and the lamb shall graze together.*[3] Everything will be restored to those days in the Garden of Eden before the Fall, except better.

Are you a future citizen of the new earth?

[1]Genesis 9:2-3   [2]Romans 8:22   [3]Isaiah 65:25a

In the beginning God created the heavens and the earth.
Genesis 1:1

Interrogative words (who, what, when, where, why, and how) are often helpful in discussing and analyzing a subject. The "what" of this discussion is creation and the "where" is Earth. The Bible primarily focuses on the "who" and "why" of creation. Evolution delves into the "when" and "how" of creation. Since evolution discounts God, there can be no "who" and thus there can be no "why" since time and chance are purposeless.

According to the Genesis account of the "how", God spoke everything into existence and that is all the detail we get and need. The "why" of creation deals with relationships. God offered mankind a relationship with Himself. He created the marriage relationship of husband and wife which in time expanded to relationships with children, friends and acquaintances.

Alexander Oparin, a Russian biochemist who died in 1980, was a proponent of the "spontaneous generation of life". Oparin argued that a "primeval soup" of organic molecules could be created in an atmosphere void of oxygen through the action of sunlight. These would combine in ever more complex ways until they formed droplets. These droplets would grow by fusion with other droplets, and reproduce through fission into daughter droplets, and so have a primitive metabolism in which those factors which promote cell integrity survive, and those that do not become extinct. I don't know how long this first wisp of life was supposed to last but obviously long enough to start the process of the very simple becoming extremely complex. For me, I need more faith to believe in that improbable series of events than God speaking matter into existence.

For they exchanged the truth of God for a lie, and worshipped and served the creature rather than the Creator.[1] The evolutionist who denies God's existence misses out on the purpose of creation: a relationship with the Creator. Pray now for your friends and family members who disregard God because of this lie. May they experience dissatisfaction with things created and long for a relationship with the Creator.

[1]Romans 1:25

1. When you consider creation and man's conscience, which has the greatest influence to convince you of God's existence? Why?

2. Do you think evolution has convinced people that God doesn't exist, or have people been looking for a reason not to believe in God and evolution filled that need? Why?

Prayer Starter: Lord Jesus, I recognize that all things were created by You and for You. When I consider all of creation I am especially thankful for ...

*And now, little children, abide in Him, so that when He appears, we
may have confidence and not shrink away from Him in shame at His
coming.*   *I John 2:28*

Today in the church of Jesus Christ, there is a fascination
with the subject of eschatology, the study of "the last things" like the
rapture and Second Coming. If you want to draw a crowd, teach
eschatology. However, when New Testament writers allude to
topics like the rapture above, they usually emphasize the need to be
ready for God's judgment on the believer's life. The Holy Spirit
wants to use the knowledge of future events to motivate and warn us,
not simply stoke our curiosity about what's ahead.

Biblical scholars disagree as to whether the rapture occurs
before, during, or at the end of the seven-year tribulation period.
Regardless, Paul describes a time when Christ will descend from
heaven with a shout and the dead in Christ will rise first. Believers
who are alive at the time will be caught up together with the dead in
Christ and meet Jesus in the air.[1] John desires that those who are
already dead in Christ and those who are alive at the rapture will be
confident when they meet Him in the air.

Which believers will shrink away in shame? They will be
those who have not abided in Him. How can you know if you have
abided in Him? *He who abides in Me, and I in him, he bears much
fruit.*[2] Have you been employing your spiritual gifts in the life of
your church? Have you been sharing your faith with lost friends,
family, and neighbors? A day of accounting is coming.[3] Are you
ready?

[1] I Thessalonians 4:13-18   [2] John 15:5   [3] Matthew 25:14-30

Then the Lord said to me, "Throw it to the potter, that magnificent price at which I was valued by them." So I took the thirty shekels of silver and threw them to the potter in the house of the Lord.
Zechariah 11:13

God has revealed Himself to man through creation, man's conscience, and also His spoken, written and living Word. The prophets and other men of God spoke and wrote God's word to the children of Israel. God communicated to Israel what He expected of them. He also gave glimpses of a future Messiah who would come to be the Lamb of God that would die to pay the penalty for our sin.

The Book of Zechariah has more prophecy content proportional to the space allocated than any other prophet. He has several prophesies related to Christ's first advent as in the example above where the price paid to Judas for his betrayal was predicted. Zechariah also references the triumphal entry into Jerusalem (9:9), the only son being pierced (12:10), and the Shepherd being stricken so that the sheep (disciples) scattered (13:7). Additionally, the book has many references to Christ's second advent and end times which are yet to be fulfilled.

Arthur T. Pierson (1837-1911) stated that the Old Testament has 332 references to Christ which are expressly cited in the New Testament, either as predictions fulfilled in His life and ministry, or as previsions of His character. It is this preponderance of prophecies fulfilled in Christ's first coming that caused Peter to declare that the prophetic word has been made surer.[1]

Prior to Jesus' birth these prophecies were just words on parchment. After the Word became flesh, these written words of God received more credence because they were established as fact. Peter's admonition to us today is that we would do well to pay attention to this specific revelation of God found in His written and living Word. We can entrust our lives to this revelation.

[1] II Peter 1:19

Your lamb shall be an unblemished male a year old ... And the blood shall be a sign for you on the houses where you live; and when I see the blood I will pass over you, and no plague will befall you to destroy you when I strike the land of Egypt.   Exodus 12:5a, 13

The tenth and final plague to strike Egypt was the death of the first-born in each Egyptian household. Every Israeli household that sacrificed a lamb and applied its blood to the home's lintel and doorposts was spared. God's judgment "passed over" those covered by the blood. The story of the Passover lamb is a beautiful Old Testament picture of the future sacrifice of the Savior. Paul declared: *For Christ our Passover also has been sacrificed.*[1] Just as God had planned Christ's death on the cross from the foundation of the world, so He planned the events surrounding the Passover to foreshadow His Son's sacrifice.

The young, unblemished, male lamb was selected four days prior to its sacrifice to ensure that it remained spotless. Christ was on public display and found to be sinless. The Israelites had faith in God's promise that the blood sprinkled on the doorposts would deliver them from judgment.[2] Today those who trust in Christ's substitutionary death on the cross escape eternal death through forgiveness of their sins.

God required that every first-born be sanctified to Him since it was the first-born that was spared.[3] Christians are to be sanctified and set apart for God's use. God commemorated the Jews deliverance from bondage to freedom by requiring an annual Passover festival. Jesus was celebrating Passover with His disciples the evening before His crucifixion when He instituted the Lord's Supper as the New Testament Passover. Jesus commanded that they remember His sacrifice and their deliverance from sin by viewing the bread as His body and the wine as His blood.

Jesus said: *I am the good shepherd; the good shepherd lays down His life for the sheep.*[4] Our Shepherd became a lamb and willingly died for us. Hallelujah, what a Savior!

[1]I Corinthians 5:7b   [2]Hebrews 11:28   [3]Exodus 13:2   [4]John 10:11

My God, my God, why hast Thou forsaken me?   *Psalm 22:1a*

When David cried these words to God, he felt abandoned and wondered why his God was not answering him in his time of need. He was probably not aware that he was writing a Messianic Psalm of the suffering Savior who would come in a millennium. When Jesus cried these same words on the cross, to Him it was a rhetorical question. Jesus knew that He would experience a temporary separation as God judged the sins of the world that were placed on Him. By quoting the first line of Psalm 22, He directed our attention to the entire Psalm which portrays snippets of His crucifixion.

Verse 7 begins: *All who see me sneer at me ... saying ... let Him deliver him.* Luke records: *And even the rulers were sneering at Him, saying, "He saved others, let Him save Himself."*[1] Verse 12 continues: *Strong bulls of Bashan have encircled me. They open wide their mouth at me.* The Bible often uses Bashan as a symbol of arrogant pride.[2] So these strong bulls are another depiction of the proud religious rulers that orchestrated Jesus' crucifixion.

The physiological effects on the person crucified are described starting in verse 14: *I am poured out like water, and all my bones are out of joint; my heart is like wax; it is melted within me.* The weight of the body suspended from the hands pulls bones out of their joints, overstresses the heart, and enhances perspiration. We read in verse 16: *They pierced my hands and my feet.* This statement is a strong reference to crucifixion even though no records exist of using crucifixion during David's time.

Finally, in verse 18 we move to a statement about the soldiers presiding over the crucifixion: *They divide my garments among them, and for my clothing they cast lots.* Roman soldiers were allowed to take any clothing that belonged to the condemned. Where practical they would divide clothing along seam lines. If a robe, for example, was one continuous piece, they would cast lots. Matthew confirms that this prophecy was fulfilled in his gospel.[3]

The disciples of Jesus were convinced by the person of Christ and the fulfilled prophesies of Christ to take the gospel to the world and die a martyr's death. Dare we do less?

[1]Luke 23:35   [2]Isaiah 2:12-13   [3]Matthew 27:35

Neither their silver nor their gold will be able to deliver them on the day of the Lord's wrath; and all the earth will be devoured in the fire of His jealousy, for He will make a complete end, indeed a terrifying one, of all the inhabitants of the earth.   *Zephaniah 1:18*

The theme of the Book of Zephaniah is the day of the Lord. Zephaniah used the expression "the day of the Lord" more than any other prophet. The phrase references impending judgment on Judah for their sins but is also prophetic of end times. Specifically, end times prior to the Second Coming of Jesus Christ, through the Millennium, and the creation of a new heaven and a new earth. Included in this time frame is the total destruction of heaven and earth by fire.

Zephaniah urged Judah to repent and seek God before His judgment arrives.[1] His message is relevant today to unbelievers who need to embrace Jesus now before God's final judgment occurs. Wealthy people in Zephaniah's day as well as ours have a false sense of security and well being since they are financially self-sufficient. That is why Jesus said *it is easier for a camel to go through the eye of a needle, than for a rich man to enter the kingdom of God.*[2]

Peter also referenced the day of the Lord but his emphasis is on how the Christian should live knowing that one day everything related to this earth will be destroyed.[3] Most people want to invest their lives in something that will be here after they are gone. We start foundations, name structures after ourselves, and leave inheritances in the hope that our lives will be remembered. However, long term, the only contributions that last are those that were invested in eternal matters. At the top of that short list are the souls of humanity, whether rich or poor.

Let's ask God to use our godly living and verbal testimony to influence as many as possible to repent and seek God while they can. When all else is gone, those souls will be eternally grateful to us for taking time to care about them.

[1]Zephaniah 2:1-3   [2]Matthew 19:24   [3]II Peter 3:10-11

1. How has your exposure to Biblical prophecy over the years shaped your life? Has prophecy motivated you to be a better steward of what God has entrusted to you or have you just increased in knowledge? Do you need to adjust your focus?

2. Imagine living your life knowing that Psalm 22 described the crucifixion and applied to you. We often view Messianic prophecies as "interesting". Jesus viewed them in a different way – from the perspective of a suffering Savior. For which of the prophecies related to His coming are you especially thankful? Pause and thank Jesus now for His sacrifice for you.

Prayer Starter: Lord Jesus, thank You so much for willingly going to the cross in fulfillment of prophecy. Help me to take up my cross daily and live for You. I specifically pray for help with …

Now Jabez called on the God of Israel, saying, "Oh that Thou wouldst bless me indeed, and enlarge my border, and that Thy Hand might be with me, and that Thou wouldst keep me from harm, that it may not pain me!" And God granted him what he requested.
I Chronicles 4:10

One day I was reading through a local obituary and saw two entries that both mentioned "legacy". One entry mentioned that the two daughters would carry on the deceased's legacy; the other said the legacy of the father will live on within his family. In truth, we all desire that after our death, our children's lives will be spiritually productive, in part because of the positive influence we have had in their lives. But I sense that Jabez wanted a legacy that extended beyond his family.

The first nine chapters of I Chronicles are almost exclusively a listing of genealogical records, a legacy of family. In the midst of this seemingly endless list of names we encounter Jabez. His legacy warrants a narrative, not a list. Jabez was noted for requesting a God-sized blessing from the God of Israel. He wasn't content with just a loving family; he wanted to experience God's presence with him as God caused his influence to increase.

In the Old Testament, God blessed His people most often in material ways. In the New Testament Jesus focused primarily on spiritual blessings. What would characterize Jabez in a New Testament setting? He would certainly have a burden to see his family members saved and encourage them to grow in their relationship with the Lord. But Jabez would also look outside his tent and want to influence those around him for the gospel.

Be a New Testament Jabez. Spread the gospel in your family and then reach out to the rest of the world. Expand your legacy to include many beyond the walls of your home. Pray a God-sized prayer!

And he summoned the twelve and began to send them out in pairs; ... and He instructed them that they should take nothing for their journey, except a mere staff; no bread, no bag, no money in their belt.

Mark 6:7-8

The disciples were present when Jesus preached His Sermon on the Mount so they heard Him say: *But seek first His kingdom and His righteousness; and all these things shall be added to you.*[1] They understood that the things He was talking about were food, drink, and clothing – the basic needs of life. Jesus was giving all of His followers a promise: If you put God's business first, He will ensure your basic needs are met.

However, a promise is not claimed until it is needed. So Jesus restricts what the twelve can take with them, so that the need will exist. They are sent out with a staff and the clothes on their backs, but with no food and no money. Now they will be able to experience God's provision in their lives as they obey Christ and do God's will. This opportunity to see God provide will serve them well in the future as they minister to others and suffer want and persecution.

As we experience physical, emotional, and financial needs today, we must remember that Jesus' promise to meet our needs is conditional. When Queen Elizabeth requested a merchant go abroad on her service, he replied that his business would be ruined if he went. She responded: If you mind my business, I will mind your business. God's condition is that we seek His kingdom first – then He will take care of our business. Perhaps God allows needy situations in our lives to help us evaluate whose kingdom we are seeking to build.

[1]Matthew 6:33

And He said to them, "Come away by yourselves to a lonely place
and rest a while." (For there were many people coming and going,
and they did not even have time to eat.)   *Mark 6:31*

The disciples had just returned from preaching repentance,
casting out demons, and healing the sick. Jesus recognized they
were weary, so they got into a boat, headed for a restful time in a
solitary place. However, the people saw them going and travelled
along the shoreline following them. When Jesus came ashore, He
saw a great multitude of people coming His way.

Jesus had several options of what to do. He could have
gotten back in the boat with the disciples and fled the scene. He
could have told the crowd that His disciples needed rest and sent the
multitude home. Instead, *He felt compassion for them because they*
were like sheep without a shepherd; and He began to teach them
many things.[1] In essence, the multitude's spiritual needs trumped the
disciple's physical needs. Jesus placed the disciple's need for rest on
hold while He ministered to the crowd.

Times will occur when you make getting some rest a priority,
only to be confronted with a ministry opportunity which interferes
with your plan for solitude. Take time to pray, asking what God's
will is in that situation. But don't be surprised if God puts your rest
on hold and leads you to be involved in ministry to others.

[1]Mark 6:34b

"But in order that you may know that the Son of Man has authority on earth to forgive sins" – He said to the paralytic – "I say to you, rise, take up your pallet and go home."   Mark 2:10-11

If Jesus' healing of people was motivated solely by his mercy and compassion, He would have entered a town and announced that everyone in that town with any illness was now healed. Instead Jesus required people to come to Him and ask for healing. By asking, the individuals were admitting a need and demonstrating faith that Jesus could heal. Their faith was typically based on reports they had heard from others who had seen Jesus heal. During Jesus' three-year ministry He was considered by most as a prophet, so they were not exercising saving faith in the Messiah. Rather they relied on healing faith in a man of God.

Jesus' primary mission in coming to Earth was to heal mankind's sin-sick souls, not unhealthy bodies. He proved Himself faithful and powerful enough to heal sickness when asked, knowing that soon He would claim that his death on the cross was payment for the penalty of their sin. If an individual admits his or her need as a sinner, and asks Jesus to heal their sin-cursed soul, He will do it. Believing in His miracles laid the groundwork for believing that He also had authority to forgive sins.

Today, followers of Christ tend to be the miracle, rather than do the miracle. A Christian's life has been transformed by the power of the gospel and we are new creatures. The indwelling Holy Spirit has caused a miraculous transformation in our lives. We have become salt and light to a bland and blind world. The believer's testimony can lay the groundwork which allows a nonbeliever to receive the gift of salvation through Jesus Christ by faith.

Are we sharing our miracle with others?

For momentary, light affliction is producing for us an eternal weight of glory far beyond all comparison, while we look not at the things which are seen, but at the things which are not seen; for the things which are seen are temporal, but the things which are not seen are eternal.   *II Corinthians 4:17-18*

Paul viewed his life on earth through an eternal lens. His afflictions for the cause of Christ were many and significant but he viewed them as "momentary". Mathematically, if you formed a ratio with your age in the numerator and a twenty-digit whole number representing a portion of eternity in the denominator, its value would be essentially zero. James expressed the same thought when he said: *You are just a vapor that appears for a little while and then vanishes away.*[1] Paul lived in the present but his actions were motivated and viewed from an eternal perspective.

No one other than Paul would have characterized his afflictions as "light". When Paul defended his apostleship against those preaching a false gospel he described himself: *in far more labors, in far more imprisonments, beaten times without number, often in danger of death.*[2] He knew his trials were more numerous than most but he saw an "eternal weight of glory" awaiting him in heaven. Compared to the weighty glory he would receive in Christ, Paul chose to view his sufferings as light.

Do you view your years on earth as a whole number or as a fraction? We need the eyes of Christ to see the unseen and the heart of Christ to act appropriately. Lord Jesus, give us your eyes and your heart so that we can live each day with eternity in full view.

[1]James 4:14b   [2]II Corinthians 11:23b

1. Write below some accomplishments God has worked through you that could be considered part of your spiritual legacy.

2. If you are a follower of Christ, then you are a walking miracle since the Holy Spirit has made you a new creature. (II Corinthians 5:17) Write a change that God has made in your life below and share that miracle with someone today.

Prayer Starter: Lord Jesus, as I read and study your Word daily, remind me to live with eternity in full view. I want to trust You for a God-sized legacy and pray that my spiritual legacy will include ...

And He was saying, "The kingdom of God is like a man who casts seed upon the soil; and goes to bed at night and gets up by day, and the seed sprouts up and grows – how, he himself does not know. The soil produces crops by itself; first the blade, then the head, then the mature grain in the head. But when the crop permits, he immediately puts in the sickle, because the harvest has come."
Mark 4:26-29

Early in our marriage we had a small vegetable garden in the backyard. After planting the seeds, I enjoyed a daily visit to the garden to see if any growth had broken the soil. Once growth was visible, I was intrigued by the daily growth and the eventual blossom. The next exciting development was the blossom becoming the miniature vegetable. Finally, after weeks of growth, we harvested the food.

Jesus uses this same illustration to describe the gospel message being sown into the heart of an unbeliever. The sower, representing the Christian, has only two responsibilities: sow the seed and reap the fruit. Jesus is clear that what happens while the seed is in the soil is out of our control. The Spirit of God will mysteriously work with the word of God in the heart of the unbeliever. Our task is to sow the seed and leave the result to God.

At times we will be fortunate enough to be present when the seed is ready to produce fruit; at other times, it will be someone else's joy to reap the fruit. However, whether we sow or reap, it is God who brings about the maturity of the seed. Since our part in the kingdom of God has been clearly laid out, are we equipped to both spread the gospel seed and to lead a person to salvation when that seed spouts? If the answer is no, training is available at a nearby church! If the answer is yes, are we sowing?

When God saw their deeds, that they turned from their wicked way, then God relented concerning the calamity which He had declared he would bring upon them. And He did not do it.   Jonah 3:10

      The Book of Jonah is the first record of God sending a missionary to a foreign country. As such it shows God's heart for the lost. It also demonstrates His people's reluctance to share God's message with the lost. When Jonah first received God's command to go to Nineveh, he headed in the opposite direction, perhaps because he viewed the Assyrians as Israel's enemy. Through Jonah's experience with the whale, he went to Nineveh, but was displeased when they repented. Although he obeyed, his heart was not right. He didn't have God's compassion for the people of Nineveh.
      In each of the four Gospels and Acts, Jesus commands His followers to tell all people the Good News. Commands are meant to be obeyed. But as we obey, God wants to give us His heart for people so that our sharing is motivated by a genuine concern for their souls. When people discern that we are sincerely concerned for them, they will be much more open to what we have to share.
      Paul makes the case that while we were enemies, we were reconciled to God through the death of His Son[1]. Jesus commanded us to love our enemies[2]. Jesus demonstrated the ultimate example of loving your enemies by dying on the cross. Since enemies are included in the list of people we are to love and share Jesus with, no one is excluded. There is a natural tendency to go the opposite way from people we consider our enemies, much as Jonah did. However, we are on mission for God and He will continue to redirect us to those He cares for, even if we don't care for them. God is working to form His heart in us. Let's submit, not resist.

[1]Romans 5:10   [2]Matthew 5:44

And he said to Him, "O Lord, how shall I deliver Israel? Behold, my family is the least in Manasseh, and I am the youngest in my father's house." But the Lord said to him, "Surely I will be with you, and you shall defeat Midian as one man."   *Judges 6:15-16*

It is not uncommon in the Old Testament for individuals who receive a task from God to respond with an excuse based on perceived inadequacies. In the above passage, Gideon is tasked to be the warrior who will deliver Israel from the oppression of the Midianites. When Moses was called to deliver Israel from Egyptian bondage, he responded with several excuses as to why he was not the best man for the job.[1] Jeremiah received his call to be a prophet to the kingdom of Judah and immediately responded that he was too young and not eloquent.[2]

In all three of these incidents, God's response to the stated inadequacies was: "I will be with you." Can you think of any excuse or shortcoming that mankind can create for ignoring God's call that is not dismissed with "I will be with you"?

Today the Great Commission still calls all Christians to evangelize and disciple the lost. If you are like me, it is human nature to find excuses not to witness. I sometimes feel I would benefit from an interactive Bible. As an example, Matthew 28:19-20 would look like this: *Go therefore and make disciples of all the nations, baptizing them in the name of the Father and the Son and the Holy Spirit, teaching them to observe all that I commanded you;* (insert excuse here) _____
and lo, I am with you always, even to the end of the age.

This format would allow me to indicate my excuse for not obeying and then I could have immediate feedback from the Lord: *I am with you always.* Whatever my inadequacy is, He is more than able to compensate for it.

For the Christian, Jesus is with us through the indwelling Holy Spirit. We have the Spirit of God within and the accompanying spiritual gifts and the fruit of the Spirit – all that is needed to respond to any call from God, including the Great Commission.

[1]Exodus 3:10-12   [2] Jeremiah 1:4-8

Hear Thou in heaven Thy dwelling place, and do according to all for which the foreigner calls to Thee, in order that all the peoples of the earth may know Thy name...
I Kings 8:43a

As part of the prayer of dedication for the newly constructed temple, King Solomon includes a request that all foreigners come to know the God of Israel. Solomon was aware that God had called Abraham and created the nation of Israel to declare His name among all the nations. God used various methods during Old Testament times to reach the foreigner. In fact, several people in Solomon's ancestry were foreigners.

Solomon's great grandfather Obed was born to Boaz and Ruth. Ruth was a Moabite woman who was introduced to Jehovah God through the testimony of her husband and her mother-in-law Naomi. When Ruth's husband died, she declared to Naomi: *Your people shall be my people, and your God, my God.*[1]

Boaz's parents were Salmon and Rahab. Rahab lived in Jericho, the first city in Canaan that Israel conquered. She harbored and protected the two spies sent to Jericho and in return she and her family were spared. She was willing to risk her life for the spies because she believed the stories of their previous conquests and the crossing of the Red Sea. God had revealed Himself through these stories and she declared: *For the Lord your God, He is God in heaven above and on earth beneath.*[2]

If we fast forward six centuries we see God sending His evangelist Jonah to the city of Ninevah with a call for repentance. As a result of Jonah's preaching, the king of Ninevah declared: *Let men call on God earnestly that each may turn from his wicked way and from the violence which is in his hands.*[3]

Today, God is still calling all nations to Himself using the same three methods. He uses the personal testimony of believers, like Naomi, in one-on-one relationships with others. He uses evangelists like Jonah to share the gospel. Finally, He reveals Himself personally to people just as He did to Rahab. Through sharing the gospel, giving our resources, and praying we co-labor with God in reaching the nations for Christ.

[1]Ruth 1:16b   [2]Joshua 2:11b   [3]Jonah 3:8b

Beloved, while I was making every effort to write you about our common salvation, I felt the necessity to write to you appealing that you contend earnestly for the faith which was once for all delivered to the saints.   *Jude 3*

      The primary purpose of Jude's single-chapter letter was to challenge believers to contend for the faith. The objects of the contention were *ungodly persons who turn the grace of our God into licentiousness and deny our only Master and Lord, Jesus Christ.*[1] As a younger half brother of Jesus, Jude had the opportunity to observe Jesus his entire lifetime. When Jude concluded that Jesus was his Master and Lord, he understandably believed it with all his heart. He was not silent while some distorted the gospel message and demeaned his Savior.

      Contend conveys the idea of striving in debate or controversy. Most of the time when Christians talk to others about Christ it is referred to as "sharing your faith". Times of contention with others over the gospel message will hopefully be rare. Usually we will follow Paul's guidance and not be quarrelsome, but to be kind, patient, and gentle when correcting those who are in opposition[2].

      However, when Paul gave his farewell address to the Ephesian elders he said: *I know that after my departure savage wolves will come in among you, not sparing the flock; and from among your own selves men will arise, speaking perverse things, to draw away the disciples after them.*[3] Paul's concern was for the flock, not for those attacking the flock; contention was appropriate.

      During most of your encounters with unbelievers you will look for opportunities to share your testimony and/or the gospel message. However, when you encounter those from either inside or outside the Church whose intent is to harm the flock, contend for the faith. If you ever get good at contention, it may mean that you have crossed over from being loving to being contentious. Sometimes what may seem as an attack on the Gospel may be a person testing his own ideas or even asking for more information. Ask God for wisdom to correctly discern situations where contention is required.

[1]Jude 4   [2]II Timothy 2:24-26   [3]Acts 20:29-30

1. At which of these three activities are you strongest: sharing your testimony/gospel with others, giving financially to spread the gospel, or praying for the lost? At which are you the weakest? Is God leading you to any action?

2. Describe the last time you contended for the faith or you saw someone else do it. In hindsight should anything have been done differently?

Prayer Starter: Lord God, I want to be more involved and more effective in promoting the spread of the gospel message. I sense that You are leading me to …

And gathering together all the chief priests and scribes of the people, he began to inquire of them where the Christ was to be born. And they said to him, "In Bethlehem of Judea, for so it has been written by the prophet."   Matthew 2:4-5

Put yourself in the place of a Jewish religious leader in Jerusalem when distinguished men from the East arrive at King Herod's palace inquiring about your Messiah. The king summons you and other leaders and asks where the King of the Jews is to be born. Each one of you knows that Micah, the prophet, foretold the birthplace would be Bethlehem, so you inform the king. The king is treating these men who travelled hundreds of miles as credible, so would you also view them as trustworthy? If so, would you volunteer to travel with the Magi the five miles to Bethlehem to see if the Messiah really had been born? Since none of the religious leaders at the time went with the Magi, we have to wonder why.

Perhaps they were like many today: apathetic about spiritual truth. The chief priests were not interested in a Messiah who would usher in change since they were content with the status quo. They enjoyed a comfortable life with power and prestige. Change was not welcome. Thirty-some years later, they would meet the baby they once avoided. Now they talk to a governor, not a king: *Pilate said to them, "Shall I crucify your King?" The chief priests answered, "We have no king but Caesar."*[1] They still chose to serve the one who afforded them a comfortable lifestyle.

Today, many unbelievers at Christmastime will be comfortable with where they are in life and are not seeking spiritual truth. However, some will be searching. We will not know which category they fall in until we engage them with truth of the gospel. Our mission is to offer mankind the choice of serving the King of the Jews, rather than the king or god of this world. They decide.

[1]John 19:15b

For a child will be born to us, a son will be given to us; and the
government will rest on His shoulders.   *Isaiah 9:6a*
The Spirit of the Lord God is upon me, because the Lord has
anointed me to bring good news to the afflicted ... To proclaim the
favorable year of the Lord, and the day of vengeance of our God.
                                                       Isaiah 61:1a, 2a

　　　Jesus didn't fit the Messiah profile based on the Jew's
perceived need. They wanted someone to deliver them from Roman
oppression. Thus they focused on prophecies that dealt with
Messiah as the new government ruler and executor of God's
vengeance. However, God saw that sinful man needed to be
reconciled with a holy God. So, God offered a perfect sacrifice to
atone for man's sin. The suffering savior and the conquering king
are sequential, not concurrent events.
　　　Old Testament references to the coming Messiah are often
referred to as mountain peaks of prophecy. When you observe a
mountain range from the distance, the peaks can appear in close
proximity to each other. However, a heavenly view reveals a
considerable distance between the peaks. God chose to discuss
Messiah's First and Second Advent together in the above passages.
　　　Jesus was well aware of this distinction even though others
were not. Early in His ministry He returned to His hometown of
Nazareth and was given the book of Isaiah to read in the synagogue
one Sabbath day. Jesus found the second passage above and read
until He arrived at "the day of vengeance of our God", at which
point He stopped reading. He closed the book and said *Today this*
Scripture has been fulfilled in your hearing.[1] He was announcing to
all present that He was Messiah, sent here with the gospel. He
would return later to fulfill the remainder of the prophecy.
　　　Today many are still asking God to meet their perceived
needs without recognizing that their primary need is forgiveness of
sin and a personal relationship with Jesus Christ. Let's ask God for
sensitivity to their stated needs and boldness to share Jesus as the
answer to their real need. The days we have to share are precious
because His Second Coming draws near.

[1]Luke 4:14-21

But when the fullness of the time came, God sent forth His Son, born of a woman, born under the Law, in order that He might redeem those who were under the Law, that we might receive the adoption as sons.   *Galatians 4:4-5*

Perhaps you have noticed that Before the Common Era (BCE) and Common Era (CE) are gradually supplanting Before Christ (BC) and Anno Domini (AD), meaning "the Year of our Lord". Many authors and publishers who want to be sensitive to non-Christians are now using BCE and CE to eliminate the direct reference to Christ and Lord. Regardless of that trend, for the Christian, the singular event in history will be when the Son of God was born a helpless baby, lived a perfect life, and died a substitutionary death.

For the Christ follower, there was a time in his or her life when the historical event of Jesus' birth and life became personal. This person will still celebrate times related to births, graduations, marriage, promotions and retirements but the most significant of all of life's events will be the day Jesus became Lord and Savior. Life will always be viewed in terms of before Christ and life lived in the presence of the Lord. The intersection of Jesus and a believing, trusting soul changes life forever, in the here-and-now and the there-and-then.

Let's think of Common Era in this way: Once upon a time, God came to earth as a common man, lived an uncommon life, and died an uncommon death, so that man's spirit and God's Spirit could share the same body in common. The establishment can cause BC and AD to fall into disuse regarding the calendar, but personally, for the Christian, they retain timeless significance.

The first man is from the earth, earthy; the second man is from heaven. And just as we have borne the image of the earthy, we shall also bear the image of the heavenly.   *I Corinthians 15:47, 49*

Paul describes mankind using two subdivisions. The first is represented by Adam who was born in innocence, was tempted and sinned. The second is represented by Jesus who was also born in innocence since He was conceived by the Holy Spirit, not man. However Jesus always resisted temptation and never sinned, thus qualifying Him to solely occupy the second subdivision.

Adam and Jesus each had a significant impact on the rest of humanity. *So then as through one transgression there resulted condemnation to all men, even so through one act of righteousness there resulted justification of life to all men.*[1] Adam brought condemnation and death to all. Jesus offers justification and life to all.

As a result of this sinless distinction, *the last Adam became a life-giving spirit.*[2] God, the Father, accepted the sacrifice of the spotless Lamb, the Son, as the one-time payment for the penalty of our sins, resulting in the offer of justification. All who accept this gift receive a pledge,[3] the Holy Spirit, Who serves as the guarantee of eternal life.

We bear the earthy image in that we have Adam's sinful nature. However with the indwelling of the Holy Spirit we have power over the old man and can walk as a new man or woman. Are you living under the curse of the first Adam or the blessings of the second Adam?

[1]Romans 5:18   [2]I Corinthians 15:45a   [3]II Corinthians 5:5
[4]II Corinthians 5:2

And to Salmon was born Boaz by Rahab; and to Boaz was born Obed by Ruth; and to Obed, Jesse; and to Jesse was born David the king. And to David was born Solomon by her who had been the wife of Uriah;   Matthew 1:5-6

  Matthew and Luke are the only two gospel writers who provide genealogies of Jesus, both through Joseph, His step-father. Matthew refers to five women in the genealogy, three of whom are mentioned in the above verses.   The term "blue blood" refers to a descendant from noble or aristocratic ancestors. If anyone ever qualified as a blue blood it was Jesus Christ, the Son of God. Yet, God in His sovereignty allowed some less than noble people in the ancestry of the man who would fill the role of Jesus' earthly step-father. The inclusion of these individuals was simply the grace of God at work in human history.

  Rahab was a harlot in Jericho who risked her life to protect two Israeli spies, thereby saving her life and those of her family when Jericho was destroyed.[1] Ruth was a Moabite. Marriage to foreigners was forbidden but Ruth submitted herself to Jehovah God and received God's grace.[2] Bathsheba, the wife of Uriah, was lured into an adulterous relationship by David.[3]

  In God's sight we are all red-blooded and red is the Biblical color of sin. *Though your sins are as scarlet, they shall be as white as snow.*[4] God's grace has been extended to all sinners; He shows no favoritism. There is no one who has been adopted into the family of God through belief in Christ, who cannot be used in a significant way to advance the kingdom of God. Eternal life with God and a meaningful life on earth are available only through the grace of God. Rejoice if you are in God's family and share the Good News with others!

[1]Joshua 2   [2]Ruth 1:16   [3]II Samuel 11   [4]Isaiah 1:18

1. Do you remember a time in your life when you transitioned from Before Christ to living in the presence of the Lord? If not, why not ask Jesus to be your Lord and Savior this Christmas season?

2. For many the focus is now on Santa, gifts and parties. Since the holiday name hasn't yet been changed to Clausmas, let's be vocal about the Christ of Christmas. Who has God put on your heart to share Christ with this season?

Prayer Starter: Lord Jesus, thank You for your willingness to leave heaven and come to Earth for a sinner such as me. Help me as I seek to speak your Name to …

Praise the Lord, for the Lord is good; Sing praises to His name, for it is lovely. For I know that the Lord is great, And that our Lord is above all gods.   Psalm 135:3, 5

God's attributes have been characterized and cataloged in several different ways. One approach is to list non-moral and moral attributes. Non-moral are those that belong to God exclusively like His sovereignty and omnipotence. Moral attributes also belong to God but limited manifestations of these are seen in mankind like His love and truthfulness.

A common prayer taught to children as they learn to say a blessing over food highlights God's greatness and goodness as the Psalmist does above. Greatness encompasses the non-moral attributes and goodness summarizes the moral attributes in a very broad sense.

When things go badly in life we can sometimes get angry with God. We may even say: How can a loving God allow that to happen? Or, if God is all powerful, why didn't He stop that? We attack in words both the non-moral and moral attributes of God. However, we are really questioning the goodness of God since all actions originate from the heart.

In the parent-child relationship, the child often doesn't understand or agree with the actions of the parent. Hopefully, however, the parent's will prevails because the parent is the mature and wise one who knows what is best for the child. The same is true in our relationship with God. When we don't understand why something happened we need to remember that our Father is the wise parent. He sees the past, present and future from the perspective of His non-moral attributes. Isaiah recorded: *My thoughts are not your thoughts, neither are your ways My ways, declares the Lord.*[1] Since God's thoughts and ways encompass both his moral and non-moral attributes, He sees events from a different perspective than we do.

The Bible declares that God is good. When we are tempted to come to a different conclusion we need to trust our wise Father. An all-powerful, sovereign, loving, truthful God can be trusted.

[1] Isaiah 55:8

I, the Lord, am your God, Who brought you up from the land of Egypt; open your mouth wide and I will fill it. But My people did not listen to My voice; and Israel did not obey Me. So I gave them over to the stubbornness of their heart to walk in their own devices.

Psalms 81:10-12

The description of the relationship between God and mankind in the Old and New Testament is the same. God longs to have a relationship with His creation but mankind refuses.

Genesis records the creation of man and woman and the eventual disobedience from which sin entered the world and created a breach in the relationship between God and man. Evil increased until God judged the world and saved only Noah and his family. Later in Genesis God initiated a relationship with Abraham and his descendants, the children of Israel. When they grew into a nation, He delivered them from slavery in Egypt, after which Israel still rejected God's favor and pursued their own interests.

In the Old Testament, He continued to pursue them through His prophets. In the New Testament, He sent His Son, Jesus Christ, to pay the sin debt for mankind. Christ's death on the cross provided a permanent means to be reunited in fellowship with God if we make Jesus the Savior and Lord of our lives.

Listen to the heart of God from verse 13 of the above passage: *Oh that My people would listen to Me, that Israel would walk in My ways!* Listen to Paul's description of the action this God took: *But God demonstrated His own love toward us, in that while we were yet sinners, Christ died for us.*[1] Have you responded positively to God's offer of reconciliation? If not, why not?

[1]Romans 5:8

You shall not do what is done in the land of Egypt, where you lived, nor are you to do what is done in the land of Canaan where I am bringing you; you shall not walk in their statutes.   Leviticus 18:3

The exodus of Israel from Egypt involved God's judgment on two unbelieving, immoral peoples: Egyptians and Canaanites. The upcoming judgments were foretold when God tells Abraham about 600 years earlier: *I will also judge the nation (Egypt) whom they will serve...then in the fourth generation they shall return here (Canaan), for the iniquity of the Amorite is not yet complete.*[1] The Amorites were the first nation that Israel fought as they journeyed to Canaan. Amorites were representative of all the nations of Canaan.

God worked providentially through Joseph to provide food and shelter in Egypt during the famine for Jacob's family of seventy. God promised Jacob that his family would grow to be a nation in Egypt and would eventually return to Canaan, the promise land.[2] God timed the exodus to coincide with when the sins of Egypt and Canaan could no longer be tolerated by a just God. It is reminiscent of the time God destroyed the earth by flood because *the earth was filled with violence.*[3] In this case, however, the specific sins mentioned following the above verse are primarily sexual sins, including homosexuality and bestiality. The sacrificial offering of children to Molech and profaning God's name are also referenced.

Palestinian excavations have uncovered evidences of infant skeletons in burial places around heathen shrines. Eighty years prior to the exodus, Egypt ordered the murder of all male Israelite children because it was an expedient way to control the Israelite population. God spared Moses' life during those dark days, but it is impossible to know how many children were killed in Egypt.

God is patient and just. However, at some point God's patience gives way to His judgment, and we don't know what that teetering point is. Consider the sins listed above: violence, sexual immorality, infanticide, and profaning God's name. Based on how the nations are doing today in these categories, one wonders how thin God's patience may be. Even so, Lord Jesus, come.

[1]Genesis 15:14a, 16   [2]Genesis 46:2-4   [3]Genesis 6:11,13

For we do not have a high priest who cannot sympathize with our weaknesses, but one who has been tempted in all things as we are, yet without sin. Let us therefore draw near with confidence to the throne of grace, that we may receive mercy and may find grace to help in time of need.   *Hebrews 4:15-16*

Someone has said that mercy is not getting what you deserve and grace is getting what you don't deserve. Those who have trusted in Christ as their Lord and Savior have received both mercy and grace. Mercy, since they are no longer bound for hell which they deserve. Grace, because they have received an abundant life on earth and eternal life with Jesus in heaven which they don't deserve. However, the author of Hebrews reminds us that the offer of mercy and grace does not stop at salvation.

Mercy is compassion. Since Jesus was exposed to every temptation we experience, he is sympathetic and compassionate toward us in our failures. When we fall short of even our own expectations, we tend to beat ourselves up because that is what we deserve. Instead, we need to confess our sins and shortcomings immediately, and ask for mercy and forgiveness.

Grace is unmerited favor. The apostle Paul begins all his epistles with the phrase "grace to you" or its equivalent. Today, I suspect our favorite phrase is "God bless you", but I think "grace" had special meaning to Paul. After all, he was the recipient of major doses of God's grace in his life. Grace abounded to him in giftedness, protection, endurance, provision and many other areas. He knew that God's grace in his life allowed him to have the impact on the world for Jesus that he had. We need that same grace in our lives if we are to accomplish the mission that God has given to each of us.

Grace and mercy meet at the cross and provide salvation to all who gratefully receive the gift provided by Jesus.   G
However, grace and mercy are still available to the   MERCY
Christian in need of them. Let's boldly go to Jesus   A
even now and receive mercy and grace to help in   C
time of need.   E

The grace of the Lord Jesus Christ, and the love of God, and the
fellowship of the Holy Spirit, be with you all.   II Corinthians 13:14

Over the centuries the concept of the Trinity has been discussed at length. In 325 AD, the Council of Nicaea adopted the Nicene Creed which confirms belief in one God, the Father; one Lord Jesus Christ; and the Holy Ghost. Three persons in "one being" is a mystery which we will never fathom this side of heaven. Instead of getting worked up over trying to explain the Trinity, we should simply give thanks since each Person of the Trinity is involved in our salvation, as Paul indicates above.

We are introduced to the concept of the Trinity on the first page of Genesis: *Then God said, "Let Us make man in Our image, according to Our likeness..."*[1] Two chapters later we read of the fall of mankind and sin's entry into the world. Just as God the Father initiated the creation of mankind, God so loved the world that He gave His only begotten Son to deal with the sin problem. Those who believe in Christ's atoning death on the cross receive forgiveness for sin and are sealed with the presence of the Holy Spirit in the believer's life. Our salvation was initiated by the love of God, accomplished by the grace of Jesus, and preserved by the fellowship of the Spirit. Each Member of the Trinity plays an integral role in our salvation.

Doubt and confusion will inevitably creep into our minds as the finite tries to comprehend the infinite. Instead of becoming frustrated or perplexed over the concept of the Trinity, simply be thankful that the infinite Triune God decided to invade the world of the finite to reunite us with the Father, the Son and the Holy Spirit.

[1]Genesis 1:26

1. One listing of God's non-moral attributes would be: sovereign, eternal, omniscient, omnipresent, omnipotent, and immutable (unchanging). Moral attributes are: righteous, just, love and truth. Which of God's attributes do you need to rely on today to help with your greatest need? Why?

2. God's mercy prompts forgiveness and His grace empowers us. How have you relied on His mercy and grace in recent days?

Prayer Starter: God, I am amazed that Someone like You pays any attention to someone like me. Help me to know You more intimately and rely on You more consistently. Right now, I need help with …

Footholds

Do not give the devil a foothold.   Ephesians 4:27 (NIV)

The weapons we fight with are not the weapons of the world. On the contrary, they have divine power to demolish strongholds.
                                          II Corinthians 10:4 (NIV)

A foothold can lead to a satanic stronghold. You have probably experienced a situation where you tried to close a door but the person outside sticks his foot in the door so it won't close. We tend to play with sin the same way. We leave a door in our life ajar so we can experiment with an enticing sin. We have no intention of opening the door further, but Satan establishes a foothold. The foothold grows until the sin has taken up residence in our lives.

Jesus described Satan as the father of lies.[1] Satan whispers: "This sinful activity will be fun and you can control it." Eventually, the bondage and the guilt override the fun. You then realize Satan has lied to you. Fortunately it is never too late if you involve Jesus. Whether the addiction is alcohol, drugs, tobacco, pornography, immorality, or gambling, Jesus has power to demolish the stronghold.

Solomon asked: *Can a man take fire in his bosom, and his clothes not be burned?*[2] He was referring to immorality, but the principle applies to any sin. It is impossible to embrace sin and not be burned. The longer you embrace the sin, the more powerful Satan's stronghold in your life.

Confess the sin confidentially to a Christian friend and seek help. The circumstances and consequences of the sin will eventually be revealed. Better for you to uncover it, than someone else.

[1]John 8:44   [2]Proverbs 6:27

And the Lord said to Gideon, "The people who are with you are too many for Me to give Midian into their hands, lest Israel become boastful, saying, 'My own power has delivered me.'"   *Judges 7:2*

The Book of Judges spans a period of roughly 300 years, beginning after the death of Joshua and ending prior to the arrival of the prophet Samuel, the last judge. Judges records the activities of twelve men and one woman who were designated by God as judges of Israel. The following cycle is played out time and again throughout Judges: Israel rebels against God; God subordinates them under an enemy country; Israel repents; God raises up a judge to deliver them.

In our passage, Gideon has been appointed as the judge to deliver Israel from the Midianites. Gideon raised an army of 32,000 Israelites to battle Midian, but God reduced the army to 300 soldiers so there would be no doubt Who was responsible for the upcoming victory.

The availability of God's grace is inversely proportional to our perceived strength and self-confidence. If we sense a need to be dependent on God as we are on mission for Him, God's grace increases. When we feel self confident, God's grace is diminished because we don't perceive a need for it.

God purposefully places us in situations in which we feel weak and inadequate so we will rely on Him and He will get the glory. However, we tend to avoid taking on a task for God when we feel inadequate. Understand, that is exactly where God wants us. When we feel insufficient for the God-given task, we spend more time on our knees in prayer and God shows up in a mighty way. God delights in situations where it is one percent us and 99 percent Him, just as it was with Gideon.

Scripture Index

Scripture Index

Scripture Index

Scripture Index

Made in the USA
Charleston, SC
30 November 2015